COLONIAL
HINDUISM

THE OXFORD CENTRE FOR HINDU STUDIES MANDALA PUBLISHING SERIES

General Editor
Lucian Wong

Editorial Board
John Brockington
Avni Chag
James Madaio
Valters Negribs

The Oxford Centre for Hindu Studies Mandala Publishing Series offers authoritative yet accessible introductions to a wide range of subjects in Hindu Studies. Each book in the series aims to present its subject matter in a form that is engaging and readily comprehensible to persons of all backgrounds – academic or otherwise – without compromising scholarly rigor. The series thus bridges the divide between academic and popular writing by preserving and utilising the best elements of both.

COLONIAL
HINDUISM

An Introduction

Amiya P. Sen

MANDALA
San Rafael Los Angeles London

For Partha da (the late Parthsarathi Gupta) and
Narayani di (Narayani Gipta), my teachers and well-wishers.

CONTENTS

PREFACE

Far from being frozen in time, Hindu civilisation has, like any other, changed continually throughout its long history. Yet in studying Hinduism we cannot lose sight of two important realities: firstly, the continuities in Indian life and thought run deep though they are not always immediately apparent; and secondly, in the history of Hinduism there have been phases of accelerated change and of deeper implication for the everyday life of the Hindu. The period in Indian history coinciding with the British colonial occupation of India represents one such important period. The face of Hinduism changed more rapidly and with more far-reaching results in the course of the nineteenth century than in the preceding millennia. The primary objective of this book is to acquaint you with the nature and extent of this change.

This book is especially addressed to those new to the study of the cultural and religious history of modern South Asia, and of the numerically dominant religious community of the Hindus in particular. Precisely because it caters to the needs of such a readership, and hopes to provide an informative as well as instructive introduction, my intention throughout has been to keep the book simple and accessible, unburdened by copious notes and references. Supplementary readings have been suggested at the end of each chapter, which will enable the interested reader to gain additional information on the subject under discussion. To aid the assimilation of the material covered in the book, questions aimed to facilitate further reflection upon and discussion of core thematic issues are provided at the end of each chapter. Those new to the subject will also find the glossary of technical terms at the end of the book useful.

This book is the work of a historian of ideas. It was written with the purpose of recounting some of the key concepts and processes that were actively at work in India during the nineteenth and early twentieth centuries – the period that coincides with the establishment of British colonial rule in India and its eventual overthrow. In hindsight, this historical moment could be said to have produced two major consequences. First, it entailed a deep intertwining of the political with that which was fundamentally social and religious in nature. A concerted political struggle against British imperialism had to be founded on greater social and religious cohesion of Hindus. Second, both the impulse to social and religious reformation and the birth of patriotic feeling among Hindus at this time were products of the dynamic and long-drawn-out engagement of modernity with tradition that followed in the wake of the establishment of British rule in India.

The nature of the material and moral challenges posed by the West to the Hindu mind differed in many ways from that posed by previous civilisations and cultures. This was even admitted by the Hindus themselves. In the nineteenth century, some Hindu thinkers observed how even five hundred years of Indo-Muslim rule had not affected Hinduism or Hindu ways of life to the same extent as a century of British rule. In this regard, it can be noted that the Muslim conquest of India was essentially a military one, producing no fundamental change in respect of the economy, society, polity, and culture. In contrast, the British carried strong ideological baggage, with roots in developments in early modern Europe. For instance, rightly or wrongly, they believed that modernity was a course of historical development that every society was bound to follow, and that Providence had ruled that the developed nations of Europe should work to elevate the 'benighted' nations of Asia and Africa in the scale of human civilisation. British colonialists used this argument to legitimise their control over Indians and their interventions in social and religious matters concerning Indian subjects.

This book is primarily concerned with the Hindus of British India, not those inhabiting states ruled by native rulers or princes. However, it is important to make a passing reference to the implications for the social experience of the Hindus entailed by this political distinction. On the whole, something like a social or religious reformation occurred in the native states without much opposition from the Hindus. Some Indian states were able to introduce social legislation earlier and with greater success than were British Indian legislatures. This, as we shall have occasion to see, is largely explained by the inverse relationship that developed between social and political reforms in British India. Native Indian states were able to control the growth of Indian nationalist sentiments more effectively than the authorities in British India. In the case of the latter, a burgeoning Hindu nationalism stood in the way of the changes contemplated in Hindu social and religious practices. Nationalists distrusted intentions behind British-initiated reform and adopted a far more conservative approach to change in the name of defending tradition.

I take this occasion to express my gratitude to the Oxford Centre for Hindu Studies Continuing Education Department for extending to me the twin invitations to prepare an online course of study on colonial Hinduism (which interested readers may choose to pursue) and to further support this programme by preparing an informative textbook that will suitably equip them for this purpose. I would also be greatly remiss if I failed to thank all those involved in the Oxford Centre for Hindu Studies Mandala Publishing Series for kindly agreeing to publish this monograph.

Needless to say, errors of fact or argument are entirely mine.

Amiya P. Sen
Gurgaon

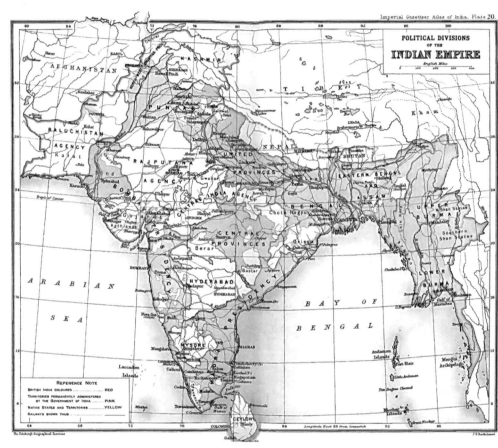

Map of the territory and political divisions of British India.
(Imperial Gazetteer of India, 1909)

INTRODUCTION

It will be useful to open with a brief overview of what this book on 'Colonial Hinduism' aims to study. There is reason to believe, as I consistently argue throughout this book, that an inchoate, amorphous 'Hinduism' did exist even before the consolidation of British colonial rule in India, although it may not have been known by that name. On the other hand, colonialism itself produced changes in Hindu society and culture of a nature and on a scale hitherto unprecedented. Much of Hindu life and thought visible today was vitally shaped during the course of the nineteenth century when colonialism in India was at its peak. By comparison, the Vedic gods and goddesses of antiquity are now either all dead or else forsaken.

Broadly speaking, one may understand colonialism in two related ways. On the one hand, it may be taken to be a system aimed at exploiting India's material resources by an invading, alien power, to its own advantage. Earlier in its history, India had been conquered, albeit only partially and for brief periods, by other invaders, for instance the Greeks, Scythians, Turks, Pathans, and Mughals. Of these, the Mughals were able to rule the Indian subcontinent the longest and over much of its territory, but they eventually ceded political and military control to the European powers who had settled in India. The original objective before these European powers was securing profits from trade and commerce, mainly through the export of Indian cottons and other raw materials to Europe. This trade was a source of great profit to the various European mercantile companies carrying out brisk trade with India. It eventually also determined the context of the British conquest of India for traders: chiefly, the British soon came to realise that commercial gains were best gained through assuming military control over a politically fragmented or disunited country. This, they were progressively able to secure through superior military skills and weaponry, as well as new forms of commercial enterprise and organisation.

Importantly enough, none of the early invaders converted their Indian empire into a colony or subjected the conquered people to a system of rigorous colonial exploitation, primarily because their objectives were very different. Whereas earlier invaders had treated land as the chief economic resource, European traders paid greater attention to trade and manufacture. This shift in the nature of enterprise or attention is best understood in the light of the extremely important historical changes that had occurred in Western Europe in the course of the seventeenth and eighteenth centuries. In Britain, for example, in a series of successive revolutions, an agrarian revolution fed into a commercial revolution and, eventually, the well-known Industrial Revolution. British markets expanded and so did the human population. New machines that had been put in place by the eighteenth century and that replaced human labour required a regular availability of raw material and overseas markets as potential consumers of British manufactured goods.

The British colonisation of India was an exploitative system which the conquering British imposed upon the Indians primarily to meet conditions growing out of the new economic and commercial system. This was characterised by complex and multiple processes of exploitation. This included, in the first place, capturing Indian markets for the forced sale of British manufactured goods, subordinating Indian agriculture, commerce, and industry to the interests of the British Empire, and transferring very large sums of Indian revenue to finance British enterprise back home. India was systematically drained of its wealth solely in order that a greater political, military, economic, and financial control could be maintained over it by an alien power. It was made to pay for its own enforced occupation by a colonising power. The Mughals, who ruled the subcontinent over 200 years, did not similarly impoverish the country. Under their rule Indian revenues were ploughed back into the Indian economy itself.

The second way of viewing colonialism is as the production of an ideology or a body of thought that facilitated this very process of exploitation. To put it bluntly, it relied on creating and disseminating a cultural system which only helped legitimise domination in the name of bringing modernity and progress to an allegedly 'benighted' people. The colonisers were quick to realise that only after Indians grew sufficiently familiar with the English language, habits, and ways of life could they be expected to patronise English products imported from the manufacturing centres of Birmingham, Manchester, and Lancashire. Only after Indians were persuaded to acknowledge the moral and intellectual 'superiority' of the West could they be better persuaded to accept that British rule was, by its very nature and intentions, enlightened and emancipating. In colonial India, the spread of English education and its ready acceptance by a section of the native population helped considerably to justify and strengthen colonial rule in India. There was a substantial body of educated, upper-class Indians who supported the idea of continued British rule and collaborated with the British ruling class in matters of everyday governance. This, in turn, produced internal complexities in the way Indians understood the nature of colonial rule.

This book is concerned primarily with the second of the two aspects outlined above, which we shall seek to understand by critically examining the unique moral and material challenges presented by the contemporary West to the Indian mind in the nineteenth century and the Indian responses to them. Seen from this perspective, colonial Hinduism does seem to represent an indigenous discourse, both accepting and contesting certain new ideas and values following from the Western cultural and ideological presence in India. In the Indian context, as we shall consistently argue, religion often became the site of the sharpest and most animated debates affecting the lives of colonised Hindus. Often a 'reformed' Hinduism was taken to be the very foundation of a modern Hindu identity.

As the numerically largest religious community in India and the first to constitute a modern Asian intelligentsia, the Hindus naturally represent an important object of study within the history of this region. Of the several religious communities in South Asia, the Hindus were the first to develop an acute sense of self-reflexivity and the willingness to take on board the significant social, economic, and political changes occurring around them. Even under Indo-Muslim rule, they had shown a strong cultural and professional adaptability to altered ways of life. Mughal revenue offices were thronged by certain Hindu castes and, until such time as Persian was derecognised as the official language for administrative purposes by the British, Hindus readily adopted the language their rulers enforced.

The Muslims, by comparison, were much slower to adapt themselves to the consolidation of British rule and, for a long time, even actively opposed both the transfer of political power in the subcontinent and the institutions of new learning. Here, it is important to note that modernisation among Muslims had to carefully tread two related paths. On one level, it had to adapt to accepting the moral and material benefits that accrued from associating themselves with the new political order. After the 1830s, knowledge of the English language and continuing exhibitions of loyalty to the English were effective ways of surviving and succeeding in an otherwise hostile and competitive world. On another level, Muslims were also forced to more clearly define their cultural and religious identity, especially in relation to the numerically dominant and professionally more successful Hindus. This followed from the fact that a large percentage of Indian Muslims, especially in areas like Bengal or Bihar, were converts from either Hinduism or Buddhism. Hence, a fundamental problem that arose for this community by the late nineteenth century was that of purging Islamic thought and practice of 'un-Islamic' influences that had been disseminated through their Hindu neighbours. An identical problem was to later confront the Sikhs in relation to Hindus. For the Hindus, on the other hand, ushering in modern changes was more a matter of critical reflection on the self and negotiating the new 'other', represented by the British ruling class. Rightly or wrongly, in the nineteenth century several Hindus were heard to say how even 500 years of Muslim rule had failed to stir them as intellectually or culturally as British colonial rule had within 100 years of its inception. Colonial Hinduism was the product of intense, internally generated debates within the Hindu community itself with little or no reference to other religious communities. The enemy in this case was seen to lie within the community and not outside.

This book invites you to understand the Hinduism of the colonial era not simply as a new religious system but also as the cultural and political self-expression of colonised Hindus, trying to defend themselves against powerful, alien, and alienating influences. It speaks of how, inspired and deeply influenced by modern Western notions of nationalism and the rights of self-determination, educated Hindus began to draw points of comparison between their 'glorious' past and their 'depressing' present, in which they had been placed under great duress. In looking back at their past, whether real or imagined, they discovered a new pride in race and ways to combat their moral guilt at being subjugated. They similarly began to resent the act of political subjugation itself. It was thus that the new Western-educated Hindu intelligentsia realised that the most effective way of meeting modern-day challenges was to modernise Hinduism itself. In circumstances in which they had been deprived of political or economic power, forging some sense of cultural and religious unity seemingly held out new promises. For it was only a reformed faith, cleansed of its irrationalities and superstitions, that could effectively speak for a subjugated yet proud people, provide them with a new identity suited to modern-day challenges, and enable an ancient civilisation to secure a firm foothold in a rapidly changing world.

Hinduism: Conceptual and Historical Problems of Definition

Currently, the term 'Hinduism' is taken to denote the religion followed by people who call themselves 'Hindus'. However, this was not always the case. Evidently, the term 'Hinduism' originates in the English language, so it follows that the term had to have been invented either by the English themselves or else by English-educated Hindus. In either case, this could equally be a convenient designation used by the English for a religious community in India for which such a general designation was needed, or a new manner of self-description for English-educated Hindus. Now, the English presence in India, though visible even in the seventeenth century, became numerically and politically significant only about 200 years later. Also, since the term 'Hinduism' is a manner of description it has to be assumed that, regardless of who put it into common use, it must have originated in a specific historical context and determined by certain emerging social and cultural needs. In this chapter it will be argued that pre-modern Hindus had no concept resembling 'Hinduism' nor, apparently, any need for it. That a new self-definition became necessary under the conditions imposed by colonial rule cannot be doubted, and the invention or the increasing use of the term 'Hinduism' would just as well reflect this change. However, this is very different from the argument, advanced by some scholars, that 'Hinduism', i.e. the religion of the Hindus, was born only in the nineteenth century, making it perhaps the youngest of world religions. We must not confuse fact with concept. Admittedly, 'Hinduism' was not a convenient shorthand that pre-modern Hindus employed to describe their religious beliefs or practices, but this should not lead us to the conclusion that these Hindus altogether lacked a religious world which they could call their own. This chapter will also try to demonstrate that pre-modern Hindus had not developed a concrete or deterministic notion of society and culture in which religion itself was understood as distinct from other aspects of human life. Sometime in the 1880s, Bankimchandra Chattopadhyay (1838–1894), a prominent thinker and author from colonial Bengal, was to write thus to a friend:

> With other people religion was only a part of life; there are things religious and there are things lay and secular. To the Hindu his whole life was religion. To the Euro-

pean, his relations to God and to the spiritual world are things sharply distinguished from his relations to man and to the temporal world. To the Hindu, his relations to God and his relations to man and to the temporal world are incapable of being so distinguished. They form one compact and harmonious whole . . . . All life to him was religious and religions never received a name from him, because it had never for him an existence apart from all that had received a name.[1]

The same letter goes on to argue how, in all the historical and literary records of pre-Muslim India, there were no references to either the word 'Hindu' or the expression 'Hindu religion'. It would be wrong to infer from this, as Chattopadhyay warns us, that there were no Hindus in pre-Muslim India or that they had no religious life worth the name. Such an inference, he sarcastically comments, would be comparable to that drawn by the early Englishman in India who, failing to find an exact parallel to the word 'gratitude' in the Bengali language, concluded that the people who spoke that language must be unfamiliar with that human virtue itself![2]

With respect to Hinduism, an equally apt example is the use of the commonplace term 'reform'. This argument will be further developed later, but a brief reference here will not be out of place. In the nineteenth century, the term 'reform' was generally taken to indicate progressive and positive changes introduced into contemporary thought or practice. Now, there is reason to believe that the equivalents of this term in

---

1 Bankimchandra Chattopadhyay, *Letters on Hinduism* (c. 1882). Reproduced in *Bankim Rachanavali* (*Collected Works of Bankimchandra*), vol. III, ed. Jogesh Chandra (Calcutta Sahitya Samsad, 1969), 230.

2 Ibid., 230.

Indian languages began to be used only during the nineteenth century. Should this, then, suggest that pre-nineteenth-century Hindus lacked the concept of reform or even the intentionality of change? Prima facie, this would be belied by the several dissenting social and religious movements which had occurred in India since the days of the Buddha and Mahavira and which aimed at introducing important and radical changes in the ways in which people were accustomed to look at God, and at their fellow humans.

Speaking of the origins of the term 'Hinduism' naturally suggests a specific time frame. It was certainly not in use in the early years of the eighteenth century when the English were just emerging as the new rulers of India, supplanting a weakening Indo-Muslim rule. At the time, the English language was not commonly used by Indians for it served no important or practical functions. But these conditions had visibly changed by the early nineteenth century, when British political power in India was firmly in place and institutions of new learning were beginning to replace the old.

The British East India Company decided to assume the political and administrative responsibility of ruling India by the end of the eighteenth century; understandably, this led to important shifts in official policy. New rules of governance required the use of new skills and strategies through which to retain territorial control and effectively administer the Indian people. Confronted with the vast diversity in Indian life, the new rulers increasingly found it useful to resort to an aggregation of castes and communities, of social and cultural habits, of trades and occupations, of bodily frames and character in order to make governance relatively easier. By the 1870s, the colonial state had introduced the census in India, which not only provided a great mass of vitally useful information but also significantly shaped future administrative policy. It is reasonable to assume that bracketing social groups or communities under one descriptive label encouraged the ruling class to assume certain qualities about their subjects: it suited European officials, merchants, and missionaries to assume that Hindus had to be idolatrous by habit or that all idolaters would justly qualify to be called Hindus.

For a long time, the ways in which the British ruling class observed or understood India and Indians were fashioned by their own knowledge and experiences back in Britain. In other words, they tended to judge or evaluate Indian life through categories of understanding that they were familiar with in their own societies. For example, European missionaries and other peoples who worked in India were prone to understand Indian religions through biblical terms of reference. However, over time, closer observation and greater acquaintance with the particularities of Indian life made them rethink and modify these categories. They soon realised that Western institutions could not easily be replicated in India, and when wrongly introduced could produce misleading or undesirable results. Indian society, therefore, had to be understood on its own terms and administered largely in the light of established local traditions. One aspect of this life, which they acknowledged as important but initially failed to comprehend, was religion.

Religio, Religare, and Religion

The term 'religion' is now commonly used in both academic practice and everyday conversation. However, the meaning and application of the word have undergone significant changes over time. 'Religion' is derived from the Latin *religio*; it first designated an inherited cultural tradition comprising rites and rituals that came naturally to people. This is the sense in which the Roman scholar Marcus Tulius Cicero (*c.* second century BCE) appears to have used it. However, the meaning and understanding attached to the term radically changed in

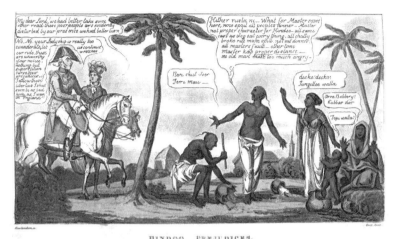

An early nineteenth-century satirical etching of Governor General and Lady Hastings encountering Hindus.

the early years of the Christian era, as best evidenced in the views of Lucius Caecilius Lactantius (*c.* third century CE), a Christian apologist and adviser to the Emperor Constantine. Lactantius claimed that *religio* itself was derived from *religare*, 'to bind together'; thus the act of binding was based on an uncompromising worship of the 'True' religion as distinguished from the 'false' worship of pagan ritualism and superstition. Implicitly, this posited the view that there could be only one 'True God' whom alone men and women were obliged to worship. Hereafter, *religio* began to be treated as a covenant between God and humankind; 'religion', a term derived from *religio/religare*, became a matter of following a particular set of beliefs and doctrines identified with Christianity.

This eventually led to another important development. Since faith now revolved around a particular set of doctrines, the 'correct' interpretation of these doctrines became crucial, leading to a new emphasis on texts and commentaries subsequently written on these texts. The European Reformation of the sixteenth century strengthened both of these tendencies, and over time they were considerably intensified by the success of print culture, which popularised both the act of pious reading and the notion of an infallible 'Scripture'.

It is not at all difficult to see the connection between such developments occurring in Europe and those in India. Since missionaries coming to India, and the British ruling class itself, were predominantly associated with the Anglican Church, certain notions about God and religion visibly coloured their assessment and understanding of Indian religious life. For instance, it was quite natural for them to compare Hindu idolatry to pagan practices, which they named 'heathenism'. In 1729 the Vicar of Beenham in Berkshire (England), the Reverend Thomas Stackhouse, devoted an entire section to 'heathen idolatry' within a huge compendium on religious practices outside Christian Europe called *A Compleat Body of Speculative and Practical Divinity*. In works of this genre, the power and influence of brahmin priests in India were compared with the 'tyrannical' hold that the early medieval church and papacy had over common Christians. Influenced by the institutions and religious culture of post-Reformation Europe, it was assumed that Indian religious communities, too, had to be defined in relation to their belief in a single God, a central organisation, a historical founder, and a common scripture. That they did not find these to actually apply to a vast majority of Hindus caused no small confusion.

Compared to the religion of the Hindus, Islam was relatively easier to understand. For one thing, being a Semitic religion, it shared many traits with Judaism and Christianity familiar to Europeans travellers to India: traders, missionaries, and Company officials. In contrast, the problems with understanding the Hindus were manifold. As early European accounts of India bear out, the Hindus, quite puzzlingly, appeared to be both monotheists and polytheists. While many of them endorsed the idea of an absolute Supreme Being, in practice they were found to worship multiple gods and goddesses. What added to the confusion was the discovery that these divinities could be said to be both formless and endowed with form; they were believed to carry human attributes but also taken to be without them. Europeans were indeed intrigued by the discovery that within the religion of the Hindus there was space for both a personal god, to whom a devotee could relate in everyday life, and an Impersonal Being, who was the object of purely meditative and mystical contemplation. Many Hindus appeared to frequently visit temples and travel on old pilgrim trails, but others lived for long periods in enforced isolation, hidden in dense forests and inaccessible mountain caves, entirely dissociated from public life and apparently following no common religious rules. Europeans also noticed how Hindus would identify themselves with a particular religious cult and uphold the cultic deity to be supreme yet worship other deities, even those considered to be relatively inferior in status. Quite clearly, early Europeans in India failed to understand how, within a given religion, there could be such baffling diversity.

Our underlying argument is that the Western understanding and use of the term 'religion' is inept and inadequate in fathoming the ways in which Hindus conceived their religion. Here we should be aware that all religions are known to evolve and change over time. A once-unified religion may quite easily take multiple forms, possibly as part of a historical process. Even world religions like Christianity, Islam, or Buddhism are not exceptions to this rule. However, this situation is distinct from that of a religious and cultural system which was plural and somewhat indeterminate in conception, even to begin with. Early Indic religion, including

Brahmanism and Jainism, reveals a philosophical inexactitude and an open-ended approach to Truth which allowed the possibility of perceiving Truth itself in multiple ways. This is clearly distinguishable from the firmness or inflexibility with which Western civilisations drew boundaries around religion and religious life. A verse in the *Rig Veda,* the oldest surviving text to originate in the Indian subcontinent, reads: *ekam sad, vipra bahudha vadanti,* which translates as 'Truth is One though the wise conceive it in plural ways' (*Rig Veda* I.164.46).

AN ARRAY OF CONFLICTING PERCEPTIONS

The interesting feature to emerge from a review of the literature related to Hinduism in the last 200 years is the air of recurring debate and difference that characterised it. Prima facie, such differences appear to have affected the understanding of both Europeans and Indians, whether belonging to the academic world or outside.

In 1970, the British historian of modern India Peter Marshall edited an important collection of eight essays, originally appearing between the years 1767 and 1790, which in his opinion point to the British 'discovering' Hinduism in the eighteenth century.[3] Some forty years later, an Australia-based scholar, Geoffrey A. Oddie, was constrained to speak in a very different way. Curiously, Oddie speaks of an 'imagined' Hinduism.[4] Admittedly, this represents an important paradigm shift in our understanding of just how non-Hindus related to

---

3 P. J. Marshall (ed.), *The British Discovery of Hinduism in the Eighteenth Century* (Cambridge: Cambridge University Press, 1970).

4 Geoffrey A. Oddie, *Imagined Hinduism: British Protestant Missionary Constructions of Hinduism, 1793–1900* (California and London: Sage, 2006).

Hindus. However, such acute differences may also be detected earlier and outside the world of scholarship. We have noted above how Europeans, regardless of whether or not they visited India, assumed that all those who called themselves Hindus must be organically related by ties of religious belief or practice. To a great extent, as also earlier noticed, they were predisposed to do so, given their own knowledge and experiences. However, the assumption that Hindus must be willing participants in an organically unified religious system became increasingly difficult to sustain in the light of greater social exposure and closer observation. Even Christian evangelists working in India, and otherwise united in their objective to win over Indian converts, did not always share the same opinion about just what constituted Hinduism. Two instances may be cited here to illustrate our point.

First, missionaries working in various parts of India often came upon mutually conflicting facts or observations. Some among them argued that Hinduism was essentially a system dominated by brahmins, who were experts in the matter of religious knowledge and in the performance of everyday ritual practices, but others were quick to notice that there also existed a popular Hinduism which did not always conform to Brahmanical beliefs or practices. Quite evidently, the lower castes or classes appeared to worship a very different set of deities and even followed a discernibly different ritual calendar. While evangelists working in Bengal or more generally in north India took Hinduism to be philosophically dominated by the school of Vedanta, or pantheism,[5] as they loosely called it, this was actively contested by those stationed elsewhere. In southern India, for instance, Bishop Robert

---

5   A term first coined by the Irish thinker, John Toland (1670–1722), author of the work *Christianity Not Mysterious* (1696).

Caldwell (1814–1891) doubted if even a small percentage of the local population were at all familiar with that school of thought. Others, who had a deep acquaintance with local languages of the south like Tamil or Telegu, disagreed with the claim, strongly put forward in the late eighteenth century by Orientalist scholars like Sir William Jones (1746–1794), that the entire religious world of the Hindus was contained within Sanskrit scholarship. A British civilian based in Madras, Francis Whyte Ellis (1770–1819), showed that the grammar of Tamil, spoken by a good percentage of people in the region, was very different from that of Sanskrit. This dismantled the theory, strongly advocated by Jones, that the unity of Hindu religious culture could be understood through the scholarly use of philological tools or language structures.

No less interesting are the differences of opinion on this issue that began to surface among modern Indians. The well-known social and religious reformer Raja Rammohun Roy (1772–1833), who is examined in greater detail in the next chapter, insisted on the inner unity (*ekavakyata*) of all Hindu scripture; the following passage is an apt example:

> the explanation of the Veda and of its commentators must either be admitted as sufficiently reconciling the apparent contradictions or must not be admitted at all. In the latter case, the Veda must necessarily be supposed to be inconsistent with itself and therefore altogether unintelligible, which is directly contrary to the faith of the Hindu of every description.[6]

---

6 Rammohun Roy, 'A Defense of Hindu Theism' (1817), in *The English Works of Rammohun Roy*, ed. Kalidas Nag and Debajyoti Burman, vol. 2 (Calcutta, 1946), 89.

Only about ten years after the Raja prematurely died in Bristol, the Brahmo Samaj, a reformist body that he had created, was rocked by a controversy surrounding the issue of *pramana*, or authority in religious life. Some members of this body, deeply influenced by the deism and scientific rationalism of post-Enlightenment Europe, refused to accept that the Vedas, hitherto revered by the Hindus as their authoritative scripture, could be justly regarded as revealed and infallible. By 1850, the Brahmo Samaj, which then best represented Hindu reformism, renounced faith in the Vedas as an unquestionable source of spiritual wisdom. Instead, the Brahmos decided on putting together their own source-book. On one level, this destroyed the perceived unity of all Hindu religious thought and practice and, at the time, would have surprised non-Hindus no less than Hindus themselves.

Hindooism (Hinduism), or What's in a Name?

The word 'Hindoo', as 'Hindu' was commonly spelt earlier, has a long history. It occurs in the *Zend Avesta*, the holy book of the Zoroastrians of ancient Iran, and in inscriptions of the Persian king Darius, who ruled in the pre-Christian era. It does appear as though in their drive towards the Indian subcontinent, the ancient Persians had crossed the river Indus, then known as the Sindhu, literally meaning 'great body of water', rendered in ancient Persian as 'Hindoo'/'Hindu'. By this term the ancient Persians, and after them the Greeks and Armenians, denoted a region and a people inhabiting the eastern banks of the Indus with whom they were only briefly familiar. At the time, therefore, the word 'Hindu' was a geo-ethnic category. The early Arabs, who had productive trade links with India, partly inherited this name and called the land al-Hind.

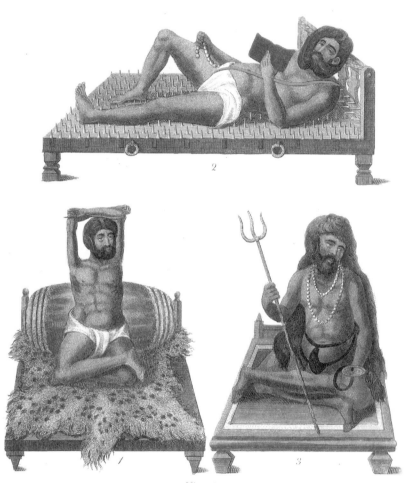

1.Parana Poori, an Oordhbahu Saniassy. 2.Purrum Soatuntr Perkasanund, a Ser-seja Saniassy. 3. A Yfogee.

An engraving of three Hindu ascetics, 1809.

An early nineteenth-century depiction of Charak Puja, or 'the hook-swinging festival,' that became an object of colonial scorn.

Until quite recently, it was generally believed that the first person to invent or use the word 'Hinduism' was Rammohun Roy sometime around 1816/1817. Within academia, this has had the effect of upholding the thesis that the term originated as a form of self-description for educated, upper-class Hindus. In 2006, Geoffrey A. Oddie, mentioned earlier, suggested that the term was first used in 1787 by Charles Grant (1746–1823), a British politician associated with the English East India Company, in his correspondence with friends Thomas Raitus and John Thomas, both located in England. The term, we are further informed, was meant to be a useful shorthand for slightly longer expressions like 'Hindoo religion' or 'Hindoo creed'. The important thing here, though, is that Grant's correspondents were expected to understand the meaning or import of the term. This, in itself, may speak for the state of mind among the contemporary British, whether based in India or in Britain, with regard to the religion of the Hindus.

Be this as it may, it is clear that Rammohun's use of the term had a more direct impact on posterity. Between 1818 and 1877 there were at least eight references to it on various platforms, both journalistic and quasi-academic. It appeared in the *Asiatic Journal and Monthly Register*, a journal published from Calcutta, in 1818, and in the *Asiatic Researches*, also published from Calcutta, in 1820; in 1829 and 1831 it was used by the Scottish missionary Alexander Duff (1806–1878); it appeared in the *Oxford English Dictionary* in 1829; and it was used by Friedrich Max Müller (1823–1900) in 1858 and by Sir Monier Monier-Williams (1819–1899) in 1877. The 1820 essay, published in the *Asiatic Researches* by one John Crawfurd (1783–1868), a Scottish physician and colonial administrator, is particularly interesting since it employed the term 'Hinduism' in relation to the religious beliefs of a certain section of the Balinese people who were not Indians either in terms of their ethnicity or geographical location. If anything, this suggests that by Crawfurd's time, the term Hindu was not simply a geo-ethnic term related to a community or a specific locale but also a religious and cultural system.

HINDUISM: THE 'CONSTRUCTIONIST' VIEW AND ITS CRITICS

It is commonplace that in the social sciences, intellectual and interpretative trends often reflect changing political moods. In the past many cultures were preoccupied with locating unity even within visible streams of diversity. This was typically the case in the nineteenth and early twentieth centuries, when people in many colonised countries were deeply affected by the new ideologies of democracy and self-determination. In colonial India itself, this sentiment was deliberately used to project a deep-rooted and long-standing political unity within the Indian peoples capable of fighting British imperialism and colonialism. Quite conveniently, this glossed over the fact that there were many frictions and fissures underneath this proclaimed unity. In truth, not all sections of the Indian people openly or equally shared the nationalist sentiment and their approaches or choices were often determined by their specific class or community interests.

Such moods or approaches changed in a post-colonial world. Rather than treat nationalism or the nation-state like a powerful ideological juggernaut that rode roughshod over small, dissenting voices, people preferred to adopt a more pluralist approach rooted in the complex multiplicities of everyday life. Thus, the local and the provincial now became important in the study of politics compared with larger political formations. Small was now seen as more beautiful, imposing structures as authoritarian, exclusionary, and ugly. Something similar occurred also in the field of cultural and religious studies. The concept of an old and unified Hinduism eventually gave way to more critical views which challenged both the antiquity of the religious and cultural system known as Hinduism as well as the view that it had a long or continued historical existence. In recent times, this view has been identified, for lack of a better expression, with the 'constructionist' view. This view was so called because its underlying argument was that the religious complex given the name 'Hinduism' was not something that naturally evolved over time but was synthetically and hastily constructed in response to certain pressing cultural and political needs. Importantly, too, these needs were seen to originate in concerns that were not really religious in character. Though originating in the West, this view has also had many Indian supporters.

This critique is generally believed to have originated in a seminal work of the Canadian scholar of comparative religion W. C. Smith (1916–2000) called *The Meaning and End of Religion: A New Approach to the Religious Traditions of Mankind* (1962). In this work, Smith was able to demonstrate how the concept of 'religion' did not always aptly define a community of believers, if only for the reason that the concept itself was European in origin and really had no corresponding term in non-European cultures. Terms like Buddhism, Hinduism, Confucianism, and Shintoism were all invented in modern times and by people who were not known to be their practitioners. Even Christianity and Judaism acquired these names from outside their own traditions. The only exception, as Smith rightly argued, was Islam, which was a term that occurs in the Quran itself and was not invented by a non-Muslim. At the time Smith was writing, he would not have known that the Hindu Rammohun had also used the term 'Hinduism' fairly early. Even so, as now proven by recent research, the fact remains that it was used even earlier by certain British men, and it is not certain if Rammohun arrived at the term independently of these influences.

What, in essence, is the constructionist argument? Of the many scholars who support this line of interpretation, a representative example is the 1995 essay by the German Indologist Heinrich von Stietencron (1933–2018). Based on the study of a Shaiva text from early medieval Kashmir, the *Somashambhupaddhati*, Stietencron argues that:

> Hinduism . . . is really a label surreptitiously foisted upon what is essentially a loose collection of discrete, sectarian cults which, in thought and practice, were far removed from one another. The text in question, we are told, upheld a particular cultic god and came down heavily upon those located outside the cult. Liberation was assured only to those who worshipped Shiva in a particular ritual form.[7]

Prima facie, it is difficult to deny that sectarian conflict has been a recurring feature in the religious life of South Asia, on occasions even leading to violence and loss of life. In 1790, for instance, at the Kumbh gathering held every six years at Nashik (in Maharashtra), as many as 12,000 Shaiva (Naga) and Vaishnava ascetics lost their lives, battling over the first right to take a holy bath in the local river. According

---

7   Heinrich von Stietencron, 'Religious Configurations in pre-Muslim India and the Modern Concept of Hinduism', in *Representing Hinduism: The Construction of Religious Traditions and National Identity*, ed. Vasudha Dalmia and Heinrich von Stietencron (New Delhi: Sage Publications, 1995).

to newspaper reports, acute differences broke out between the two communities as late as 2015. In eighteenth-century Bengal, Vaishnavas desisted from using the word *kali* (Bengali for ink) because this reminded them of the fearsome Shakta goddess Kali. They preferred to use the Persian word *syahi* instead. Writing in the 1880s, Bankimchandra Chattopadhyay, referred to earlier, observed that there was greater affinity between Islam and Christianity than between Shaktas (worshippers of the Goddess) and Vaishnavas (votaries of Vishnu).[8] He also observed that the tendency to use a common descriptive term for Hindus arose from the fact that internal differences in thought or practice within the religion practiced by Hindus were imperceptible to non-Hindus. Hence, it could very well be the case that the British inherited some incorrect assumptions about Hindus from the Indo-Muslim rulers who preceded them.[9] When arguing this, Bankimchandra evidently had a specific purpose: he wanted to draw a distinction between the 'authentic', qualitatively superior Hinduism as practised by the upper castes or classes and that practised by the common people, which, in his understanding, was no more than 'rubbish accumulated over ages'. In the face of hostile criticism of Hinduism from colonial officials and missionaries, it was his intention (and that of men belonging to his class) to argue that what was commonly seen to be a part of Hinduism did not actually belong to it.

Importantly, Bankimchandra adds that there was just as much truth behind the common appellation 'Hinduism' as there was error. The use of the term 'Hinduism' could

---

8   Chattopadhyay, *Letters on Hinduism*, 230.

9   Ibid., 231.

draw some justification from the fact that, notwithstanding immense variety in thought or practice, the various Hindu sects originated in a common body of thought. This explained some important doctrinal similarities between them. That apart, their most revered scriptures were all written in a common language, Sanskrit, and were the work of a special sacerdotal class. In a sense this reiterates the position adopted by the Orientalist Horace Hayman Wilson (1786–1860), who, in his well-known work *Sketch on the Religious Sects of the Hindus* (1828, 1832), noted how, even when the expression 'Hindoo religion' was used in a collective sense to describe the worship of an immensely diverse range of divinities, there was a kind of unity that straddled this.

In Bankimchandra's analysis, the difficulty in separating the grain from the chaff lay in the fact that over time matters like Hindu social usage or ethics were also mistakenly put on the level of scripture. 'Everything Hindu', he complained, 'was merged into that whirlpool of things – the Hindu religion'.[10] Bankimchandra concluded on the note that, as a religion, Hinduism had both fixed and immutable principles that were good for all ages – the 'eternal verities', as he called them – as well as mutating beliefs and practices which arrived and went away over time. From this it followed that an analytical distinction between the two was vital to the project of defining true and authentic Hinduism.

Arguments matching the 'constructionist' view were qualified in other ways by near contemporaries of Bankimchandra. In 1893, Guru Prosad Sen (1842–1900), an influential writer of the time, argued that Hinduism was more a social than religious organisation and that, so long as a Hindu followed certain social rules related to caste or

---

10 Ibid., 233.

ritual conformity, it did not really matter just where his faith lay.[11] This echoes the verses attributed to the Hindu yogi and mystic Gorakhnath (*c.* eleventh century CE): 'I am a Hindu by birth, I am a yogi in my maturity, and by intellect I am a Muslim. Recognise, oh Kazis and Mullahs, the path accepted by Brahma, Vishnu, and Maheshvara.'[12] Even the Christian evangelist John Nicol Farquhar (1861–1929) was to observe:

> Although Hinduism has many gods, many theologies and many sacred books, a man may remain an orthodox Hindu without believing in any god or any theology and without acknowledging a single sacred book . . . .
> The divinities thus reverenced vary all over India, there is no uniformity. Nor are there any theological conceptions he need hold: an orthodox Hindu may be an atheist, an agnostic or Christian in his conception of the world.[13]

If anything, this confirms the doctrinal flexibility within Hinduism and helps us to understand better why, in actual practice, the religion of the Hindus could have been a loose conglomeration of beliefs and practice until this was deliberately changed with the advent of colonial Hinduism. It was more suited to be called an orthopraxy than an orthodoxy.

In recent times, the critique of the constructionist view is best represented in the writings of the scholar of religious

---

11 Guru Prosad Sen, *An Introduction to the Study of Hinduism* (Calcutta: Thacker, Spink, and Co., 1893).

12 *Gorakh Bani*, ed. Pitambardutta Barthwal (Allahabad : Hindi Sahitya Sammelam, 2004), 26.

13 J. N. Farquhar, *The Primer of Hinduism* (London: Oxford University Press, 1911), 150.

studies David N. Lorenzen. In an essay titled 'Who Invented Hinduism?', originally published in 1999 and republished since, Lorenzen makes a series of critical points. First, why, if the term 'Hindu' is merely a geographical term, were Muslim invaders in India or their descendants not also known by the term 'Hindu'? Lorenzen's argument alerts us to the possibility that the tendency manifest in political Hinduism (Hindutva) since the 1940s to manipulatively identify all inhabitants of India as Hindus may have been built on an older argument. It is partly because older commentators found geographical location to be such an important marker of Hindu identity that ideologues like Vinayak Damodar Savarkar (1883–1966), considered the progenitor of political Hinduism, insisted that non-Hindus, too, be made to identify themselves with a common 'holy land' called Bharata or India.

The related question, so far without a satisfactory answer, is why the Hindus chose to call Muslim invaders by their ethnic labels such as the Tazik, Turushka, Parasika, or Yavana, and not the religious label 'Muslim' or 'Islam'. This is especially true of Sanskrit literature. The historian of early medieval India B. D. Chattopadhayay lists at least seventy-five Sanskrit references to Muslims but only one uses the term 'Mussalmana'. In Guru Prosad Sen's understanding, this was primarily because the Hindus never quarrelled with the religious beliefs of others nor enquired into these. For the Hindu, as Sen argues, the more important question was whether a person was religious (*astika*), not the nature of their religious affiliation. The tenth-century Hindu religious classic the *Bhagavata Purana* argued that devotional culture had the potency to liberate all people, even 'barbaric' tribes such as Shakas, Kiratas, Hunas, or Pulindas, not to speak of socially marginalised Hindus. The researches of Joseph Thomas O'Connell (1940–2012) establish the fact that in Vaishnava hagiographies from medieval Bengal, the use of the term 'Hindu' occurs clearly in only confrontational contexts. I have myself found references to the term 'Hinduyani' ('the Hindu identity or culture') in Krishnadas Kaviraj's early seventeenth-century Vaishnava text the *Chaitanya Charitamrita*, which recounts how the Muslim Kazi of Nadia (Nadia was the birthplace of the Vaishnava saint and mystic, Krishna Chaitanya (1486–1533)) issued an order prohibiting all religious processions organised by the Vaishnava-Hindus.

By comparison, the polemical use of the word 'Hindu' is indeed much more pronounced in the vernacular literature of India, for two possible historical reasons. In the first place, vernacular literatures showed a spectacular growth and development from about the fifteenth century and more accurately portrayed changing social and cultural sensibilities. Second, the growth of vernacular literature more closely corresponds to the consolidation of Turkish rule in North India. Lorenzen cites the instances of the mystic poet Kabir, from Benares, Tukaram, from Maharashtra, and Vidyapati, from the Maithili-speaking region in eastern India, to demonstrate how Hindus progressively developed a sense of the Muslims being a religious community different from their own. While Kabir and Eknath (from Maharashtra) show some disenchantment at how Hindus and Turks are equally misled by a sense of religious self-righteousness or dogmatism, Vidyapati's *Kirtilata* (*c.* fifteenth century) actually reports acts of cultural violence perpetrated by Turks on Hindus, especially on the brahmin caste. The Turks are seen to destroy Hindu temples and construct mosques in their place. Arguably, such reporting or representation would not have been possible without some sense of religious boundaries developing in contemporary India. It might not also have escaped the notice of Hindus that their notions of God being present everywhere and in everything could not be reconciled with the Islamic idea of a transcendent God. This would suggest that the religious sense of the word 'Hindu' could have co-existed with the ethnic and the geographical even in pre-modern India.

About a decade after Lorenzen published his work appeared another important contribution to the ensuing debate. In this instance, the emphasis was on researching the intellectual history of Hinduism more than social or political developments within it. In 2010, Andrew J. Nicholson, another scholar of religious studies, ably contested the view that the forging of Hindu unity, whether real or imagined, was a phenomenon unique to colonial India. This directly controverts the view articulated by the literary and cultural historian Vasudha Dalmia that between them, Christian missionary, Orientalist, and Hindu reformist conceptions of Hindu religion and culture coalesced to create notions of a unified Hindu thought and praxis.[14] Nicholson's work demonstrates that the process of unification, at least on the level of thought, was already underway between the twelfth and sixteenth centuries CE. Apparently, this exercise could be carried out without employing a common descriptive terminology for the new religion or philosophy being so fashioned. Understandably, this unity was forged within the world of *astika* philosophy; this had precedents in the way Brahmanism battled the *shramanic* traditions of Buddhism and Jainism, which disregarded the authority of the Vedas. Nicholson attributes the success of this enterprise to the work of the *c.* fifteenth- and sixteenth-century scholar Vijnanabhikshu, who argued that even

---

14 Vasudha Dalmia, 'The Only Real Religion of the Hindus: Vaishnava Self-Representation in the Late Nineteenth Century', in *The Oxford India Hinduism Reader*, ed. Vasudha Dalmia and Heinrich von Stietencron (New Delhi: Oxford University Press, 2007).

The Great Banyan, Sibpur Botanical Gardens, West Bengal.

mutually conflicting Hindu philosophical schools such as the Vedanta and Samkhya could be brought together to produce a higher unity. It is interesting that Vijnanabhikshu, who himself belonged to the *bhedabheda* ('unity in difference') school of the Vedanta, produced a seminal commentary on Patanjali's *Yoga Sutra* (*c.* fifth century CE) and more intangibly influenced the course of Advaita Vedanta (non-dualist Vedanta) in nineteenth- and twentieth-century India.

This line of argument even appears to have influenced some earlier scholars, as, for instance, Julius Lipner, a scholar based in Cambridge (UK) who, quite aptly and evocatively, drew modular parallels between the complex religious structure of Hinduism and the 'Great Banyan': 'Like the (Great Banyan) tree Hinduism is an ancient collection of roots and branches, one indistinguishable from the other, microcosmically polycentric and macrocosmically one, sharing the same regenerative life-sap.'[15] Lipner's work helps us to understand how different religious or philosophical conceptions may originate within the same culture and that we may better understand such complexities if we do not habitually prejudge or predetermine the nature of a religion.

---

15 Julius Lipner, *Hindus: Their Religious Beliefs and Practices* (London: Routledge, 1994), 4–5. There is reason to believe that the metaphor had been used even earlier with similar intentions. Speaking at the Vedanta Society of New York in the early years of the twentieth century, Swami Abhedananda, a brother disciple of Swami Vivekananda of the Ramakrishna Order, said the following: 'It [Hinduism] stands like a huge banyan tree, spreading its far reaching branches over hundreds of sets, creeds and denominations . . . .' Swami Abhedananda, *India and Her People*. New York: The Vedanta Society, 1906, 51.

CONCLUSION

In this chapter we have examined in some detail the following questions:

- What is the historical origin of the terms 'Hindu' and 'Hinduism'?
- Can Hinduism justly be called a religion in the commonly accepted sense of the term?
- Does Hinduism deserve to be treated as a descriptive term for the religious beliefs and practices collectively followed by the Hindus?

At the end of our deliberations it would be reasonable to arrive at the following conclusions:

- The term Hinduism first came into vogue and increasingly appeared in common usage only by the close of the eighteenth century. However, this should not lead us to believe that there was nothing that qualified to be called a religion as practised by the Hindus prior to that time. It would be more correct to say that until the modern era, Hindus did not feel the necessity to conceptualise themselves as a community defined exclusively along religious lines. Historically, the need to do so arose in significantly altered social and cultural circumstances when another community (the Muslims), that was more clearly and self-consciously constituted along religious lines, assumed political power over large parts of the Indian subcontinent. The new ruling class believed in the religious conversion of non-Muslims; this in turn forced the latter to change their approach or strategy in negotiating with the Indo-Muslim state and the Muslim ruling class accordingly. Traditionally, a Hindu was determined by the act of birth. Hinduism itself did not seek to convert non-Hindus in a religious sense. Hindu missionaries, as shown below, did not emerge until about the close of the nineteenth century. The new threats posed by Islam called for greater internal unity among Hindus and the need for a clearer self-understanding and self-definition. It would be only reasonable to say that this process was repeated under British colonial rule, albeit for a somewhat different set of reasons. For one, British India witnessed a greater political, administrative, and economic cohesion and unity. The spread of English as the language of the new Hindu social elite, the rapid success of print culture, and radical improvements in transport and communication greatly facilitated the wider social and cultural unity of the Hindus. The use of the label 'Hinduism' to describe the religion followed by a people anxious to protect their sense of the past and their contemporary identity thus became more pressing under such circumstances.

- Not enough is known about the pre-modern past of the Hindus to definitively conclude that the exclusionary spirit evident in the early medieval text the *Somashambhupaddhati* on which Heinrich Stietencron hangs his thesis typically represented the Hindu's understanding or approach to religion. The discovery of more texts of this genre would be required to radically alter our commonplace perceptions about the pre-modern religion of the Hindus.

- The error underlying the early European characterisation of Indian religious life lay in unimaginatively transplanting Western categories of understanding to Indian conditions. When W. C. Smith argued that Hinduism did not qualify to be called a religion, what he had meant to say was that the category of religion, originating in Western historical experience, could not satisfactorily explain the conceptual categories known to other cultures, as, for instance, Hinduism in India. Pre-modern Hindus clearly did not conceive their religious life in the same way as Europeans. For the former, to provide an apt example, monotheism could well co-exist with polytheism, and a personal god with the abstract and impersonal. Doctrinal diversity, in other words, was always possible within this culture.

• Like every other historical religion, Hinduism has evolved over time; hence, beyond a certain point it is futile trying to separate the 'authentic' from 'accretions' within Hinduism. In the next chapter we shall examine how some colonial Hindus attempted to do precisely that, albeit under certain compelling circumstances. It is undeniable that the way modern Hindus looked at certain important components of their religion and culture was different from that known in pre-modern times. However, this only upholds the view that Hinduism is not so much a given product as a continuing process.

Discussion Topic:
The Construction of Hinduism

• How and why did early European assessments about the religion of the Hindus differ?

• To what extent is the term 'Hinduism' a just descriptive term for the religion of the Hindus?

• What is the 'constructionist' view on the origin and use of the term 'Hinduism'? In what ways did this view depart from the older understanding of the term?

• Why did some scholars come to critique the 'constructionist' view of Hinduism? Do you find such arguments valid?

Further Reading

David Lorenzen. *Who Invented Hinduism?* New Delhi: Yoda Press, 2006 (Chapter 1).

P. J. Marshall. *The British Discovery of Hinduism in the 18th Century.* Cambridge: Cambridge University Press, 1970 (Introduction only).

Arpita Mitra. 'Hinduism' (Historiography). In *Encyclopedia of Hinduism and Tribal Religions*, edited by P. Jain et al. Dordrecht: Springer, 2019.

Brian K. Pennington. *Was Hinduism Invented? Britons, Indians, and the Colonial Construction of Religion.* New York: Oxford University Press, 2005.

Geoffrey A. Oddie. *Imagined Hinduism: British Protestant Missionary Constructions of Hinduism, 1793–1900.* California and London: Sage, 2006 (Introduction and Conclusion).

Raja Rammohun Roy (1772–1883).

I
RAMMOHUN ROY AND THE STIRRINGS OF NEW HINDUISM

This chapter will attempt to understand the crucial changes that began to occur in the everyday life of the Hindu following the establishment of British rule. This will cover the history of early intellectual and cultural exchanges between India and Britain, which produced two overlapping movements: attempts on the part of the British ruling class, first, to understand India's past history and society and to study its people and their manners or habits, and, second, to open up to Indians the scientific and philosophical knowledge of the modern West, the new ways of social and political organisation that had been developing in Europe since the Enlightenment. Understandably enough, this produced a creative response from Indians themselves. Exposure to Western knowledge and ways of life simultaneously produced in them a critical approach to their own history and tradition and an eagerness to imbibe what was good, instructive, and useful in Western societies.

This chapter will examine the following:

- *The intellectual and cultural movement, generally called 'Orientalism', which made a serious attempt to study Indian history and culture, and to introduce these in a meaningful way to interested circles in Europe.* It was this movement that first created a greater awareness among Indians about their own history and an appreciation of the worth of its achievements. In the process, it also awakened in them a sense of urgency to do away with irrational and regressive ideas and institutions and to strengthen all that was good and instructive in their own civilisation.

• *The Indian response to the intellectual and moral challenges presented by the contemporary West.* This relates mainly to the Hindus, who were quicker to awaken and respond to these challenges than the Muslims. In early modern India, the man who most creatively and comprehensively represented this response was Raja Rammohun Roy.

THE NATURE OF CULTURAL CHANGES UNDER BRITISH COLONIAL RULE

One important feature that differentiated British rule in India from the preceding Indo-Muslim rule is that the former invented an ideology or a theory with which to justify their colonial occupation of India. Rightly or wrongly, they associated themselves with a historical mission by virtue of which they claimed to visibly enhance the quality of life in the people over whom they ruled. By comparison, the ruling classes in the pre-modern era ruled the country primarily by virtue of their superior political and military power: they were essentially invaders and political adventurers who left their own homeland in search of better fortunes. India, with its famed riches and persisting pockets of political disunity, consistently attracted this class of men. This perceptible difference in the nature or origin of foreign rule over India was to have an important bearing on the way the Hindus came to perceive pre-British rule and the British. Not surprisingly, for a long time, educated Indians fully believed in the 'civilising mission' that the British claimed to be carrying out in India. A good number of them even took the nature of British rule to be 'providential'.

Allowing for rare exceptions, the preceding Indo-Muslim state had not shown any noticeable inclination to intervene in the social and religious life of the Hindus. Conversion of non-Muslims to Islam was allowed and encouraged, but this was essentially a change of faith without the accompanying intellectual convictions that were new and refreshing in some ways. On this question the approaches of the colonial state and the Christian missionaries working in India were markedly different. Evangelists projected Christianity not only as a superior religion but also as capable of significantly improving a person's moral and intellectual status. For instance, it was argued that embracing Christianity would allow Hindus to free themselves of various kinds of social oppression commonly perpetrated in the name of caste, class, or gender. Though their primary objective was to convert Indians to Christianity, Christian missionaries also believed that a secular, modern education would equally contribute to better prepare Hindus for modern life. In British India, they were at the forefront of an educational movement that included training Indians in both modern Western and Indian knowledge. Through educating the 'native', they hoped to awaken in him or her a new conscience. On its part, the colonial state insisted on a secular education and linked this to the emergence of the modern citizen. The birth of the new Hinduism, it has to be said, owes considerably to both these seemingly different but interrelated influences. From the evangelists, the Hindu learned the virtues of piety, a morally upright life, and the spirit of social service; from the secular education imparted in modern schools and colleges, the importance of education in character building, an honest calling, and the courage and conviction to fight irrationalities, dogma, and superstition.

As suggested in the previous chapter, one of the aspects of Indian life upon which the attention of the ruling class was riveted was religion. The early British response to Hinduism was a mix of curiosity, wonder, and revulsion. The unfamiliar had its own intellectual attraction and many Europeans devoted long years to the study of Hindu religion and culture. At the same time, they also increasingly came to believe in the notion of the 'white man's burden', which assumed that the superior culture of Europe in both religious and secular aspects was morally obligated to free the 'benighted' Hindu from all forms of ignorance and superstition. This naturally required them to go beyond mere curiosity and information seeking to the position of interested and meaningful intervention.

The Hindu nationalist leader Bipinchandra Pal (1858–1932) once observed that the sense of individual liberty and freedom that British rule brought to India could not have survived in the face of orthodox hostility had they not been adequately strengthened by the new public concern with religion. By this he meant that it was the formulation of new and 'reformed' religion, based on a modern concern for reason and social usefulness, that most effectively represented a break with the past. Rammohun Roy, generally taken to be the 'father of modern India', whose life and work is briefly studied here, took religion to be the site of the most fundamental changes for the Hindu.

However, religion was the domain over which the colonial state had gained no direct control – nor did it wish to do so. For a long time, the British chose not to intervene in the religious or cultural practices of their Hindu and Muslim subjects, as a matter of official policy. The legal abolition of cruel social practices, like *sati* (the self-immolation of Hindu widows), had to await important ideological changes within Britain itself and commitment from Indian crusaders like Rammohun himself. Similarly, it was only after 1813, and under considerable pressure from several interested forces in Britain itself, that the government of India allowed Christian missionaries to enter British Indian territories with the aim of religious preaching.

Even so, Hindus could not overlook the recurring criticism that missionaries levelled against certain 'irrational' and 'inhuman' practices that allegedly sullied the name of Hinduism. Short of giving up their ancestral faith and accepting an alien one, Hindus were thus left with two important tasks to accomplish. First, they realised that it would be to their advantage to argue that some ideas or practices that were obviously crude or socially ruinous were inauthentic and did not actually belong to 'true' Hinduism. Second, it was important to demonstrate that their religion, too, was capable of embracing modernising changes. In the nineteenth century, the Hindus were quick to realise that the initiative for reform, rather than being forced upon them from the outside, was best generated by Hindus themselves.

The Orientalist Interlude

The man who first personified many of the aspirations articulated by modern Hindus was Raja Rammohun Roy: reputedly, he was the 'pioneer of all living advance: religious, social and educational'.[16] This assessment, though just and appropriate, conceals one important fact. The aspirations of modern Hinduism that Rammohun embodied actually predate him, even though he was the first to effectively articulate them. To more fully understand this phenomenon, we shall have to go back to the point in time when Rammohun himself would have been only a young boy of about twelve.

Bengal, as well-known, was the Indian province to first come under British rule. In hindsight, it could be said that this had a paradoxical effect on the contemporary Hindu–

---

16 John Nicol Farquhar, *Modern Religious Movements in India* (New York: The Macmillan Company, 1915).

Bengali mind. Some Hindus soon developed a great liking for European ideas or ways of life. Over time, however, this growing familiarity also produced a cultural reaction. Many were puzzled and offended by new ideas or practices which they found very different from their own. This explains why nineteenth-century Bengal witnessed the creation of both an influential, anglicised class which readily aped English manners or customs and a class which angrily rejected these.

On their part, the British considered it expedient to win the support and confidence of the people over whom they ruled. One way in which they believed they could win this support and also secure their own political interests was to promote the study of the history and culture of their subjects. They believed that understanding a people and their culture was the key to effectively ruling over them.

Rooms of the Asiatic Society in 1828.
(From a lithograph by Savignhac and Pearson.)

Premises of the Asiatic Society, c. 1828.

An important landmark in Indo-British relations was the foundation in 1784 of the Asiatic Society of Bengal, a colonial institution that still survives in independent India. Founded in the British Indian capital of Calcutta, this gave expression to an intellectual and cultural movement that aimed at creatively building bridges of understanding between the Western and Indian civilisations. These efforts were also deeply influenced by the intellectual and cultural environment in contemporary Europe. Enlightenment Europe had developed a keen sense of rationalism and cosmopolitanism which produced both a critical attitude towards European culture itself and a gripping curiosity in relation to cultures outside Europe. Writers and scholars of the time admired the richness and antiquity of the cultures in India and China. This was typified by the French Enlightenment scholar Voltaire (1694–1778).

In India, this culturally adaptive movement is associated with a group of scholars called the 'Orientalists', after the fact that they were deeply interested in understanding the 'Orient', a concept both geographical and cultural. Geographically, the 'Orient' stretched from Turkey in the west to China in the east – in effect, the large landmass known as Asia. Culturally, Orientalism was associated with the study of non-European people who, apart from exhibiting very different physical features, were presumed to follow dissimilar life styles, speak very different languages, and follow unique religious thought or practices. Impressions about India and about Indians had travelled to Europe long before the Orientalists were even recognised as a group. Such impressions were carried over by traders, adventurers, Christian missionaries, and political or diplomatic personnel representing their respective countries. Mostly, such writings reveal bizarre impressions not founded on fact or actual observations. However, over time, pure speculation and unverified information gave way to more accurate and scientific observation. These opened up new vistas of knowledge about non-European peoples. Strange as this may now appear, much information about India was made known to Indians through Western writings. Even in the late eighteenth century, Hindus had little knowledge of their own past and even less curiosity. The Orientalists were the first to impart to Hindus a sense of their own history and, more importantly, a pride in their past. In modern times, they were among the earliest to study Indian flora and fauna, track down some hitherto unknown or ruined Indian monument from antiquity, discover ancient manuscripts relating to the religious and cultural life of the Hindus, retrieve ancient Hindu treatises on polity, government, astronomy, and medicine, and, perhaps most copiously, recover the rich treasures of ancient Sanskrit literature.

These Orientalists were employees of the East India Company, professionally engaged with day-to-day administration in India; with rare exceptions they were all based in Calcutta. Belonging mostly to aristocratic families back in England or Scotland and benefitting from a classical education, they served the judicial, military, diplomatic, and civil wings of the Company's government in India. Most of them developed a passion for studying the history and culture of the country they had temporarily made their home. This made them the true inheritors of the liberal and universalistic spirit of the European Enlightenment.

Between them, these men contributed significantly to the recovery of India's ancient heritage and greatly influenced the intellectual and cultural movement that began in nineteenth-century Bengal, commonly known as the 'Bengal Renaissance', of which Rammohun was to be an integral part. Rammohun himself benefitted substantially from the work of the Orientalists. For instance, he fully accepted the concept of a lost 'Hindu Golden Age' that some of the Orientalists promoted; he was also in their debt in matters of scholarship.

Sir William Jones (1746–1794).

William Jones (1746–1794), the founder of the Asiatic Society, mastered three classical Oriental languages (Sanskrit, Persian, and Arabic), translated Sanskrit plays of Kalidasa, advanced an influential theory on the common source for Indo-European languages, and helped compile digests on Hindu law. Henry Thomas Colebrooke (1765–1837) was the first European scholar to study the Vedas, the oldest and most authoritative of Hindu religious texts, and anticipated both Rammohun and Governor General Lord William Bentinck in arguing against the practice of *sati*. John B. Gilchrist (1759–1841) was the first to prepare an Urdu dictionary and a book on grammar. Henry Pitts Foster (1766?–1815) prepared the first modern Bengali dictionary, and Nathaniel Brassey Halhed (1751–1830), the first modern grammar of the Bengali language. Without such valuable contributions, some modern Indian vernaculars might not have developed as rapidly or effectively as they did in the years to come.

The Orientalists also helped recover India's historical past. F. Gladwin (1744?–1812) produced the earliest historical account of Akbar's India gleaned from Persian texts. Colin Mackenzie (1754–1821) collected over 1,500 manuscripts from South India and authored one of the earliest modern accounts of the Jains and Jainism. Jonathan Duncan (1756–1811), the

HENRY THOMAS COLEBROOKE.
Founder, 1823 ; Director, 1823–37.

A bust of Henry Thomas Colebrooke (1765–1837).

Company's Resident at Benares and later Governor of Bombay, discovered the Buddhist site of Sarnath. As early as 1795, a diplomat by the name of Samuel Davis (1760–1819) wrote a paper on the astronomical calculations of the Hindus. Charles Wilkins (1749–1836) was the first to translate the Hindu religious classic *Bhagavad Gita* into English and, with the help of some Indian assistants, invented the first Bengali typeface. This invention contributed significantly to the success of the printing press and to vernacular print culture in colonial Bengal. James Prinsep (1799–1840), founder editor of the *Journal of the Asiatic Society of Bengal,* the official journal of the Asiatic Society, deciphered the Brahmi and Kharoshthi scripts, which made it possible to read inscriptions associated with the Maurya dynasty and reconstruct the political history of early India.

Some scholars have doubted if the Orientalists at all contributed to the modernisation of India. They assumed that their classicism and romantic attachment to the past was inconsistent with modernisation. In the 1820s and 1830s, this was also the perception of an influential section of the British press and public who had been blinded by the pejorative views of Indian civilisation carried back to the European continent. The ideology of utilitarianism, which was very influential at the time, saw little or no value in studying or supporting older cultural traditions. Very soon, such critical perceptions produced in both India and Britain a lengthy and meaningful controversy over the issue of suitably modernising Indians. One camp, generally identified as the 'Anglicists' and differing from the Orientalists, argued that modernisation was possible only through the active promotion of the English language as the medium of instruction, replacing the 'antiquated' knowledge systems of the Orient. One of their principal spokespersons, Thomas Babington Macaulay (1800–1859), who later secured a victory for the Anglicists, was to famously claim that a single shelf of books in any European library contained more knowledge than that available in all Oriental libraries put together! The Anglicists also claimed that it was simply providential that an 'enlightened' country like Britain had taken upon itself the noble task of emancipating a backward India. For the colonial Indian government and their supporters back in Britain, this marked the beginning of persistent attempts to justify the British conquest and occupation of India in cultural terms.

Such views or perceptions treat the Orientalists and their work quite unjustly. Scholars now admit that even Orientalists took Western knowledge and the English language to be decidedly superior. Neither did they deny the fact that Europe was the birthplace of the modern science and technology that had revolutionised Britain's society and economy, making her the most advanced nation in the contemporary world. In their political thinking, too, Orientalists fully supported British colonial rule and thought that the interests of Britain's Indian Empire should not be compromised in any way. Nevertheless, there remained some important differences between the two camps. First, the Orientalists did not propagate Western values or culture among Indians to the same extent as the Anglicists. They were far more empathetic to Indian culture itself and pained by the unjust or misplaced words of criticism sometimes directed against it. Some of them, like Horace Hayman Wilson (1786–1860), are suspected to have gone to the opposite extreme of supporting certain Hindu practices in which change was justly called for. Wilson disliked British reformist interventions in Hindu social and religious practices on, for instance, the question of legally abolishing *sati*. This placed him in opposition not only to the Anglicists but also to some Indians like Rammohun, who campaigned against the practice. In the controversy over educational policy in India, too, Rammohun and the Orientalists were on opposite sides. In 1823, Rammohun pleaded with Governor General Lord

Amherst not to spend state resources in promoting traditional Hindu studies. At the time, however, the Orientalists were a very powerful group and Rammohun's request was turned down, leading to the inauguration of the Calcutta Sanskrit College in 1824. Further, the Orientalists viewed the West itself not so much as the site or source of modernity but rather as facilitating the modernising process. They wished to modernise the Hindus but were equally keen to ensure that this occurred according to the Hindus' own value system. In short, they did not want Western education to produce an alienating effect on the Hindu mind. They did not confuse Westernisation with modernisation, unlike the Anglicists.

RAMMOHUN ROY AND THE BREAK WITH THE PAST

It is no coincidence that Rammohun was possibly the first Hindu to use the term 'Hinduism' in his writings. There is an important reason underlying this. Arguably, Rammohun soon realised that in order to reform a religion one had to assume an inner unity of faith and practice. In other words, a reformer had first to identify and isolate a particular religion *as* a religion, then associate it with an identifiable body of practitioners before he could think of introducing suitable changes. It is not improbable that he perceived how important the unity of the medieval Christian Church was to Luther and the Reformation.

Rammohun himself was not a product of English-language schools; on the contrary, he had learned English when serving Company officials and through persistent hard work. William Digby, one of his employers, testifies to how Rammohun developed an immense interest in developments occurring in contemporary Europe and how, to gain some knowledge of these matters, he started the habit of reading English newspapers. At first, his success was modest, but he persevered; by the time he settled down in the colonial town of Calcutta in 1814, he could write an elegant English prose which won him the praise of even Englishmen. From this time onwards, the Raja devoted all his attention and energies to the cause of India and Indians.

Rammohun's outstanding qualities were his activism and enormous breadth of intellectual interest. He is known to have engaged with and commented upon religion, politics, law and jurisprudence, commerce and agriculture, gender equality, and improving the conditions of the Indian peasantry. Freedom and self-determination were important to him. When, in the early 1820s, the news of the successful Neapolitan revolt against Austrian occupation reached him in Calcutta, the Raja threw a public reception to commemorate the event. On the way to England in 1830, when his ship anchored at Aden, Rammohun caught sight of a French ship also anchored nearby, and the sight so excited him that he tried to board the ship himself with repeated cries of 'Vive la France!' Unfortunately, he injured himself in the attempt.

Rammohun would have concurred with the English thinker and natural scientist William Paley (1743–1805) in the belief that God wanted human beings to be happy. Contrary to the orthodox spirit exhibited by his own class at the time, he had the liberality to suggest that the Hindu tradition had the flexibility to adopt and accept what was good in other traditions. The Raja consistently tried to oppose the xenophobia and insularity of the Hindu orthodox by reminding them that India was but a small part of the world and could not remain isolated from the swift and sweeping currents of change. India's degradation he put down to several factors: the disunity created by the caste system, the lack of physical vigour resulting from following an animal-free diet, an enforced self-isolation, and the reluctance to keep abreast with the changing times. He was the first brahmin to have defied the conventional taboo on sea voyages and, when in England, freely mixed with English aristocrats and the labouring poor – the 'great unwashed', as the British press called them. Rammohun believed in free trade among nations, by which he also meant free travel and exchange of ideas across peoples and nations. In modern times, he was the first Indian to express the utopia of a world without borders. Finally, he was also the first Indian to acquire an international reputation in his lifetime. Scholars and churchmen in England and the United States knew of him and of his work even before he travelled to the West.

RAMMOHUN'S LIFE

It is customary to associate the name of Rammohun with the law prohibiting *sati*, passed by the colonial government in 1829. This was no doubt a radical and courageous step to take; it so greatly alarmed and offended the Hindu orthodox that for a time the Raja, fearing assaults upon his life, walked the streets of Calcutta in the company of armed bodyguards. In truth, however, his courage and radicalism was displayed even more in the field of religious thought and practice. In contemporary Calcutta, an orthodox brahmin pundit by the name of Mritunjay Vidyalankar (1762–1819) is known to have anticipated Rammohun in arguing that the practice of *sati* had no sanction in the Hindu tradition. Interestingly, however, the two were on opposite sides when it came to defining Hinduism.

Rammohun was born in 1772 to an orthodox brahmin family of Radhanagar, district Hoogly, in the present Indian state of West Bengal. His ancestors, in serving the Indo-Muslim state in the capacity of revenue officials, learnt Persian and adopted the manners and customs of a Persianised elite. Rammohun himself preferred to dress in that fashion. It has also been suggested that he travelled to Patna (now located in the present Indian state of Bihar, but then a part of Bengal) to learn Persian and Arabic. This seems unlikely, as arrangements for learning these languages existed locally too: a *madrasa* (school for Muslims), which taught these languages, is known to have been established in Calcutta by 1781. Similar stories of doubtful authenticity were also in circulation in the Raja's lifetime. Rammohun himself tells us that even as a young boy of sixteen he was turned out of the ancestral house for producing a tract condemning Hindu idolatry, and subsequently wandered around in Tibet and other 'distant lands' for a few years until called back by a relenting father. There is also some evidence to the contrary, however. In 1796, when he was twenty-four, Rammohun willingly inherited a share of his father's property on condition that he would contribute to the daily worship of the family deity at Radhanagar. This practice he continued until 1814, when he made over his share of property to a nephew. This throws doubt on his supposed sharp and irreconcilable differences with contemporary Hindu practices very early in his life.

Rammohun was never a direct employee of the East India Company, but he served Company officials in the capacity of a *divan* (private secretary). In 1793, when the British introduced the concept of private property in land, the value of land increased phenomenally and many wealthy Hindu Bengalis, including Rammohun himself, began to invest in it. Quite uncharacteristically for a brahmin, he also practiced usury, lending money at fairly high rates to Company servants, who often lived beyond their means. Over the years this helped him to amass a small fortune. By the time he settled down in Calcutta in 1814, his monthly income from all sources was about 10,000 rupees, a very high sum at the time. He used a part of this fortune to purchase properties in Calcutta and thereafter never worked for a living. The Calcutta gentry looked up to him as a respected citizen and clearly a man of substance; Rammohun returned the favour by patronisingly associating them with his manifold activities. This is evident from the two bodies or institutions he founded.

The first of these, the Atmiya Sabha (literally, 'association of kindred souls'), founded in 1815, was a private club whose members met occasionally to discuss matters of social and cultural interest affecting Hindu society. The issues of *sati*, infanticide, education, and the general condition of women were among the subjects discussed in such meetings. In 1828, he founded the Brahmo Sabha, later renamed the Brahmo Samaj, a religious reform institution which propagated monotheism and the importance of moral correctness in human life. The Brahmo Sabha, too, comprised mainly his friends and acquaintances. In 1821 he, in collaboration with William Adam (1796–1881), started the Calcutta Unitarian Society, which aimed at popularising Unitarian worship as opposed to orthodox Trinitarian Christianity. The details of this controversy, which lasted between 1820 and 1822, do not concern us here. Suffice to say that in so trying to depart from mainstream Christianity, Rammohun brought upon himself the ire of several missionary figures of the time, including his good friend, William Carey of Serampore. The Serampore missionaries were no less cross with Adam, whom they described as the 'second fallen Adam'! In 1830, a year after he had persuaded Governor General Lord William Bentinck to legally prohibit *sati*, Rammohun was commissioned by the then Mughal emperor, Akbar II, a pensioner of the East India Company, to plead for an enhanced pension on the latter's behalf with the authorities in Britain. It was the emperor who also conferred upon him the title 'Raja'. Rammohun had plans to travel to the USA but died prematurely at Bristol in 1830 of a sudden attack of meningitis. He was buried in the town of Bristol; his friend and patron, Dwarkanath Tagore (1794–1846), the grandfather of the poet Rabindranath (1861–1941), later built a splendid structure over his grave.

Rammohun's Religion

Rammohun's earliest thoughts on religion are to be found in an undated Persian work called *Manzaratul Adiyan* (Discourses (or Debates) on Various Religions). The manuscript of this work was never found and the book never printed, although its existence is known from the local Zoroastrians' objections to it. The *Manzaratul Adiyan* preceded his better-known *Tuhfat ul-Muwahidin* (A Gift to Monotheists), dated around 1803–1804, a Persian text of about fourteen pages with a short introduction in Arabic. The *Tuhfat,* too, was little known until after 1884, when it was published in an English translation.

The *Tuhfat* appears to have been deeply influenced by the unorthodox Muslim sect of the Mutazalites. The Mutazalites were rationalists in their belief and denied the act of revelation; they were thus comparable to the European Deists of the seventeenth and eighteenth centuries. It is possible that the *Tuhfat* was influenced by two similar works: the twelfth-century Arabic *Kitab al-Milal-wa-al-Nihal* (Book of Religion and Philosophy), by Shahstrani, and the seventeenth-century Persian work *Dabestan-e Mazahib* (School of Religions), whose authorship is uncertain. Both these works are valuable sources of information on contemporary religion and culture.

In hindsight, it appears that even when borrowing from such works, Rammohun's radicalism went beyond them. For instance, the Mutazalites believed neither that God authored the Holy Books nor in *pirs* (Sufi spiritual guides or teachers) or prophets. They also took scriptures to be humanly created, but whereas the Mutazalites accepted the authority of the Koran, Rammohun did not. Interestingly, Rammohun's authorship of such early works also proves that rationalism in matters of religion first came to him through non-European sources and only further developed in the company of European friends or scholars. Rammohun taught himself the philosophical and scientific thought of contemporary Europe; in opposing orthodox Hinduism he often invoked the names of Francis Bacon (1561–1626) and John Locke (1632–1704).

The *Tuhfat* was not critical of Hinduism in particular. Rather, somewhat in the manner of Voltaire himself, Rammohun alerts us to the misuse of religion in public life. In his *Tomb of Fanaticism* (1767), Voltaire had likened the uncritical human mind in matters of religion to the ignorant ox which unthinkingly allows itself to be yoked. Similarly, Rammohun argued that falsehood had to be common to all religions since these were humanly mediated. It is important to bear in mind, however, that Rammohun remained a staunch theist who believed in a Creator God: atheism was unacceptable to him, and even idolatry, which he otherwise severely opposed, he found better than disbelief in God and Providence. Reportedly, his opposition was not to religion per se but to its 'perversion'.

At a rough count, Rammohun authored (at times in collaboration with a close follower or under a pseudonym) about thirty-eight tracts and pamphlets in all, twenty-five of which were in Bengali. This number pertains to his writings on Hinduism alone, excluding tracts that he wrote on Unitarian Christianity. His published writings included two commentaries in Bengali on the *Vedanta Sutra/Brahma Sutra*[17] of Badarayana (*c.* 300 BCE–400 CE), called the *Vedanta Grantha* and the *Vedantasara* respectively, both published in 1815. These were later published in English as *Translation of an Abridgement of the Vedanta* (1815). In addition, between 1816

17　A core text for all followers of the Vedanta school of philosophy; this has been the subject of many commentaries ever since the ninth century CE, with quite different readings. Importantly, one way or another, these differences developed in relation to the interpretation of Shankara, which was philosophically non-dualistic.

and 1818 he translated five Upanishads (*Isha*, *Kena*, *Katha*, *Mundaka*, and *Mandukya*) into Bengali. Of these, four were also later produced in English translation. He was drawn into frequent polemical exchanges with orthodox Hindus located both within and outside Bengal. His opponents included local pundits like Mritunjay Vidyalankar and Kashinath Tarkapanchan (1788–1851), two Hindu apologists from Madras (Sankara Sastri and Subrahmanya Sastri), and two Vaishnava religious leaders belonging to the Bengal school of Vaishnavism, one of whom remains anonymous and the other, unknown, was a writer who called himself 'Kabitakar'.

At this point, a brief explanation of the term 'Vedanta' is required. It is a compound of two words, 'Veda' and '*anta*', the latter meaning 'end'. Literally, therefore, Vedanta denotes the end of the Vedas, corresponding to the body of philosophical literature called the Upanishads; chronologically, the Upanishads were the last to be produced within the whole corpus of Vedic literature. But the term 'Vedanta' is also used to suggest the 'quintessence of the Vedas'. Indeed, the Upanishads have consistently been taken to represent the best of Hindu philosophical wisdom.

Rammohun used the words 'Veda' and 'Upanishads' interchangeably. By 'Vedas' he always meant the Upanishads; it is doubtful that he was at all sufficiently acquainted with other components of the Vedic canon, such as the Samhitas (hymns, *mantras*, litanies, and prayers), the Brahmanas (commentaries on Vedic rituals), or the Aranyakas (a loose combination of philosophy and ritual). This is not surprising since ethnic Bengal was always deemed to fall outside the Brahmanical heartland. In the nineteenth century, Orientalists could not procure a single reliable manuscript copy of the *Rig Veda* in Bengal and had to turn to the private collection of the Maharaja of Jaipur.

Vedanta is one of the six orthodox (*astika*) philosophical schools in Hinduism, so called principally because they acknowledged the authority of the Vedas. Today, of all the Hindu schools of philosophy, Vedanta has produced the largest body of literature. The most prominent Vedantic philosopher in early India was Acharya Shankara (*c.* ninth century CE), who gave it a distinct philosophical character. Shankara was an Advaitin, or a non-dualist in philosophical matters that is, he took the one metaphysical Principle called Brahman to be the basis of all Reality, including the phenomenal world (*jagat*) and all forms of life (*jiva*) within it. Advaita Vedanta did not admit a creator God, and creation itself was understood in somewhat mystical terms. Vedanta, as interpreted by Shankara, did not accommodate a personal God to whom one could relate emotionally. There was no space here for devotion since, given the single nature of Reality, man was in essence the same as God. Only ignorance kept him from realising this Truth.

For Shankara the higher, esoteric knowledge of the Vedas was permitted only to the three upper *varnas* (classes) of brahmin, *kshatriya*, and *vaishya*, and categorically denied to the lowest *varna* (*shudra*) and to women. It is important to note here that though Rammohun situated himself in the spiritual lineage of Shankara and regarded himself as an Advaitin, he differed from this tradition in some significant respects. For instance, he believed that women and *shudras* too could have equal access to the *shruti* (the Vedic canon).

An important change that occurred within modern Hinduism was the rapid success of the printed book and an expanding market for books. By the second half of the nineteenth century, the success of social and religious reform greatly depended on the production of tracts and pamphlets and of cheap editions of major religious texts, some of which even became available in Indian vernacular translations. Rammohun himself launched this important enterprise.

Having settled down in Calcutta, he chose to translate and publish literature that had hitherto never been treated as public knowledge. Astonishingly, he chose to translate *shruti* not only into Bengali but also into English. This was a major departure from tradition and outraged orthodox upper-caste Hindus. The latter objected not so much to Rammohun's promoting the worship of one God, or even his attacks on idolatry, since these were known in the Hindu tradition itself, but rather his opening up 'sacred' knowledge to classes from whom this had been hidden for centuries. Their objection was more social in nature than doctrinal. Rammohun's work simultaneously challenged the religious doctrines as well as the social organisation of the Hindus. For instance, if the sacred books were to be opened up to all, the caste system itself would be the first casualty. He also had some sectarian critics, including Vaishnavas who were aghast at his critique of the Bengali Vaishnava mystic Chaitanya (1486–1533) or, more generally, of Radha-Krishna worship.

At this point it would be useful to summarise the religious ideas of Rammohun Roy:

- God was unknowable through the faculties of the human mind but this did not imply his non-existence. The existence and nature of God may be aptly known from his works in nature.
- God was one and without a second (*advitiya*) or equal.
- His omnipresence could not be reduced to any form, human or otherwise.
- Idolatry or image worship was not only doctrinally in error but also the cause of social evils, such as the enforced burning of widows (*sati*), caste practices, and polygamy.
- Contemporary Hinduism and its common practices represented certain vested interests at work – for instance, brahmin priests, *gurus*, or theologians.

- Moral principles were a part of the adoration of God; Rammohun admitted that in this respect Christianity was relatively superior to Hinduism.
- While religion had to be rational, reason could not be taken to be a reliable guide under all circumstances.
- Truth and true religion did not necessarily solely belong to men of wealth or power, to high names, or to lofty places.
- Religion had to have a social face.
- The consequences of our good and bad actions were experienced in our worldly life itself. They did not follow death, nor were they related to some Day of Judgement.

A closer examination of these ideas or principles will lead us to certain interesting conclusions. We have already noted how selective Rammohun was with respect to Vedic literature, but he also confused monism (accepting a single order of Reality) with monotheism (the worship of one God). He declared himself an Advaitin but composed prayer songs addressing the impersonal Brahman as 'Father' of spiritual life. For a Vedantin, or practitioner of the Vedanta, Rammohun also understood religion in uncharacteristically utilitarian terms. This led his first biographer, Kissorychand Mitra, to describe him as a 'religious Benthamite'. In a letter of 18 January 1828, written to an English friend, Rammohun associated religion with securing 'political advantage and social comfort'. For him, religion obviously had non-religious functions to perform. One of these was to be a good citizen and socially responsible: 'The Vedas, coinciding with the natural desires of social intercourse . . . require of men to moderate their appetite and regulate their passions in a manner calculated to preserve their peace and comfort of society and secure their future happiness'.[18]

---

18 *Brahmanical Magazine*, IV (1823).

And again: 'A sense of duty compels me to exert the utmost endeavour to rescue them [the Hindus] from the imposition of servitude and promote their comfort and happiness'.[19]

It is noticeable how Rammohun quite unreasonably connects idolatrous practices with evil and criminal instincts in men. In a work that he authored in 1816, he took Hindu idolatry to be worse than any known pagan forms of worship. The following is an excerpt from the text:

> My constant reflection on the inconvenient or rather injurious rites introduced by the peculiar practice of Hindoo idolatry, which, more than any other pagan worship destroys the texture of society, together with compassion for my countrymen has compelled me to use every possible effort to awaken them from their dream of error and by making them acquainted with their scripture, enable them to contemplate with free devotion the unity and omnipotence of Nature's God.[20]

The Hindus, he similarly argued in his translation of the *Isha Upanishad*, were more concerned with following dietary restrictions than the prevention of murder, theft, or perjury.

Another important quality in Rammohun's religious thought is his unconcealed religious materialism. There was something of the ancient Vedic *rishi* (sage) in the Raja, who would not hesitate to beseech the gods for gifts of a son or cattle: 'A votary of God obtains his desired objects; anyone

---

19 Rammohun Roy, *A Second Defense of the Monotheistical System of the Vedas in Reply to an Apology for the Present State of Hindoo Worship* (Calcutta: 1817).

20 Rammohun Roy, *Translation of an Abridgement of the Vedanta or the Resolution of all the Vedas etc.* (London: T. and J. Hoitt, 1817).

seeking honour and advantage shall revere him.'[21] Importantly, Rammohun discouraged asceticism and valorised the life of the pious householder (*brahmanishtha grihastha*).

Some of Rammohun's critics felt that his religious beliefs were of an indeterminate nature and could not be identified with any of the established world religions. A critic based in Ganjam (now in the Indian state of Odisha) remarked that he was neither Christian nor Mussalman nor Hindu. This was later echoed by some students in Calcutta who alleged that Rammohun's strength lay in the fact that he meant all things to all men. That the Raja distanced himself equally from orthodox Christianity and traditional Hinduism is clear from the remark he once made before Bishop Thomas Middleton, Lord Bishop of Calcutta. Confident that Rammohun's critical attitude towards his ancestral religion would soon lead him to accept Christianity, the Bishop sent the Raja a congratulatory message in anticipation. To this Rammohun shot back: 'My Lord, I have not given up one error to embrace another!' That, at least for social purposes, he remained a Hindu all his life is clear from the fact that he never gave up the sacred thread that brahmins habitually wore, not even on his deathbed. In Britain, when invited to public feasts or dinners, the Raja was known to accept only rice and plain water.

Rammohun's Brahmo Sabha was for all practical purposes a Hindu religious organisation even though it claimed to be universalistic in its spirit or vision. In the early 1840s, when the mantle of running this organisation fell on Debendranath Tagore (1817–1905), father of the poet Rabindranath and a close follower of Rammohun, orthodox brahmin pundits from southern India were known to privately chant Vedic hymns in a secluded room so that they could not be overheard by

---

21 Commenting on *Mundaka Upanishad* III.1.9.

non-brahmins present. Debendranath heard the then minister (*acharya*), Pundit Ramchandra Vidyabagish (1786–1845), reciting verses in praise of Hindu *avataras*, quite contrary to the beliefs of Rammohun himself. Even in the Raja's lifetime, the Brahmo Sabha was associated with only one non-Hindu, Gholam Abbas, who accompanied the singing of hymns or songs in praise of Brahman (*Brahma sangit*) on *tabla* and *pakhawaj* (both kinds of drum). This remained the general situation until the 1840s, when some young radicals pushed Debendranath to the brink of meaningful reform.

Rammohun was hopeful that his countrymen would readily accept the error or follies that they had fallen into with respect to their religious life. He was also sure that his efforts would be duly appreciated by posterity: '…a day will arrive when my humble endeavour will be viewed with justice – perhaps acknowledged with gratitude'.[22]

CONCLUSION

This chapter has tried to bring out the historical context in which new thoughts or visions about Hinduism began to take shape in the early nineteenth century. The context was determined as much by a new political and cultural environment created by colonial rule as new patterns of thought. This self-expression on the part of Hindus was greatly encouraged by the Orientalists, who brought alive many hidden or unknown aspects of Indian history and culture, created a sense of pride in Hindus, and also encouraged the idea that for the Hindus, religious reform was the key to a new definition of the self.

---

22 Cited in Amiya P. Sen, *Rammohun Roy: A Critical Biography* (New Delhi: Penguin Viking, 2012), 1.

Understandably, such developments affected only the upper crust of Hindu society and people whose exposure to modern English education created in them a critical attitude towards their own tradition. Debates and differences that developed around new definitions of Hinduism originated in these classes and were limited to them. Such debates rarely permeated the lower castes or classes, who were denied the benefits of both a Sanskrit and a Western education. Rammohun had virtually no interest in popular culture; on the contrary, he was aghast at upper-caste cultures borrowing elements of religious life from the popular. The worship of images, pilgrimages, 'obscene' festivities, a blind dependence on the services of priests, astrologers, ritual experts, or soothsayers he took to be 'corruptions' carried over from a 'lower' culture which seriously called for reformist intervention.

In some ways, Rammohun inherited the more positive approach to understanding or appreciating Indian culture that was created by the combination of sympathetic Orientalists and scholarly missionaries. He agreed with these people in arguing that the ancient civilisation of the Hindus had been corrupted over time and had to be restored to a state of purity and authenticity. He also concurred in the view that modernisation was a task incumbent upon Indians which they could perform by suitably drawing upon the example of contemporary Europe. This, in his view, required important changes in contemporary Hindu society.

It was more in respect to his methods than in the analysis of the contemporary situation that Raja Rammohun Roy differed from both Orientalists and missionaries. Compared to the Orientalists, he preferred introducing a modern school curriculum sooner and more directly; he was also more impatient towards the irrationalities and malpractices within Hinduism. With regard to missionaries, he differed both in terms of aims and the methods of securing them. Rammohun's response to Bishop Middleton proves that he did not necessarily view Christianity to be a superior religion in all respects.

Rammohun was moved by a sense of cultural pride associated with Indian civilisation and, in a larger sense, the civilisation of Asia. It is not commonly known that he was the first Indian to emphasise the Asiatic origin of Christ. Over time, this gave birth to two important arguments that became integral to the self-understanding of modern Hindus. First, Hindus were now heard to argue that both India and the West suffered backwardness in one form or another. Admittedly, India lacked in material progress but the West was poor in matters of spirituality. From this also followed that the West had as much to learn from India as India from the West. This, the Hindus after Rammohun hoped, would help place a politically defeated country like India on an equal footing within the community of great nations.

DISCUSSION TOPIC:
RAMMOHUN ROY AND THE NEW HINDUISM

- Why did religion become the site of social and religious transformation in respect to colonial Hinduism?

- Who were the Orientalists? What was their contribution to the intellectual and cultural awakening of the Hindus in the eighteenth and nineteenth centuries?

- Why does Rammohun Roy deserve to be called the pioneer of the Renaissance in nineteenth-century India?

- What were the chief features of Rammohun's critique of contemporary Hindu religion and society?

FURTHER READING

David Kopf. *British Orientalism and the Bengal Renaissance: The Dynamics of Indian Modernization, 1773–1835.* Berkeley: University of California Press, 1969.

Amiya P. Sen. *Rammohun Roy. A Critical Biography.* Delhi: Penguin Viking, 2010.

The Life and Letters of Rammohun Roy. Compiled and edited by Sophia Dobson Collet. Edited by Hem Chandra Sarkar. 2nd edition. Calcutta: R. Cambray & Co., 1914.

Keshabchandra Sen (1838–1884).

II
A REFORMED RELIGION
FOR THE HINDUS 1:
THE BENGAL AND BOMBAY
PRESIDENCIES, *c.* 1830–1890

An integral part of colonial Hinduism was its engagement with 'reform'. In this chapter we shall attempt to understand the complex meanings attached to this term, which was both a concept and social practice. The first part of the chapter will be devoted to a discussion of the major ideas or assumptions underlying the concept of reform and the subtle inner variations in meaning. The second part will undertake a detailed examination of the operative history of reform in two of the three 'Presidencies', which were large divisions created in British India for administrative purposes. Here, we will focus on reform work carried out in the Bengal and Bombay Presidencies.

THE PARADIGM OF 'REFORM'

It is now common practice to distinguish 'Reform Hinduism' from pre-modern attempts at reforming, or changing for the better, certain social and religious ideas or practices associated with the Hindus. Scholars now generally accept the view that 'Reform Hinduism' originated in nineteenth-century India and was the work of the newly emerging, Western-educated class. For the purposes of definition, 'Reform Hinduism' is also taken to assume and accept a sharp separation between Indian 'tradition' and Western 'modernity'. Modern Hindu reformers, concentrated mainly in the three Presidency towns of Calcutta, Bombay, and Madras, are believed to have consciously employed ideas and methods borrowed from the contemporary West to produce progressive changes to their social life or religious life.

This chapter seeks distinguish pre-modern attempts at changing elements of society or religion from those that occurred under colonialism. It is argued that mere attempts at changing some thought or practice did not constitute 'reformism'. The term 'reform' carried the undercurrents of a modern ideology which needs to be examined and better understood.

Let us begin by admitting that the intention to change contemporary society or religion goes back a long time. Even in the pre-Christian era men, like the Buddha and Mahavira expressed dissatisfaction with the existing conditions and wished to change them. However, they did not describe themselves as 'reformers' nor did their contemporaries call them by that name. In the context of South Asia, the English term 'reform' and its vernacular equivalents began to be commonly used only in the nineteenth century. Interestingly enough, it was only then that the Buddha himself, and the medieval *bhakti* saints like Kabir, Nanak, or Chaitanya, came to be known as 'reformers' and their work as acts of 'reform'.

It should also be acknowledged that, contrary to what has often been assumed, the work of reform did not always mean dramatically changing the 'traditional' into the 'modern'. The work underlying reform was, more often than not, slow and affected by several complexities. Assuming a sharp distinction between tradition and modernity overlooks two interrelated facts: first, it ignores how a particular tradition is capable of modernising through a dynamism born within itself, and second, it also wrongly leads us to the belief that what occurs in the modern era never carries within it elements of the old and the traditional. This chapter and the next will therefore also address, however briefly, those attempts at change as were not directly inspired by Western ideas and, at least initially, not carried out by Western-educated people.

There are of course good reasons why any comparison between the two models of reformist changes outlined above must be approached with due care and caution. When assessed in terms of the impact it made or the number of writers and publicists it produced over a length of time, one of these models clearly outweighs the other. The sheer volume of literature available on 'Reform Hinduism' is many times more than that which is available outside it. Qualitatively, too, the literature produced by the Western-educated reformers reveals a greater complexity and engages with a greater variety of issues or questions.[23]

THE IDEOLOGICAL MOORINGS OF REFORM

From the fact that the term 'reform' came to be commonly used only in the nineteenth-century, it may be reasonably deduced that the term carried with it certain new ideas or understanding. Directly or indirectly, the new concern for reform was influenced by certain key ideas surfacing in post-Enlightenment Europe: for instance, the emphasis on reason or reasonableness, on humanism, utility, and practicality, the tendency to question older dogmas and beliefs, and an intellectual curiosity about the world and about human

---

23 For a recent in-depth critique of the concept of 'reform' and its binary-producing consequences for the study of colonial Hinduism, see Brian A. Hatcher, *Hinduism Before Reform* (Cambridge: Harvard University Press, 2020).

life in it. Enlightenment thought was particularly critical of contemporary European religion, and this sharpened anti-clericalism and the critique of religious intolerance. Importantly, it also gave rise to new conceptions of God and religion. One conception which made a deep impact on the contemporary Hindu mind was that of Deism or Natural Religion.

Deism was known in Europe even before the Enlightenment. Some seventeenth-century English thinkers and scientists were known to be Deists. Deism did not believe in Revelation and argued that the created world better revealed God and his intentions than the 'Word' of God. From this it followed that scriptures were humanly produced and hence carried fallacy and error. It did admit a creator God but assigned Him a more passive role than earlier. The Deist's God was not involved with the everyday working of the world but was a distant, impersonal God who, having created the world, withdrew Himself from its active care. The English Deist William Paley, mentioned earlier, famously compared the world to a watch and God Himself to the watchmaker who ceased to have any interest in his creation. This implied that human beings themselves were to take active care of the world and of life in it. It now fell upon humankind to suitably fulfill the desired goals of human 'improvement' and 'progress'. It was thus that 'reform', as a conscious attempt to better the human condition, became the moral responsibility of the individual person.

THE NUANCES OF REFORM

A closer examination of the history of Hindu reform reveals several internal conflicts and tensions. First, it should be accepted that 'reform' was both a static and an evolving concept. On one level, it meant a principled and continuing commitment to progressive changes. Practically, however,

*Deists compared the world to a watch and God to the watchmaker, who had
ceased to have any interest in his creation.*

such commitments often weakened and failed to produce the
desired changes. The following passage from Bankimchandra
Chattopadhyay is typical: 'Let us revere the past but we must,
in justice to our new life, adopt new methods of interpretation
and adapt the old, eternal and undying truths to the necessities
of that life.'[24] Here, Bankimchandra appears to accept two
mutually conflicting ideas. On one hand, he is keen to adopt
new methods of interpreting the past in keeping with visibly
altered needs or circumstances. On the other, he confuses us
by suggesting that older truths could also be *adapted* to altered
circumstances. Now, if 'truths' could be so adapted they
could not also be 'eternal' and 'undying'. However, the clear

---

24 Bankimchandra Chattopadhyay, *Letters on Hinduism*, in *Bankim
Rachanavali*, ed. J. C. Bagal (Calcutta, 1969), 236.

confusion here has an explanation: apparently, Bankimchandra accepts a notion of tradition that is both fixed and moving in time. While locating the sources of 'purity' or 'authenticity' of his tradition in a given historical past, he believes that notions of what is 'true' or 'pure' in tradition could be redefined in keeping with changing needs.

Reformers could not always agree on the specific object of reform or the pace and extent to which reforms could be carried out. In the matter of religious reform, they could not always agree on just which particular text to take as their source book. For instance, not everybody admitted the Vedas as the religious authority for the Hindus. Later on we shall see how the Brahmo Samaj in Bengal gave up faith in the Vedas and composed their own source book. Bankimchandra found the attempt by Dayananda Saraswati, the founder of the reformist body the Arya Samaj, to establish Hindu religion and philosophy entirely in the Vedic canon to be plainly 'anachronistic'. The Aryas retaliated by calling the Brahmos too idealistic. Even within Bengal itself, Rammohun and Bankimchandra represented two very different approaches to the question of religious authority. While Rammohun was sharply critical of Puranic[25] religion, Bankimchandra contributed to a Puranic revival. Whereas Rammohun had dismissed the Puranic god Krishna as 'lecherous', in Bankimchandra's writings he emerged as the ideal warrior, diplomat, and statesman.

25　The Puranas comprise one of the richest sources of Hindu history, mythology, religion, social usage, and ritual codes. Certain concepts or themes like *bhakti* are best explicated in this literature. The Puranas were also sectarian in character and valorised the worship of various Hindu gods and goddesses, chief of which were Vishnu, Shiva, and Devi (Shakti).

While, in theory, reform implied a willingness to change irrational practices, not everything requiring change became a part of the reformist agenda. Reformers also made strange exceptions in matters that were otherwise deeply interrelated. For instance, they supported the education of young girls but were reluctant to send them to school. They were prepared to see women acquire university education but disapproved of their marrying late or choosing their own husbands. Many reformers also went back on their commitments and failed to set personal examples. Some brahmin reformers took off their sacred thread as a mark of protesting caste but ensured that their daughters were married to brahmin grooms. Others who consistently supported the cause of widow marriage (traditionally in Hindu society, upper-caste widows were forbidden from remarrying) did not agree to marry widows themselves.

In the modern West, the work of social reform was far wider in scope and included a broad range of issues. In nineteenth-century India, by comparison, it was limited to primarily two subjects: the condition of (Hindu) women and the inequities of the caste system. By themselves, these were indeed important issues since they touched upon questions related to both Hindu social organisation and religious life. Even so, the importance attached to either varied from province to province. In nineteenth-century Bengal, there were no meaningful organised movements that aimed at reducing the social oppressions in the name of caste, primarily because caste inequities in this province were relatively weaker than elsewhere in India. In contrast, Hindu reformers in Bengal showed a preoccupation with issues related to women; in part, this followed from their accepting new social theories which claimed that the state of a civilisation could be judged by the way that civilisation treated its women.

In Bengal, religious questions were more frequently raised than social questions. After Rammohun, many members of the

Rao Bahadur Mahadev Govind Ranade (1842–1901).

Brahmo Samaj were heard to say that the Samaj was primarily a religious organisation, not a social body. Not surprisingly, this led reformers from elsewhere in India to look at Bengal with some concern. The reformer from Maharashtra, Mahadev Govind Ranade, accused Bengali reformers like Keshabchandra Sen of being obsessed with religious questions at the expense of the social. However, this accusation cannot be wholly supported, since the Brahmos also led in the field of women's education, producing the first female graduates in India. They were also at the forefront of the local temperance movement, promoted widow marriage and inter-caste marriages, and supported the first Special Marriage Act (India Act III of 1872), which deemed marriage not to take place on religious lines. On the whole, though, a Brahmo was more often identified by his religious piety and passion. After 1870, Keshabchandra himself went back on women-related reform and dedicated his life to conducting religious experiments.

The situation elsewhere in India was quite different. For some early Hindu reformist associations in Bombay, membership was contingent upon a person radically breaking caste rules by accepting water from a Muslim and eating bread baked by a European baker. Caste was a more important issue in western India and in the south, so the direction that reform work took in these areas was different. In Bengal, where the emphasis was on propagating a new religious consciousness, the brahmin and upper castes invariably took the lead and were seldom challenged by the lower castes. This was because in matters of religious faith the brahmin had traditionally been the authority figure. In Maharashtra or the Tamil-speaking region, by contrast, the brahmin hegemony was strong but often challenged by socially radical, lower-caste movements, which preferred the path of a revolutionary break with the past over gradual and cautious reformism. Whereas reform for upper-caste reformers was expected to follow the 'line of least resistance', lower-caste reformers like Jotiba Phule (1827–1890) and Bhimrao Ambedkar (1891–1956) preferred revolution to easy-paced reform. They also argued that since social malpractices drew their strength from religious sanction, the latter had to be completely rooted out.

REFORM AND REFORMERS IN BENGAL

Under British rule, the fortunes of Bengal rose substantially. Employees of the East India Company and their Indian collaborators profited greatly from investments in trade, brokerage, usury, and sundry services. By the close of the eighteenth century, the British had also introduced sweeping changes in agrarian relations. Land was now recognised as private property and a new propertied class called *zemindars* had been created. The new landed elite, which included some of the most prominent families in nineteenth-century Calcutta, were patrons of culture. There was also a fast-emerging service class drawn essentially from the three upper castes of brahmins, *baidyas*, and *kayasthas*. The common name given to them in the local language was *bhadralok* (genteel people). It was this class which constituted the earliest English-educated intelligentsia in Bengal and formed the backbone of the cultural movement called the Bengal Renaissance.

Contemporary accounts speak of the great importance and urgency shown by Hindu Bengalis in acquiring knowledge of the English language. At the time, English-language education was available in the several local free schools, mostly set up by Scottish philanthropists like David Drummond (1785–1843) and David Hare (1775–1842). The rising demand for English-language learning indicates the growing employment needs of the Bengali *bhadralok*. After 1837, when English had replaced Persian as the language used for administration and in law courts, and by when the Anglicists had won a victory over the Orientalists in matters of educational policy, knowledge of the English language became essential for securing employment in government offices or in private mercantile firms. But over time, such knowledge also became a mark of respectability and cultural distinction. In 1824, Reginald Heber (1782–1826), Bishop of Calcutta, who had invited some prominent Hindus of the city to his birthday party, was pleasantly surprised to hear them speak English freely and gracefully. Two schoolboys of central Calcutta by the names of Nitai Sen and Advaita Sen enjoyed great respect in their locality even though they spoke the language quite ungrammatically. However, English-language education was not merely an avenue to employment under the government but also served other intents and purposes. Young men appear to have been equally enthused by the idea of broadening their mental horizons through adopting a modern educational curriculum and patronising new institutions of learning. The Bengali nationalist leader Surendranath Banerjee (1848-1925) once said:

> We are essentially intellectual people . . . . There is indeed innate in us, a deep, passionate hankering after knowledge, in whatever shape, in whatever form, it may happen to be presented to us . . . . William Digby has likened this process of ours to the interest commonly characteristic of the Athenians of old times.[26]

Comparing their own ideas and achievements to points of excellence in the history of classical Europe was a recurring feature with educated Bengalis.

---

26 *Speeches and Writings of Surendranath Banerjee* (Madras: G. A Natesan & Co., 1940), 88.

This is amply borne out by the history of the Hindu College founded in 1817. The Hindu College, actually a school, was entirely the creation of the affluent Hindus of the city. It did not receive any grants from the government and charged students a monthly fee of five rupees at a time when the average monthly salary for an Indian was no more than twenty-five to thirty rupees a month. This reveals the great enthusiasm that some Hindus showed towards the value of the new learning as also the social class to which they belonged.

The idea behind establishing the college was to impart to students modern and 'useful' knowledge of the West through lessons in English literature and language, politics, history, geography, and basic mathematics. But it outgrew that narrow purpose and resembled for a time an academy from ancient Greece where a free and engaging dialogue ensued between

Henry Louis Vivian Derozio (1809–1831).

teachers and pupils. The institution employed some of the finest teachers available at the time, including Captain David Lester Richardson (1801–1865), famed for his teaching of Shakespeare, and Henry Louis Vivian Derozio (1809–1831), a man of Portugese descent and perhaps the most popular young teacher that the city of Calcutta has since known. Students of the Hindu College were quite aware of their role in ushering in a new intellectual era. In the words of one, Kissorychand Mitra (1822–1873), 'like the top of the Kanchanjunga [they] were the first to catch and reflect the dawn'.

Some, if not all, boys studying at the Hindu College came to be called 'Derozians' after the fact that they were students of Derozio, as well as his followers. They were also given the name 'Young Bengal', modelled after 'Young Italy', comprising the followers of the Italian nationalist and revolutionary Joseph Mazzini. Both groups shared a youthful rebelliousness, even though the latter was more politically active than the other.

The Derozians focused their energies on either eagerly soaking up the new political and social theories emanating from the West or overturning some of the settled Hindu beliefs and practices. The writings of the English-born American political theorist Thomas Paine (1737–1809) were a rage with them, and unscrupulous booksellers of Calcutta sold Paine's works at five times the stated price. The Derozians themselves ran several journals (*Jnaneshwan, Parthenon, Bengal Spectator,* and the *Reformer*) and founded debating clubs like the Academic Association and the Society for the Acquisition of General Knowledge. These clubs periodically held meetings in which student members would read papers on pressing social issues.

However, the Derozians' methods relied very largely on personal protest, not the collective. They disregarded taboos of food and drink, rejected common customs, and questioned traditional wisdom. In doing so it was their intention to shock the Hindu orthodoxy. Openly defying food taboos, Hindu students of the College ordered beef broth in restaurants and relished *kebabs* sold by Muslim hawkers. Several Derozians drank habitually with the result that some of them developed serious ailments. A journal from contemporary Calcutta, the *Oriental Magazine* of October 1843, found them 'cutting their way through ham and beef and wading to liberation through tumblers of beer!'

What greatly offended and shocked orthodox society was their open defiance of Hindu social conventions. The Derozian Radhanath Sikdar (1813–1870) declined to marry a minor girl; his fellow student, Rasik Krishna Mallik (1810–1858), refused to swear by the Holy Ganges in a court of law, and yet another, Madhavchandra Mallik (n/k), declared, as reported by the *Bengal Harakaru* of 13 October 1831, that if there was anything that he hated from the bottom of his heart, it was Hinduism. Eventually, this so offended orthodox society that they persuaded the Management Committee of the Hindu College, comprising wealthy, conservative, and influential residents of Calcutta, to take corrective action. On the basis that Derozio himself was to be blamed for such sacrilegious acts, they removed him from the post of teacher in 1829. Derozio died soon after of cholera and his radical views on religion were so unpopular that it became difficult to secure even a decent burial place for him at the local cemetery.

The Derozians were not a homogenous group, and not all of them took to open rebellion. Some were content with a passing skepticism and did not openly defy society or tradition. At times they were also guilty of hypocrisy. One, by the name of Prasanna Kumar Tagore (1801–1886), declared himself to be opposed to idol worship but privately celebrated the annual Durga *puja*.

One way or another, the most pressing engagement of Derozians was with religion, and with Hinduism in particular.

Within this group were atheists and agnostics but also people who chose to renounce Hinduism. Three students of the Hindu College, Krishnamohan Bandyopadhyay (1813–1885), Gyanendramohan Tagore (1826–1890), and Madhavchandra Mallik (n/k), embraced Christianity, while others like Rajnarayan Basu (1826–1899), Shib Chundra Deb (1811–1890), and Ramtanu Lahiri (1813–98), became well-known Brahmo evangelists.

The most serious charge that both liberal and conservative Hindus levelled against the Derozians was that they had advanced too far and too rapidly in the name of a reformed Hinduism. The Brahmo leader Keshabchandra Sen addressed them in the following words: 'You started from disbelief in idolatry and superstition but landed in disbelief and skepticism. You doubted Hinduism but brought yourself to doubt religion altogether'.[27]

While in the eyes of contemporary Calcutta society the Derozians were a group of young boys misled by the rush of Western ideas, this view should be suitably qualified. Derozio himself was a talented poet who composed patriotic poems praising the country (India) where he was born. One of his students, Kashiprasad Ghosh (1809–1873), disputed the negative characterisation of Indians in James Mill's *The History of British India* (1817), and another, Udaychandra Addy (n/k), preferred Bengali over English when addressing public meetings. Notwithstanding their excesses, the Derozians represented a moral improvement over the preceding generation of the newly rich who had spent their lives in laziness and debauchery. The greatest virtue in Young Bengal was their moral uprightness. At the time, a Hindu 'College student' was taken to embody honesty and truthfulness.

---

27 Keshabchandra Sen. 'Young Bengal, This Is for You' (1860).

THE BRAHMO SAMAJ:
ITS PRINCIPLES AND PRACTICES

The Brahmo Samaj was the first body born of Reform Hinduism to establish a pan-Indian presence. It inspired similar reformist organisations outside Bengal and created the earliest religious missionaries in modern India who worked among a variety of social groups. Brahmo social and religious ideals were also carried over by Bengali migrants posted elsewhere in British India. This was most visible in the North-Western Provinces and the Punjab.

The word 'Brahmo' is cognate with 'Brahman', the metaphysical principle representing Supreme Reality/Absolute/God that features prominently in the writings of Rammohun. With the advantage of hindsight we may say that, regardless of recurring changes in their religious views, there were three core doctrines to which the Brahmos after Rammohun remained faithful: first, they upheld the concept of monotheism, or the worship of one God who was just, compassionate, and omnipotent; second, they strictly rejected the worship of idols or images in any form; third, they disapproved of the offices of both the *guru* and the priest. The Brahmos replaced the *guru* with the Acharya, or the Minister who conducted services. With certain other issues, the Brahmos were more flexible and agreed to change their position from time to time. For instance, under the leadership of Keshabchandra, they admitted the 'Motherhood' of God and even adopted typically Hindu-Vaishnava practices like public devotional singing on the streets (*sankirtana*).

During its history, the Brahmo Samaj suffered two successive schisms in 1866 and 1878 respectively, though not so much on account of doctrinal differences. Interestingly enough, these had more to do with non-religious issues, as, for instance, the question of democratic functioning or the pace at which reform was to be carried out.

The institutional foundations of the Brahmo Samaj developed during Rammohun's lifetime. The Brahmo Church was inaugurated on 23 January 1830; since then, this day has been annually celebrated as Maghotsava (literally, 'the festival falling in the month of January/February of the Bengali calendar'). In Rammohun's time, the Brahmos, less than a dozen in number, held weekly prayer meetings on a Saturday. This had to be later shifted to a Wednesday since the Raja's friends were reluctant to give up weekend entertainment for the sake of dull *upasana* (congregational worship)! Before leaving for England, the Raja left a Trust Deed for his followers which laid down the basic principles of the new body: it encouraged the adoration of God without resorting to any form of sectarian or idolatrous worship. A closer look at the document, however, reveals certain inner complexities. Thus, all people irrespective of their colour, creed, or sex were welcomed and no criticism was to be directed against any religious beliefs they held. At the same time, image worship was not permitted within the premises, which amounted to a rejection of certain forms of worship. For some, this might have meant following double standards in religious life: members could well have been idol-worshippers at home but shunned such worship when inside the Samaj. This was soon to cause some problems related to organisation and discipline within the community.

Hereafter, it became increasingly necessary to get Brahmos to agree to constitute a separate community and scrupulously follow all religious and social practices specific to that community. The transformation of the Brahmo Sabha (literally, 'gathering'), founded in 1828 by Rammohun, into the Brahmo Samaj ('formalised religious community') was largely the work of the Maharshi Debendranath and his successor in office, Keshabchandra Sen. Between them, they gave the Brahmos a new religious source book, a new set of rituals, a formal

Maharshi Debendranath Tagore (1817–1905).

Brahmo identity, and, above all, the courage and conviction to set themselves apart from the parental Hindu community. In 1843, twenty-one individuals, including Debendranath, were formally initiated into Brahmoism by the then Minister, Acharya Ramachandra Vidyabagish. In 1847, the term 'Brahmodharma' was formally adopted to describe the religion of the Brahmos. Still later, in 1866, Keshabchandra made the Brahmos sign a covenant pledging their loyalty to Brahmo ideals and to the Brahmo Church. Such Brahmos henceforth came to be called covenanted (*anushthanik*) Brahmos.

An early challenge faced by Maharshi Debendranath and his companions came from the Christian missionaries; this arose from the fact that at the time, Brahmoism was based on the philosophy of Vedanta as expounded in the Upanishads.

The missionaries found the Vedantic God to be neither a creator God – hence not worthy of reverence – nor a source of moral inspiration. Such charges Debendranath and his co-workers tried to answer in the discourse titled 'Vaidantic Doctrines Vindicated' (1845).

In the 1840s, the Maharshi was increasingly troubled by the presence of certain 'atheists' (*nastika*), as he called them, among his close companions and co-workers. Some of them were members of the Tattvabodhini Sabha, a society founded in 1839. Among the editors of the Sabha's journal, the *Tattvabodhini Patrika*, was a fierce rationalist by the name of Akshaykumar Dutta (1820–1886). Dutta was a staunch deist, a man of science, and quite discomfited by the Brahmos establishing their faith on the Vedic canon (*shruti*). Akshaykumar raised several questions that troubled Debendranath. For one, he alleged that the *shruti* was internally inconsistent and spoke

Akshaykumar Dutta (1820–1886).

with many voices. Around 1845–1846, Debendranath sent a team of scholars to Benares to closely study Vedic literature. On their return, the scholars supported Akshaykumar, forcing Debendranth to take the extremely courageous step of giving up the Vedas as the authoritative source book for Hindus. At the time, this must have looked like a moral victory for Akshaykumar, but it shocked most Hindus. The *shruti* was now substituted by a work called *Brahmodharmagrantha* (1849–1850), synthetically culled from a variety of sources including the Upanishads, Puranas, and Tantra.

Some other interesting facts about the Maharshi should be mentioned here. First, he distrusted Western Christianity but was drawn to contemporary European philosophy and mysticism, being particularly fond of the French mystic François Fenelon (1651–1715). Second, he was greatly captivated by the Persian mystic poetry of Saadi and Hafez (*c.* thirteenth–fourteenth centuries CE), which he would often recite in a state of rapture. Third, the Maharshi's life was marked by a strong spiritual quest and he refused to judge religion by measures of social utility: 'We are not among those who seek both God and this world; this world is acceptable to us only after we have made our acquaintance with God'.[28] He lacked the religious materialism of Rammohun.

The Brahmo theologian who soon surpassed even Debendranath in his thinking and rhetoric was Keshabchandra Sen. It was with Keshab that the fortunes of the Brahmo Samaj had risen, and it was with him again that it went down in public regard. Keshabchandra was the first non-brahmin Brahmo Minister; with him the emphasis on social questions became quite pronounced. He supported female education,

---

28 Debendranath Tagore, *Brahmodharmer Vyakhyan* (An Exposition on Brahmoism, 1861; reprinted Calcutta, 1965), 172.

assigning to the woman and wife new roles within the domestic economy of the Hindus. Keshab encouraged inter-caste marriages and widow marriages and, quite extraordinarily, decided to seat men and women together at prayer meetings. There was also a new emphasis on promoting vernacular literature and journalism, and a number of new papers and journals started under his inspiration, including the *Sulabh Samachar*, a Bengali daily priced at an insignificant one *paisa*. Night schools were opened for working men, and drinking of spirits among all classes seriously discouraged.

Keshab was a gifted orator and delivered a series of lectures and sermons which enthralled an audience comprising a good number of Englishmen. In the 1860s, two of his lectures, 'Jesus Christ, Europe and Asia' and 'Asia's Message to Europe', were highly acclaimed both in India and abroad. With Rammohun, he was the Brahmo leader who emphasised the Asiatic origins of Christ, thereby rejecting Eurocentric views of Christianity, proclaiming Asia to be the seat of major world religions, and creating an early form of pan-Asian consciousness. Over the years, Keshabchandra also became a great follower of Christ and Christianity, and this became a matter of suspicion even among Brahmos. What compounded matters was the fact that Keshab commanded the loyalty and respect of the younger generation of Brahmos. The conservative Debendranath felt threatened by the 'reckless' speed at which the Keshab party wished to carry out reform. Matters came to a head when, in November 1866, about 200 Brahmos seceded to form a new church, which they called the Bharatvarshiya Brahmo Samaj, with Keshab as their leader. This was the first of the two schisms within the movement. Debendranath's camp renamed itself the 'Adi' or the original Brahmo Samaj, and insisted on retaining links with parental Hindu society.

In 1870, Keshab travelled to England at the invitation of the British Unitarians and spent some productive months meeting noted public figures and alerting the British press and public to the urgency of Indian reform in several matters. Around the same time, he also met the Hindu mystic Ramakrishna Paramahamsa, a priest serving a temple complex located a few miles north of Calcutta. Ramakrishna appears to have influenced Keshab in two important ways. He strengthened Keshab's experiments in borrowing from several religious traditions. Keshab now also conceptualised God as 'Mother', as known to certain sub-traditions within Hinduism. Such eclecticism eventually led to the establishment of the New Dispensation Church, or the 'Nababidhan' around 1879–1880,

Keshab's daughter, Maharani Suniti Devi of Cooch Behar, c. 1885.

which tried to syncretise ideas and imageries taken from various religious traditions. The experiment failed as dramatically as it had arisen, but with Keshabchandra there also began the serious study of comparative religion. One of his followers, Girishchandra Sen (1835–1910), produced the first Bengali translation of the Koran.

The issues which made Keshab quite unpopular as a religious leader had little to do with religion itself. He was accused of an 'authoritarian' style of functioning that would not tolerate difference or dissent. But the event that seriously damaged his reputation and qualities as a leader was the controversy surrounding the marriage of his daughter, Suniti Devi. In 1872, Keshab had helped enact a law under which Brahmo girls could not marry below the age of fourteen. In 1878, Keshab married his daughter to a Hindu from the princely state of Cooch Behar in north Bengal, even though she had not attained this legal age. His political views, too, now came in for sharp criticism. Keshabchandra had long been known for his loyalty to British rule, and those who had once been inspired by his charisma now felt let down by his reluctance to support patriotic sentiments. Taken together, these issues led to the second schism in the Samaj. A number of young men severed their relations with Keshabchandra on 15 May 1878 and founded a new body called the Sadharan Brahmo Samaj. With its incorporation of the word *sadharan* ('common, public'), the name clearly carried a message of greater openness and democratic ways of functioning. Most members of the Sadharan Samaj were young and involved with political agitation. Some of them, like Bipinchandra Pal (1858–1932), Ashwini Kumar Dutta (1856–1923), and Krishna Kumar Mitra (1852–1936), were militants who suffered varying jail terms. After 1878, the Sadharan Brahmo Samaj was the most active of the three wings of the Brahmo Samaj. It produced several theologians, scientists, philosophers, political workers, teachers, and scholars.

In the early years of the twentieth century, the most sophisticated expression of Brahmo religious and spiritual ideals came from the poet Rabindranath Tagore. Tagore composed evocative religious songs and poetry marked by a deep sense of piety. Tagore was neither a theologian nor a philosopher but felt drawn to the mystic poetry of the wandering Bauls of Bengal. Towards the closing years of his life, he distanced himself from the regular working of the Brahmo Samaj and chose to express his spiritual anguish in very abstract terms. A good instance of this was the public lecture he delivered at Oxford in 1931 and to which he gave the title *The Religion of Man*.

Bankimchandra Chattopadhyay (1838–1894).

Reason and Reaction in Colonial Bengal: The Life and Work of Bankimchandra Chattopadhyay

By the 1880s, the intellectual and cultural environment in Bengal had changed perceptibly. After the first flush of excitement had worn off, many Hindus wondered if they had indeed overreached themselves. Many now began to clearly react to the ways of Young Bengal and, subsequently, of the Brahmo Samaj. Both these groups appeared to comprise 'denationalised' upstarts. Educated Hindus now increasingly expressed reservations about the acclaimed 'superiority' of Western thought and culture. Being subjected to foreign rule was bad enough in itself, but with that arrived also the fear of being uprooted from one's cultural world. By the third quarter of the nineteenth century, this transformation in intellectual and cultural attitudes was best exemplified by Bankimchandra Chattopadhyay.

Bankimchandra belonged to a family of respectable and professionally successful brahmins. In 1858, he was one of the two men to first graduate from the newly opened Calcutta University, the first modern university to be set up in India. Thereupon he was nominated to the post of Deputy Magistrate, an office the British conferred upon people whose competence and loyalty they trusted.

Service under the colonial administration considerably diluted the faith he once had in the progressive nature of British rule: soon Bankimchandra used his immense literary gifts to persuade his fellow Bengalis to critically reassess the new political and cultural world in which they were placed. Bankimchandra was India's first successful novelist, and he used this innovative literary form to create new waves of thought and feeling. He also made a considerable contribution to the development of Bengali prose and vernacular journalism.

The *Bangadarshan,* the Bengali monthly that he launched in 1872, soon became a popular and greatly successful vehicle for disseminating new thoughts on a wide range of subjects, including art, politics, science, literature, society, religion, and everyday relationships. In his day, Bankimchandra was perhaps the best read in the history, philosophy, and literature of Europe, but he did not accept any of this uncritically. On the contrary, he was consistently engaged with the question of how a Hindu would best learn from the West without culturally uprooting himself. Like Rammohun before him, Bankimchandra believed that British rule would liberate India from social prejudices and superstition and ought not to be overthrown until such time as Indians had raised themselves to the level of their political masters.

Bankimchandra observed with great acuity shortcomings among Hindus in matters of intellectual thought and forms of social organisation. In his *Essays on Hinduism* (n.d.), he noted how Hindus had failed to develop an inductive line of reasoning based on actual observations which alone could produce a scientific temperament. He also effectively employed the newly developing disciplines of history, sociology, and cultural anthropology to suitably instruct his readers. For instance, he demonstrated how several Indian festivals, long taken to be religious in origin or character, were actually based on agrarian cycles of production.

Bankimchandra's most important interventions, however, were in the matter of defending Hindu religion and culture and this took broadly three directions. First, he condemned archaic and irrational definitions of Hinduism, and argued for giving Hindu scriptures not a fixed but a contemporaneous meaning. Second, Bankimchandra contested European projections of Hinduism and, more specifically, the possibility of European scholars and observers understanding Hinduism better than the Hindus themselves. This led him to oppose both the Indologist Max Müller (1823–1900) over the interpretation of Vedic deities and the Calcutta-based scholar Rev. William Hastie (1842–1903), who had accused educated Hindus of being idol-worshippers. Third, Bankimchandra contributed to the revival of Vaishnava devotional culture in modern Bengal. His chosen ideal was Krishna: the figure drawn not from the Puranas or folk culture but from the *Mahabharata*, where he was portrayed as an accomplished warrior and statesman. In his retelling of the Krishna narrative, he was clearly influenced by the works of Ernest Renan and David Strauss (*The Life of Jesus*, 1863, 1865) who had tried to recover the historical Jesus from the figure surrounded by myths, miracles, and legends. In another major work (*Dharmatattva*, 1888), he took *dharma* as an organising principle in society.

Bankimchandra's reinterpretation of Hinduism was addressed to a particular class. This was the class of Western-educated, middle-class Hindu Bengalis who disapproved of obsolete and irrational elements within contemporary Hinduism but were reluctant to sever their connections with parental Hindu society. His writings gave this class of Hindus food for thought and ways of reconciling a just pride in tradition with the willingness to work towards modernity.

Bankimchandra's thought has often been labelled as 'revivalist'. However, the term is inappropriate, since his writings do not reveal hatred of the foreigner or the socially reactionary tendencies visible in some of his contemporaries. Unlike others, he never openly abused non-Hindu traditions, nor did he empathise with Hindu missionary organisations which were emerging in his time and which opposed a new social order.

Social and Religious Dissent in the Colonial Hinterland: Nineteenth-Century Odisha and the Mahima Dharma Movement

British rule was less successful in penetrating the outlying areas of the Bengal Presidency like Odisha, where new social ideas or institutions were accepted less readily and, for that reason, changes met with greater resistance. Odisha became a part of British India only in 1803 and remained a relatively underdeveloped hinterland for a long time. Higher education arrived here with the foundation of the Ravenshaw College in 1868, and even ten years later, this was the only institution of higher learning in Odisha. Professional colleges were set up still later. This produced a relatively smaller class of intelligentsia and over a longer period of time.

Modern-day Mahima ascetics at Joranda Gadi, Dhenkanal.

Not surprisingly, therefore, in colonial Odisha the inspiration for changes in the status quo first arose not from a modern intelligentsia but from illiterate, dissenting lower castes or tribes who had challenged older social hierarchies and ways of religious life. Medieval Odisha, for instance, had been home to the faiths of Vaishnavism and Buddhism, which had attracted lower castes and the socially marginalised.

Around 1826, there appeared at Puri, the famous pilgrim town associated with the Jagannath cult, an ascetic by the name of Mukunda Das, later popularly known as Mahima Gossain. In all probability Mukunda was a Vaishnava mendicant or recluse who had been travelling in Odisha for some time past. Officials stationed at Puri saw him as a troublemaker. In 1873, he clashed with the local authorities but somehow escaped prosecution by fleeing Puri. He died in 1876 and was buried at Joranda (Dhenkanal district of Odisha). This burial spot

*Late nineteenth-century etching of the entrance to
the Jagannath Temple in Puri, Odisha.*

later became the nucleus of a new monastic order dedicated to Mahima Swami; it is currently the most important centre of the Mahima Dharma movement.

The expression Mahima Dharma literally means the '*dharma of glory*'. In some respects, the movement deviated from mainstream Hinduism. Mahima Gossain's followers took him to be a reincarnation of *Alekh* (after the Sanskrit *alakshya*), the unseen and indescribable Absolute. This indicates influences from the older tradition of Nirguni Sants and Nath Yogis, who invoked the expression '*alakh niranjan*' ('the stainless Absolute'). Ascetics of the Joranda Ashram later used this invocation to declare their conformity to Vedanta Hinduism.

Sometime before his death, Mahima Gossain chose a man of tribal origin named Bhima Boi (1850–1895) to be his spiritual successor. After the death of his *guru*, Bhima assumed leadership of the movement, setting up an independent centre at Khaliapali (Bargarh district, Odisha) in 1877. Eventually, however, the two *ashrams* at Joranda and Khaliapali respectively came to represent two dissimilar faces of the movement.

Bhima himself led a stormy life. The Indian Census Reports of 1911 state that in March 1881, he and his followers attempted to storm the Jagannath Temple at Puri and take it under their control. Some followers of Mahima Dharma regarded Lord Jagannath to be a disciple of Mahima Gossain himself. Such claims were clearly aimed at gaining some legitimacy for a radical, dissenting movement.

Bhima's life and work are contentious and debated within the Mahima tradition. For one, it is not clear if he was an ascetic or a householder. However, there is no reason to doubt that he attracted female followers, one of whom later came to be revered in the tradition as his Divine Consort. Bhima was certainly a gifted poet whose compositions (mostly included in his two best-known works, the *Stutichintamani* and the *Bhajanamala*) reveal a generous borrowing of older terms known to both Hinduism and Buddhism. Several terms were borrowed from the Tantric-Yogic traditions, indicating the use of mystic and meditative practices. The emphasis on songs and on spontaneous devotional music (to the exclusion of philosophical texts) loosely connects this movement with the popular cults of the Bauls, Sahajiyas, and Fakirs, which roamed many parts of eastern India in good numbers.

Bhima Boi spurned the common Hindu practice of image worship and frowned upon pilgrimages. His followers were forbidden to accept food from brahmins, princes, barbers, and merchants, ostensibly on moral grounds. In itself this is a dramatic reversal of Hindu norms since traditionally, the brahmin was the only *varna/jati* whose food was considered ritually pure and could be accepted by all castes. Claims are sometimes also made about gender equality within the movement: at the Joranda *ashram*, only males were allowed to enter and accept the status of an ascetic. The supporters of this *ashram* were mostly rich peasants of western and central Odisha, whereas the Khaliapali *ashram* was made up of tribes and marginalised castes. The Joranda *ashram* openly conformed to upper-caste religious culture, not radical dissent. This remained the profile under Vishwanath Baba, who controlled the affairs of this *ashram* from about the 1920s to the 1990s. Even at the peak of its popularity, the Mahima Dharma movement showed a greater opposition to Hindu social norms than to religious thought or practices.

When compared to the reform movements occurring in the metropolitan areas, the movement led by Mahima Gossain and his followers is easily distinguished by its class character but also certain methods of operation. It was not inspired by Western ideologies or by social and religious movements influenced by the West; rather, it drew upon the resources of an

Mountstuart Elphinstone (1779–1859).

indigenous tradition of questioning and dissent that had once characterised the anti-Brahmanical movements in medieval India. Since this movement remained essentially a rural one, recruited mainly from tribes, farming, and artisan castes, it remained largely localised. It had no press or publicists of its own, no body of literature to boast of, and no preachers of a pan-India standing. It was ignored by the British authorities and went unnoticed in the reformist Hindu press.

NEW MORAL AND RELIGIOUS IDEAS IN THE BOMBAY PRESIDENCY

The Marathas who had once controlled the territory of the Bombay Presidency were defeated in successive wars and fully annexed to the British Empire in India by 1818. Territorially, the presidency covered the bulk of Maharashtra, Gujarat, and the northwestern part of the present Indian state of Karnataka. Sind was added to it in 1843.

The last of the Maratha rulers, the Peshwa Baji Rao II, was pensioned off and the Bombay Presidency put under the administrative control of military officers appointed by the Company. The first of these, the Scot Mountstuart Elphinstone (1779–1859), was Lt. Governor of Bombay between 1819 and 1827. He was a man who respected traditional indigenous institutions, somewhat like the Calcutta-based Orientalists, and did not support the spread of modern English education for purely pragmatic purposes.

In Elphinstone's time, older educational and administrative policies were allowed to continue. Elphinstone continued the policy of honouring brahmin scholarship through what was commonly known as the institution of *dakshina*, stipends awarded annually to deserving brahmin scholars. In the 1820s, as many as fifty-one *pathshalas* (native primary schools) in Poona imparted Vedic studies. The Hindu College in Poona (founded in 1821) was exclusively devoted to the study of Hindu *shastras*, with the study of English and vernaculars such as Marathi, Kannada, and Gujarati introduced only in 1837.

At both Bombay and Poona (now Pune), social and intellectual life was dominated by the brahmins. In 1870, of the 179 students at the Elphinstone College, Bombay, about 34 per cent were from the brahmin caste alone. By the early 1880s, over 90 per cent of students at the Poona College (renamed Deccan College) were brahmins. This accounts for a significant difference in the social composition of the student community in the presidencies of Bengal and Bombay. Elphinstone himself noted that the commercial classes in Bombay had no social influence outside the city of Bombay and were not particularly interested in promoting modern education. By comparison, at the Presidency College, Calcutta, the largest single group of students was drawn from the landowning and independent professions.

The pioneer of the renaissance in Maharashtra is considered to be B. G. Jambhekar (1812–1846), who served the Elphinstone College and later the provincial Education Department. Reformist yet somewhat orthodox in his temperament, Jambhekar disapproved of Rammohun for having unduly 'forsaken' his ancestral religion. He was also the father of modern journalism in Maharashtra, founding the *Bombay Darpan* and the monthly *Digdarshan*, which may be justly compared to the role played by Bankimchandra's *Bangadarshan* in Bengal. In him are also found early anxieties about the inroads that Christianity was making among the educated Maratha youth. In 1843, he was instrumental in readmitting to Hindu society a convert by the name of Narayan Govind Paralikar.

Nineteenth-century Maharashtra saw a greater awareness of local history and society – also initiated by a brahmin. Gopal Hari Deshmukh (1823–1892) was a prolific contributor to Marathi journalism who wrote under the pseudonym 'Lokahitawadi' (literally, 'man who advocates the common good'). From the 1840s, he started contributing regularly to a variety of Marathi periodicals like the *Prabhakar, Jnanprakash,* and *Vrittavaibhava*. His best-known writing, however, was a series of a hundred letters (*Shatapatre*) that appeared in the *Prabhakar* between 1848 and 1850. Deshmukh was saddened by the lethargy, incompetence, and corruption among his countrymen and rued the fact that they took no effective steps to overcome these. In raising such concerns, Lokahitawadi served as the precursor to men like Mahadev Govind Ranade, Narayan Ganesh Chandravarkar (1855–1923), and Ramkrishna Gopal Bhandarkar (1827–1925), whose speeches and writings were soon to create a new intellectual and cultural milieu in modern Maharashtra.

The link between Jambhekar and the new crop of thinkers and reformers was Dadoba Pandurang Tarkhadkar (1814–1882), who belonged to a mercantile community. In 1844, he, together with a Gujarati colleague at Surat,

Durgaram Mancharam Mehta (1809–1876), established the Manava Dharma Sabha, an organisation intended to promote a reformed religion among his close circle of friends and acquaintances. The Sabha accepted the idea of God as the moral governor of the universe and emphasised the value of prayer; it also rejected caste, conceptualising all humanity to be tied in a common brotherhood. For a time, the transactions of the Sabha were diligently recorded by Durgaram Mehta and represent some of the earliest writings of the kind. In 1846, when Dadoba was transferred from Surat to Bombay and Durgaram, too, was soon forced to leave Surat for good, the meetings of the Manava Dharma Sabha became irregular and the body finally ceased to exist.

In 1849, when serving in the Education Department, Dadoba inspired the idea of the Paramahamsa Mandali at Bombay, though it is widely believed that he personally never attended any of its meetings. The Mandali was a body that met secretly and somewhat dramatically defied common social conventions. Membership was granted only upon accepting water served by a Muslim and eating bread baked by a European baker. The members of the Mandali rejected the infallibility of scriptures and preferred the pious adoration of God to the abstract philosophy of the Advaita Vedanta. The activities of the Mandali, not surprisingly, were hidden from public knowledge for quite some time; however, in 1860, information regarding its membership was leaked to the press and the body had to be promptly closed down.

The religious views of Dadoba were encapsulated in two works, the *Dharmavivechana* (1848) and the *Paramahamsik Brahmodharma* (1880). He is known to have seriously engaged with the work of the Swedish theologian and mystic Emanuel Swedenborg (1688–1772), as evidenced in his *A Hindu Gentleman's Reflections Regarding the Work of Swedenborg* (1879). Dadoba was also the inspiration behind student literary and debating clubs which he started in 1848 under the name of Upayukta Jnanprasarak Sabha (Society for the Dissemination of Right Knowledge).

Dadoba also set up the Prarthana Samaj (literally, 'Prayer Society'), a more public and respectable body than its precursor, the Paramahamsa Mandali. It eventually travelled beyond Maharashtra into South India and was inspired by Brahmo leaders of Calcutta, most notably by Keshabchandra Sen, who visited Bombay successively in 1864 and 1867. The society was founded in 1867 at the residence of Dr. Atmaram Pandurang (1823–1898), Dadoba's younger brother. Atmaram was among the earliest to pass out of the Grant Medical College in Bombay, co-founder of the Bombay Natural History Society, and, briefly, the Sheriff of Bombay. Other than the Pandurang brothers, all other members of this body were brahmins. The Prarthana Samaj turned a new leaf when, in 1870, both Ranade and Bhandarkar joined it. In 1880 it was joined by S. P. Kelkar (n/k), Narayan G. Chandravarkar, and Pandita Ramabai (1858–1922).

The religious ideology of the Prarthana Samaj was largely modelled on the Brahmo Samaj. It entirely accepted the Brahmo rejection of the Vedas as a work of revelation, the critique of image worship, and its strict monotheism. It stressed the role of prayer and meditation in character building and the importance of social service. Like the Brahmos, it held a weekly service on Sundays and believed in the efficacy of repentance before God for one's sinful acts. Where it differed from the Brahmo Samaj was in its pronounced effort to integrate the *bhakti* sentiments associated with the local *bhakti* movement based at Pandharpur with the modern theistic revival. In 1880, Sophia Dobson Collet, the author of the first major biography of Rammohun Roy, observed the following of the Prarthana Samaj:

Sir Ramakrishna Gopal Bhandarkar (1837–1925).

[I]t is of indigenous origin and of independent standing.
It has never detached itself from the Hindu element of
Brahmanism as many of the Bengali Samajes . . . .
It is more learned and less emotional in its tone and
far more cautious and less radical in its policy than the
chief Samajes of Bengal.[29]

Between the 1870s and 1890s, the culture of theism was
reinforced by the writings and public addresses of Ranade and
Bhandarkar, both within and outside the Parthana Samaj. In a
lecture delivered at the Samaj in 1883 titled 'Basis of Theism and
Its Relation to the So-Called Revealed Religions', Bhandarkar
claimed, much in the manner of Rammohun himself, that
all religions had elements of truth and falsehood in them.

---

29 Collet, Sophia Dobson (ed.), *Brahmo Year-Book: Brief Records of Work
    and Life in the Theistic Churches of India* (London: Williams and Norgate.
    1880).

He further argued that the function of religious belief in the development of mankind was higher than secular knowledge. Borrowing Herbert Spencer's idea of social evolution he applied it to the field of religion: in his understanding, the progressive evolution of human religious life paralleled the path of biological evolution. His basic argument, though, was for banishing atheism, and, here, he did not hesitate to fault the Buddha himself. In Bhandarkar's opinion, the Buddha's agnosticism had led to humanity's losing a friend in the personality of God. Not surprisingly, he also supported the idea of revelation, arguing that it was only natural that higher religious conceptions should be revealed to man by the Supreme Being. Bhandarkar strongly advocated the necessity for reforming Hindu religious life:

> The existing forms of (Hindu) religion, belonging as they do to the earliest stage of civilization are destined, if India is to advance, to disappear . . . . And the existing mechanical modes of worship must be entirely thrown away and the spiritual mode substituted to bring about the real reformation of the country which is so urgently required.[30]

Ranade agreed with Bhandarkar on the need for revelation. It was essentially a common revelation, he argued, that all humanity would witness, although seen in different ways. Ranade's best statement on theism occurs in an undated lecture called 'Philosophy of Indian Theism'. This lecture rejected both pantheism and polytheism as well as austerities and ascetic practices. The idea of God incarnating on Earth he found unacceptable, and visits to temples were not absolutely necessary. Ranade did not entirely reject the office of the

---

30 Ramkrishna Gopal Bhandarkar, 'The Position of the Prarthana Samaj in the Religious World' (1903).

priest; he only discouraged the idea of making it hereditary. The social events of birth, initiation, marriage, and death, in his opinion, had to be backed by some religious sanction.

Though modelled on the Brahmo Samaj, the Prarthana Samaj in Bombay was not the refuge of rebels who had severed their connections with their family or the larger community. On the contrary, it represented a respectable body of gifted and influential thinkers of the region who did not wish to confuse reform with revolution. Rao Bahadur Waman Rao Madhav Kolhatkar, who rose to the position of District and Sessions Judge, put this very well in a comparison that he drew between developments in Bombay and Bengal:

> In Bengal social reform has been in a degree impeded by the tacit requirement of conformity with the principles of Brahmoism, which is the religion of the reformers, while in Bombay, the reformers continuing as they do in the religion of their ancestors, are not estranged from popular sympathy to the degree they have been in Bengal. In Bengal the social reform has assumed the shape of a caste question, while in Bombay, the refusal of the reformer to claim a separate caste for themselves has set the whole society in a ferment. Reform is bound to live an isolated life in Bengal and to be general in Bombay.[31]

The cultural renaissance in nineteenth-century Maharashtra was almost exclusively the work of the 'new brahmins' who were

---

31 Waman Rao Madhav Kolhatkar, 'Widow Re-marriage', in *Indian Social Reform. In Four Parts. Being a Collection of Essays, Addresses, Speeches etc* (with an Appendix), Part I, edited by C. Yajneshvara Chintamani (Madras: Minerva Press 1901), 311.

ideologically persuaded by the education they had received at institutions like the Elphinstone and Deccan Colleges. Unlike the brahmins of old, they wished not to subsist on state patronage but to assume social and political leadership. However, their approach was not to unduly shock orthodox sentiments or radically break with the tradition. Ranade persistently warned reformers not to break with their past or cease all connections with the native society. In the 1880s, the Russian traveller A. P. Minayeff, who was passing through Maharashtra, noticed that the students of the Deccan College in Poona were as committed to the new social theories of Herbert Spencer as they were to the traditions of Hindu spirituality.

INTELLECTUAL FERMENT IN NINETEENTH-CENTURY GUJARAT

Like Maharashtra, Gujarat had been deeply influenced by the medieval *bhakti* movement: the very moving Vaishnava lyrics of the fifteenth-century poet Narsi Mehta cast a spell even on later political workers like Gandhi. Hindu society in this region was also influenced by the upper castes, chiefly the Nagar brahmins.

We have already referred to the work of Durgaram Mancharam Mehta and the Manava Dharma Sabha. What connects Durgaram to his intellectual successors is the pressing interest in progressive thought and literature. In the 1840s, Durgaram is known to have maintained diaries and also produced a textbook on elementary science (*Vigyan Pustak*). An early thinker from Gujarat who contributed substantively to the intellectual awakening in the region was Mahipatram Rupram Nilkanth (1829–1891), a Nagar brahmin born in Surat. Mahipatram came under the influence of both Durgaram Mehta and Dadoba Pandurang, which inspired him to be actively associated with educational work. He was an active member of intellectual bodies like the

Gyan Prasarak Sabha and the Buddhi Vardhak Sabha, which worked towards the education and intellectual training of young men. In 1860, he proceeded to England for higher training, defying stiff resistance from his community. On his return to India he was excommunicated by the brahmin community for as long as twelve years. Mahipatram braved this troubling period in his life with grace and fortitude, never going back on his commitment to the social causes to which he had committed himself. Over the years he emerged as a prominent author and writer of school textbooks, which is comparable to the efforts of his eminent contemporary from Bengal, Ishwarchandra Vidyasagar.[32]

Narmadashankar Lalshankar Dave (1833–1886) was a gifted figure from mid-nineteenth-century Gujarat and became known to posterity as 'Arvachina ma Adya' (First Among Moderns). Narmadashankar produced many works, including an anthology of poems, plays, and grammatical works; in his early life, largely spent in Surat, he was associated with voluntary organisations like the Buddhivardhak Sabha, which was pledged to spreading modern education and progressive values among young men. He contributed to modern Gujarati journalism by establishing two journals, *Gyan Sagar* (1851) and *Dandiyo* (1864). Narmadashankar was the first literary figure in the province to deliberately use words and expressions like *desh* ('nation') and *swabhiman* ('patriotic pride') to foster a sense of unity among the Gujarati people. He also coined the slogan 'Jai Jai Garvi Gujarat' ('Hail, glorious Gujarat!'), a sentiment that evokes Gujarati sentiments even today.

---

32 It is little known that Mahipatram Rupram is the author of one of the earliest travelogues written by an Indian travelling to England in the nineteenth century. This work, called *Englandni Musafarinu Varnan* (*A Description of My Voyage to England*), was published in 1862.

Traditional portrait of Swaminarayan (1781–1830).

In his social and religious views, Narmadashankar, too, was drawn to the ideals of the Brahmo Samaj and to the figure of Keshabchandra Sen in particular. This led him to question the value of antiquated scriptures, support the marriage of widows, and express anxiety at the alleged 'degeneration' of Hindu society. His *Hinduo Ni Padli* (1884) found Vaishnavas, especially those belonging to the Swaminarayan cult,[33] to be the cause of moral decadence. Some of his works take God to be formless, critique image worship, and deny the possibility of God incarnating on Earth. In addition to Brahmo influences, such views may have been reinforced by a meeting

---

33 On the Swaminarayan cult, see the next section.

with the Gujarati reformer Swami Dayanand Saraswati,[34] who was visiting Bombay at the time. However, Narmadashankar turned more conservative with age. Initially supporting female education, he later alleged that this had the undesirable effect of making women lazy and neglectful of their household duties. Similarly, he began by supporting widow marriage but later found the life of chastity (*brahmacharya*) to be better suited to widows than marriage.

Such hardening of social attitudes is also visible in Manubhai Nathubhai (1858–1898). Manubhai married an infant girl and vigorously contested the issue of widow marriage in the Gujarati Social Union. Like several Hindu reformers of his time, he believed degenerate Hinduism to have appeared with the Puranas; unlike them, he was dogmatic and distrustful of other religions. In his understanding, reform work in India had failed because it was far too influenced by the British and by Western Christianity. He also claimed that other world religions like Islam or Christianity were derived from Advaita Vedanta and that the Prophet Mohammad was really a worshipper of the Vedantic Brahman.

REFORMING HINDUISM OUTSIDE 'REFORM': THE SWAMINARAYAN MOVEMENT

In the Kathiawar region of Gujarat, a new religious order sprang up in 1801 and had reached great popularity by the 1830s. A movement that appears not to have been significantly influenced by the new ideology of 'reform', it resembled traditional religious movements strongly anchored in the personal charisma of a religious leader. Its founder, Ghanashyam Pande, took the monastic name of Sahajanand

---

34 On Dayanand and the Arya Samaj, which he founded, see Chapter 4.

Kalupur Swaminarayan temple in Ahmedabad, Gujarat, c. 1866.

Swami (1781–1830) but was widely known as Swami Narayan, after the Divine Form in which he worshipped and with which he was himself later identified.

Sahajanand, too, drew inspiration from the school of Vedanta but with certain important differences. For one, his religion was more in the nature of Vaishnava Vedanta, which developed after Acharya Shankara and infused Vedantic philosophy with *bhakti* sentiments. The teachings of Sahajanand reveal influences from the philosophical schools of both Vishishtadvaita of Ramanuja and the Pushtimarga of Vallabhacharya, both of which worshipped God in human forms. The *Shikshapatri*, one of the two core texts of the Swaminarayan cult, refers specifically to Vallabha and to his son, Vitthalanatha. The Swaminarayan community readily accepted the sanctity of divine images and of ornate, ritualistic worship, both of which later became objects of criticism by modern reformers. The Gujarati reformer Narmadashankar Lalshankar, it may be recalled, directed his sharpest invectives against the Swaminarayanis. On his visit to the Bombay Presidency, Swami Dayanand Saraswati found religious life there to be as immoral and socially despicable as that of the Pushtimargis or the Vallabhacharya sect of Vaishnavism. The views of both Narmadashankar and Swami Dayanand are very likely to have been influenced by the exposé of the Pushtimargis' scandalous sexual misconduct by the reformer Karsondas Mulji (1832–1871) in the well-known Maharaj libel case tried before the Bombay High Court in 1862.

Sahajanand's religion and that of his followers developed around impressive temple complexes. Between 1822 and 1828, Sahajanand himself organised the construction of five temples in various parts of Gujarat. Contrary to Brahmo practice in Bengal, the Swaminarayanis allowed the institution of both ascetics and lay disciples; they were, and have continued to be, a fairly large religious community. In Sahajanand's own lifetime they numbered around 3,000, by 1872, only a little short of 400,000.

Two further points of contrast between the Brahmos and Swaminarayanis may be mentioned here. With regard to caste, the position adopted by the Swaminarayanis is somewhat peculiar: while people from all castes could be recruited, the post of the Acharya or Minister was reserved for a brahmin, which obviously conformed to the older Hindu practice. The Brahmos, on the other hand, had dared to appoint the non-brahmin Keshabchandra as Acharya and some among them even formally renounced the sacred thread. Further, whereas the Brahmos were essentially recruited from English-educated, middle-class professionals, the Swaminarayan community belonged to the class of indigenous bankers, brokers, traders, and shopkeepers. As early as 1847, Swaminarayan annual income from public donation was about 175,000 rupees. Even today, it remains a highly affluent religious community within the expanding world of global Hinduism.

It is doubtful if news of developments in Bengal reached distant Gujarat in Sahajanand's lifetime. Nevertheless, like the Brahmos, the followers of the Swaminarayan religion valued ethical correctness in life. They were also strict monotheists, although their revered deity was a form of the Puranic god, Krishna, rather than the impersonal Brahman of the Upanishads. Like Rammohun, Sahajanand was personally acquainted with Christian missionaries and the rudiments of Christianity. Reginald Heber, Bishop of Calcutta, is known to have met Sahajanand and initially held hopes of converting him to Christianity. The Bishop eventually gave up these hopes, finding his acquaintance far too engrossed in 'heathen' image worship. It is quite likely, though, that an emphasis on humanitarian social service found in the early Swaminarayan community was reinforced by Sahajanand's familiarity with the work of Christian missionaries. While Rammohun relied mostly on translating Hindu religious classics and commenting upon them, Sahajanand and his disciples preferred to produce their own religious and moral texts, albeit based on older scriptures. Their principal theological text, called the *Vachanamrita* (Nectar-like Discourses), is a compilation of Sahajanand's preaching compiled by disciples between 1819 and 1829. Their moral injunctions are compiled as *Shikshapatri* (1826). This work comes down heavily against the killing of animals for food, the consumption of spirits, theft, robbery, and sexual promiscuity, and insists on the strict regulation of everyday domestic life. Generally speaking, it upholds a patriarchal social order, insisting on 'virtuous' and servile conduct on the part of women and wives even though it disapproves of cruel malpractices like *sati*. Evidently, the Swaminarayan community was eager to have its ideas or practices known to the British ruling class and possibly also counted on its support. A copy of the *Shikshapatri* was personally presented by Sahajanand to Sir John Malcolm, the then Governor of Bombay.

As a person, Sahajanand was flamboyant, polemical, and authoritarian. When on his rounds, he was known to ride a horse accompanied by armed guards. The authority and power that he wielded in his community came from the fact that he was widely regarded as an incarnation, often identified with Purushottama, the highest Divine Being.

CONCLUSION

This chapter began by examining the term 'reform' both as a concept and a practice, underlining its inner complexities. We next studied in detail the history of reform in the presidencies of Bengal and Bombay, related to the Hindus inhabiting these regions. The chapter has sought to bring out the important characteristics of what has now been identified as 'reform Hinduism' as well as some of its variations.

In the first case, reform was taken to be a distinct ideology that was vitally shaped by new ideas and values arriving from contemporary Europe. It was also associated with the emerging class of Western-educated Hindus, who, by virtue of their exposure to the new learning, were persuaded to bring about certain significant changes in their social and religious thought and practices. These men were self-conscious reformers who took upon themselves the task of suitably modernising their society. However, this chapter has also demonstrated how local conditions vitally shaped the way Hindus approached this question. Bengal, the earliest region to be brought under British control, was also rapidly influenced by ideas and values spread through a modern education. In the course of time, this produced in Bengal the paradoxical effect of encouraging a blind imitation of the West and Western ways of life followed by a strong reaction to its alienating effects. By comparison, the Bombay Presidency, which joined British India later, was more moderate in its approach. Bengal focused more on reform related to religion than to social practices. In some other parts of British India, the caste question was the subject of far more agitation.

However, insofar as reform work implied dissatisfaction with the existing state of society and religion, it also appeared in other forms. Whereas 'reform Hinduism' was principally an urban movement led by a Western-educated intelligentsia, other movements at changing the status quo occurred in the outlying areas or rural hinterlands, away from the largest or populous towns, led by different social groups. We have examined two of these movements occurring in the Bengal and Bombay Presidencies. The Mahima Dharma movement in Odisha was essentially a movement of lower-caste peasants, artisans, and tribes, while the Swaminarayan movement in Gujarat recruited its followers from the traditional mercantile classes or petty businessmen. Also, such movements relied far more on the personal charisma of their leader and did not adopt modern forms of functioning or organisation. In hindsight, these are best understood as extensions of older movements of dissent and not produced by changes uniquely brought about by colonialism. Interestingly, though, such movements were not entirely unaffected by the new social and political environment in nineteenth-century India and shared certain ideas or approaches with those led by the educated upper classes. Swami Sahajanand was aware of the presence of Christian missionaries and European officials, and Bhima Boi clashed with the colonial magistrates and the police. It is also the case that often movements started by the lower classes subsequently attracted patrons from the educated upper castes or classes. This was true of both Mahima Dharma and the Swaminarayan movement.

From this it would be reasonable to conclude that the spirit of reformism in colonial India was not created entirely by the Western impact on the Indian mind. Both Rammohun and Swami Dayanand (discussed in the next chapter) are known to have developed a rational critique of religion and society at a time when they had very little knowledge of the West. In this sense, the history of social and religious reform in colonial India was facilitated by the British colonial presence, not caused by it.

Discussion Topic: Reform Hinduism in the Bengal and Bombay Presidencies

- What were the characteristic features of 'Reform Hinduism'?

- Describe the main principles and practices of the Brahmo Samaj.

- In what ways did the work of Bankimchandra Chattopadhyay contribute to the growth of neo-Hinduism in the late nineteenth century?

- Who were the major reformers in nineteenth-century Maharashtra and Gujarat? In what ways did their work differ from that of reformers in Bengal?

- Compare the Mahima Dharma movement in Odisha and the Swaminarayan movement in Gujarat. How did these movements differ from those led by the English-educated middle classes in the Bengal and Bombay Presidencies?

Further Reading

Brian A. Hatcher. 'Remembering Rammohan: An Essay on the Re-Emergence of Modern Hinduism'. *History of Religions* 46, no. 1 (2006): 50–80.

Brian A. Hatcher. *Hinduism Before Reform*. Cambridge: Harvard University Press, 2020.

Kenneth W. Jones. *Socio-Religious Reform Movements in British India* (The New Cambridge History of India, vol. III.1. Indian Edition). Delhi: Cambridge University Press and Foundation Books, 1994 (esp. chap. 2 and 5).

Raymond B. Williams and Yogi Trivedi (eds.). *Swaminarayan Hinduism: Tradition, Adaptation, and Identity*. New Delhi: Oxford University Press, 2016.

Dayanand Saraswati (1824–1883).

III
A REFORMED RELIGION FOR THE HINDUS 2: THE MADRAS PRESIDENCY AND THE PUNJAB, c. 1830–1880

In the previous chapter we discussed some major attempts to reform Hinduism in the presidencies of Bengal and Bombay. This chapter will be devoted to the study of similar attempts in the third of the presidencies in British India, Madras, and in the North Indian province of the Punjab. This narrative arrangement will help us to maintain a thematic and historical continuity since developments in the Madras Presidency and the Punjab reveal influences from those occurring in Bengal and Bombay.

REFORM HINDUISM: A COMPARATIVE ANALYSIS OF DEVELOPMENTS IN VARIOUS REGIONS

In respect of 'Reform Hinduism', Madras and the Punjab lagged behind Bengal and Bombay. Both these regions failed to produce a movement distinctively their own and adopted instead ideas and values that originated elsewhere. The Madras Presidency was influenced by modern social and religious reform movements originating in Bengal and Bombay, like the Brahmo Samaj and the Prarthana Samaj. The Punjab was the most successful centre for the Arya Samaj, which was founded in Bombay. In hindsight, two possible explanations may be offered for this. First, modern English education took longer to take root in Madras and the Punjab, but, second and, more importantly, for reasons not as yet clear, this education, even when it succeeded, did not produce a dedicated band of reformers, as was the case in Bengal and Bombay.

The differences in social experience between Bengal and Bombay on the one hand and Madras and the Punjab on the other are also explained in part by the peculiarities of local culture and by the historical period in which they occurred. For instance, neither Bengal nor Bombay nor Madras produced a Vedic revival of the kind experienced in the Punjab. In Bengal, the Vedic tradition had always been relatively weaker, Maharashtra was more attuned to medieval devotional culture, and Madras had nurtured strong anti-Vedic sentiments in the form of popular Shaivism and Vaishnavism. Social persecution in the name of caste was far stronger in Madras than in either Bengal or the Punjab, and this had the effect of eventually dividing public opinion. Lower-caste movements in southern India keen to assert their rights against upper-caste dominance eventually adopted political methods which distracted from purely social work and weakened social reform campaigns.

Whereas reformism led by the upper castes in Bengal had begun by the 1830s, it took another forty years for this to be achieved in the Punjab. By then, the political and cultural situation in much of British India had changed significantly. In the 1880s, the Arya Samaj was able to dislodge the Brahmo Samaj from the Punjab by playing upon the allegation that the Brahmos were an excessively Westernised community with few or no roots in the national culture. In Dayanand Saraswati, the Punjabi Hindus found a messiah whose life and work suggested how even traditions could be suitably excavated to arrive at modernist conclusions. Swami Dayanand did not shun science; rather, he provoked Hindu pride by suggesting that the conclusions of modern science had all been anticipated in the Vedas. At a time when both racial slurs from the ruling class and the economic scars left by colonial exploitation were beginning to stir the colonised, such claims naturally carried a great appeal.

MODERN SOCIAL AND RELIGIOUS DEVELOPMENTS IN THE MADRAS PRESIDENCY

The territorial expanse of the Madras Presidency stretched across the Indian peninsula, measuring over 120,000 square miles and covering five distinct linguistic regions. On the east coast, the area coinciding with the modern Indian states of Andhra Pradesh and Telengana, the population was Telugu-speaking. To its immediate south were the Tamil-speaking regions, and to the immediate north, also on the east coast, were predominantly Odiya-speaking areas. On the west coast there were Malabar and the native states of Travancore and Cochin, ruled by Indian rulers, all of whom spoke Malayali. To the immediate north was the Kanarese-speaking region of the present Indian state of Karnataka, which then formed the southern half of the Bombay Presidency.

The Madras Presidency had an overwhelming majority of Hindus, with Muslims, Jews, and Christians being mainly concentrated along the Malabar coast. Hindu society in this region was clearly dominated by brahmins, most noticeably in the Tamil-speaking areas, as in Madura and Thanjavur (Tanjore). Within the brahmin community of South India, the Tamil-speaking brahmins clearly dominated their Telugu compatriots educationally and professionally, while the latter in turn dominated the Odiya and Kanarese brahmins. The Tamil brahmins were broadly divided into two classes along religious lines: the Aiyengars were Vaishnavas belonging to the *sampradaya* (sect) of either Ramanuja or Madhva; their rivals, the Aiyers, also called *smarta* brahmins, were Shaivas by persuasion. This is an important classification to note since the Tamil-speaking regions of the Madras Presidency had witnessed long-standing sectarian hostility between the Vaishnavas and Shaivas in the pre-modern era; in colonial times, too, important changes occurred within Tamil Shaivism.

Modern Education and Literary Activities in the Madras Presidency

Madras was the capital town of the presidency but compared unfavourably to both Calcutta and Bombay in terms of urbanisation, improved communication networks, or matters of professional mobility. The distinctive quality about Madras lay elsewhere: in its high literacy rates and rapidly multiplying educational institutions. By the third quarter of the nineteenth century, roughly one out of every four local residents was literate. By 1882, the presidency had a university, five arts colleges, three professional training institutions, including medical and engineering colleges, and four English high schools. The student strength in schools here was about 25,000, of which about 60 per cent possessed some knowledge of English. By 1886, it had five more English colleges compared to even Bengal, and twenty-three more than Bombay.

Predictably, educational advancement in this presidency was the most noticeable among brahmins. About 73 per cent of all successful candidates passing out of Madras University between 1876 and 1881 were brahmins. Brahmin dominance in the area created resentment among non-brahmins and some worry even among the British. In 1893, a non-brahmin author writing under the pseudonym of 'Fair Play' observed that the British were only nominally the rulers of the region and that real power was vested in the hands of the brahmins. The presidency also had a sizeable number of 'untouchable' castes whose very presence in public areas was considered ritually polluting for the upper castes. Discrimination along lines of caste was particularly sharp in this province.

As in Bengal, Madras witnessed an era marked by an active Orientalist interest in Indian history and culture. The greatest contribution to this field came from the Scottish army officer Colin Mackenzie (1754–1821), aided by his Indian assistants. Mackenzie eventually rose to the position of the first Surveyor General of India. In 1817, another British judicial officer, by the name of Sir Thomas Newbolt, launched the Madras Literary Society; the society ran a journal, the *Madras Journal of Literature and Science*, which survived until about 1894.

One advantage that Madras enjoyed over the Bombay and Bengal Presidencies, at least initially, was a thriving print culture. The English acquired a wooden press from the French as early as 1761 and printed some of the earliest evangelical literature in the region. Over time, however, the printing press was turned against the missionaries when local Hindus, worried by the prospects of conversion, went on the counter-offensive. In 1842, an affluent merchant by the name of Pachaiyappa Mudaliar (1754–1794) founded a school that was named after him. This was the first school in the province to be set up without any government aid. The man who significantly complemented such efforts was the philanthropist Gazalu Lakshmanarasu Chetty (1806–1868), also belonging to the mercantile community. Chetty resisted efforts to introduce the Bible to students enrolled at Madras University. In 1844, he bought a paper by the name of *Native Interpreter*, renaming it the *Crescent*, which hereafter was actively used in the defense of Hinduism. In 1844–1845, Chetty opposed the government's move to allow converts from Hinduism to inherit ancestral property and increasingly involved himself in provincial politics. He was the guiding hand behind the Madras Native Association founded in 1852, a body that aimed at promoting Indian interests.

The public outcry over conversions reached its greatest intensity in the 1880s when the Hindu polemicist R. Sivasankara Pandiah started the *Hindu Excelsior Magazine* in 1884, the Hindu Tract Society in 1887, and the Hindu Theological High School in 1889. Of these, the Hindu Tract Society specifically aimed at countering Christian publications circulated by missionaries, publishing eleven tracts of their own by the year 1889. One of these, carrying the provocative title *Hindu Triumph: One Hundred and Fifty Contradictions of the Bible. A Handbook for Mission School Students and Inquiring Christians*, caused something of a sensation.

Attempts at Social Reform

In contrast to Bengal and Bombay, Madras failed to develop a dedicated body of social activists and reformers who could meaningfully influence public opinion. For one, the stranglehold of caste in everyday life was enormous and the possibility of social excommunication deeply dreaded. In Bombay and Bengal, educated brahmins, along with some advanced non-brahmin castes, had tried to promote social initiatives and assume positions of leadership. In the Madras Presidency, by comparison, no straight case could be made connecting the spread of modern education to a growing dissatisfaction with the older social order.

In the Madras Presidency, early attempts at instilling a sense of ethical and social responsibility in educated Hindus is evident in the Hindu Progressive Improvement Society, founded in 1852 by a man named Srinivasa Pillay. This organisation was later taken over by 1863 by Venkatarayalu Naidu, who ran a paper called the *Rising Sun*. No reform work attaining the level of a pan-Indian movement originated in nineteenth-century Madras. Rather, some movements originating elsewhere travelled to Madras, as for instance the widow-marriage campaign of Ishwarchandra Vidyasagar and the Prarthana Samaj in Bombay. By the 1860s and 1870s, there was some exchange of views between reformers of the three presidencies which continued well into the early years of the twentieth century. Many prominent Brahmo theologians from Bengal regularly toured much of peninsular India during this period. Occasionally, there was reverse traffic too. Some local young men from Madras travelled to other regions to gather firsthand experience. One such individual was Chembeti Sridharalu Naidu (d. 1874), who had been inspired by the writings and speeches of Keshabchandra Sen. By one account, the earliest reformist body in this region, the Veda Samaj, was founded at Madras in 1864. The Veda Samaj was something of a compromise between upper-caste conservatism in the province and the relatively more liberal position adopted by the Brahmos. It was subsequently renamed the Brahmo Samaj of South India.

In the third quarter of the nineteenth century, the Prarthana and Brahmo Samajes successfully extended their organisational network deep into South India. Here it is important to note that reformers outside Bengal, though otherwise sympathetic to the ideals of the Brahmo Samaj, would not always agree to take the Brahmo name. In the Telugu-speaking areas, for instance, such organisations were invariably called Prarthana Samajes. One possible explanation for this may lie in the fact that many took the Brahmo community to be excessively estranged from the parental Hindu society.

Telugu-speaking areas saw the birth of several branches of the Prarthana Samaj: between 1878 and 1909, many of these came to be established along coastal Andhra. By 1916, we hear of a centralised organisation overseeing all activities of the

Brahmos, called the Andhra Brahmo Mandali. Membership of these bodies was small, and, going by one estimate, the total membership of such organisations in coastal Andhra was under 100. Many who expressed some sympathy with reformist ideals were reluctant to openly identify with the reformed Samajes. Recruitment to these bodies was undertaken almost entirely from the new urban professionals: teachers, lawyers, and men in public service. The solitary exception to this was the Raja of Pithapuram, Rao Venkata Kumara Mahipati Surya Rau (1885–1964). The Raja supported educational movements aiming at the social amelioration of the depressed castes of the region.

A branch of the Brahmo Samaj was established in Bangalore Cantonment by an army man, Rajaravelu Naidu. In neighbouring Mangalore, a man by the name of Nirveshvaly Arsappa tried to enlist educated members of the ritually inferior Billava caste, without much success. The Billavas resented the fact that upper-caste members of the local Brahmo Samaj adopted anglicised manners and preferred to converse in English. Angered by this, upper-caste members, mostly Saraswat brahmins, eventually broke off to form a separate body called the Upasana Sabha, which was marked by a considerable toning down of reformist thought and practice. The Upasana Sabha later came to be known as the Mangalore Brahmo Samaj. A branch of the Brahmo Samaj was also established at Hyderabad in 1914, inspired by a Bengali Brahmo, Aghorenath Chattopadhyay (1851–1915), who served as the Principal of the Nizam College. Chattopadhyay was instrumental in opening a women's college as part of Osmania University.

The Prarthana Samaj movement in the presidency was weakened by the emergence of two somewhat contrary forces in the early twentieth century. One of these was the anti-colonial movement seeking greater political rights for Indians and, quite understandably, this tended to somewhat ignore purely social reform questions. The other movement aimed at the opposite and sought to secure greater rights and privileges for the relatively backward castes, trying to enlist the support of the British government to this end. Raghupati Venkataratnam Naidu (1862–1939), once a student at the Madras Christian College (founded 1837) and a prominent Brahmo who later rose to the position of the Vice Chancellor of Madras University, joined the Justice Party (founded in 1916) in order to champion the cause of the non-brahmins. This weakened unity within the social reform movement in the Andhra region.

The outstanding reformer from South India who won recognition both at home and abroad was Kandukuri Viresalingam Pantulu (1848–1919), also a brahmin. His involvement with woman-related reform has led people to compare him with the Bengali reformer and educator Ishwarchandra Vidyasagar, discussed at some length in the next chapter. However, as one of his ardent followers, Raghupati Venkataraman Naidu, was to later observe, the important difference separating the two lay precisely in their approach to religion. Vidyasagar, though culturally a Brahmanist, had little or no interest in Hinduism as a religion. Viresalingam, on the other hand, was a dedicated Brahmo whose musings and ministrations represented a reformed view of Hinduism.

Viresalingam launched the first Prarthana Samaj at Rajamundry in 1878, built the first Brahmo chapel (*mandir*) at the same place in 1887, and arranged for three Brahmo marriages between 1913 and 1918. He was also the father of modern Telugu prose; his novel *Rajshekhara Charitamu* (1878), adapted from Oliver Goldsmith's *The Vicar of Wakefield*, is generally considered to be the first in that language. He was also a successful journalist, running monthly journals, some especially for women. Viresalingam also authored books in Telegu on the subjects of history and popular science. For his valuable services rendered to society, the government conferred upon him the title 'Rao Bahadur' in 1893.

The Modernity of Tradition:
The Movement to Reform Tamil Shaivism

In the previous chapter we noted how movements aimed at bringing about changes in contemporary society could take different forms. There was reform even outside 'Reform Hinduism'. In such instances, the inspiration was local and indigenous rather than cosmopolitan. These movements were not pan-Indian in scope or objectives; instead, they wished to agitate on issues specific to a tradition and address a largely local audience.

In the mid-nineteenth century, there were two such movements, both related to Tamil Shaivism, that attained a good measure of success. One of these was centred in the sacred temple town of Chidambaram, close to Madras, and the other, in the Tamil-speaking Jaffna Peninsula in modern Sri Lanka but with active linkages with Madras itself.

The first of these is associated with Ramalinga Pillai, better known as Ramalinga Adigal (1823–1874), who inherited the old Tamil Shaiva *bhakti* tradition dating back to the eighth century CE. It was deeply theistic in tone and insisted on the dualistic separation of God and human. Understandably enough, the grace or benediction of God and a sense of man's utter powerlessness before the Power of the Divine were two of the defining features of this movement. Such sentiments came to be expressed in a wealth of popular religious poetry and songs, a feature visibly different from developments located in metropolitan Calcutta or Bombay. A popular collection of such songs called the *Thirumurai* came to be the textual basis of this neo-Shaiva movement.

Ramalinga himself composed a vast body of devotional songs and poems in praise of Shiva. These acquired great popularity and began to be sung in local shrines and temples. His songs were subsequently collected and published as

Ramalinga Adigal (1823–1874).

Thirurutpa (Divine Songs of Grace) by his first disciple, Velayutha Mudaliar. Ramalinga belonged to the intermediary caste of the *vellalars*, who usually functioned as scribes or book-keepers, but also at times as rich peasants. Ramalinga was acquainted with Tamil religious classics, although he knew no Sanskrit nor made any effort to master it. However, even as a non-brahmin, he adopted a critical but not a virulently radical attitude towards Brahmanical religion. This sets him apart from a strong non-brahmin movement that was to follow after him and which later became the basis of an anti-Sanskritic Tamil provincialism. His religious vision entailed the concepts of *samarasa* or *sanmarga,* which rejected social discrimination and supported a form of spiritual democracy that offered everybody an equal right of worship. He advocated the unity and universality of Truth and a spiritual selfhood founded on humility, brotherhood, and compassion for all (*jivakarunayam*). One of the earliest religious organisations that he founded, in 1865, was called Samarasa Vedha Sanmarga Sangam, renamed Samarasa Shuddha Sathya Sangam (Society for Pure Truth in Universal Selfhood) in 1872. Committed social service was a defining feature of this movement; this included large-scale feeding of the poor – the gift of food to the hungry was considered one of the highest human virtues. But while Ramalinga openly accepted people of all castes as his followers, he insisted on strict food habits. The consumption of fish or flesh was strictly prohibited.

Ramalinga stressed the progressive psychological development of the body and bodily consciousness. This suggests his familiarity with yogic processes. Reportedly, what made him attractive as a religious figure was the assurance given to his householder disciples that yogic power and immortality were within their capability to attain. Ramalinga equated God with *arutaparamajyothi* (Supreme Grace of Light) and instructed his followers to keep alight the perennially burning lamp representing the Supreme Being. His last days are surrounded in considerable mystery: several accounts state that he simply 'disappeared' from the room where he usually resided, with no traces of the body being found thereafter.

Ramalinga's exact contemporary, also located in the Tamil Shaiva tradition and of the *vellalar* caste, was Arumuga Pillai (1822–1877), later given the suffix 'Navalar' ('Accomplished Orator'). Though working within the same religious tradition, the two men developed acute differences with respect to doctrine and methods of work. In his attempt to bring about suitable changes in the Shaiva tradition and to defend it against attacks from non-Hindus, Navalar enjoyed certain advantages over Ramalinga. First, his reasonable proficiency in the English language enabled him to better understand

Arumuka Navalar (1822–1879).

the nature of missionary accusations levelled against Hindu religion and culture, and, second, he had the experience of working closely with Protestant missionaries themselves. For a time, Navalar was a part of a Wesleyan Mission team attempting to translate the Bible into Tamil, and this enabled him to use evangelist communicative practices to counter European evangelists themselves.

Beginning in 1841 with an anonymous article in a missionary organ called the *Morning Star,* Navalar sharpened his criticism of biblical literature and contested missionary allegations against Hinduism. He argued that the use of iconography and temple rituals was not confined to the Hindus and had been in vogue even among the ancient Israelites. In 1847, he started conducting a series of weekly public lectures called *prasangams* which urged fellow Tamil Shaivas to suitably reform their religious practices. This was supplemented by the opening of theological schools (*shaivaprakasha vidyashala*) for training men in Shaiva theology. From Jaffna, in present-day Sri Lanka, Navalar frequently crossed over to the Indian mainland to the important pilgrim centres of Thanjavur and Chidambaram. On one of these visits he acquired a printing press which he used to set up the Vidyanulambana Yantra Sala (Preservation of Knowledge Press). Navalar soon began to counter missionary allegations by alleging the use of 'corrupt' and 'vulgar' language in the Bible itself (*Bibliya Kutsita*). In 1854, he published a standard training manual for all Shaivas, *Shaiva Dushana Parihara* (literally, Abolishing Abuses of Shaivism). Navalar's literary production was enormous; in all he had about ninety-seven Tamil publications to his credit, of which as many as twenty-three were his own. In this enterprise, he had the financial backing of wealthy patrons, most of whom were from his own caste, the *vellalars*.

It is interesting that the reworking of the Tamils's Shaiva canon, the *Shaiva Siddhanta*, as it was generally called, was the work of two men who belonged to the non-brahmin community of *vellalars*. Some scholars have therefore interpreted social and doctrinal differences between Ramalinga and Navalar as an instance of intra-*vellalar* differences, but such differences were also sharp and significant. In 1869, in a work called *Poliyarutpa Muruppu* (Critique of Pseudo Divine Verses), Navalar accused Ramalinga of being a demagogue and of insidiously replacing traditional Shaiva preaching by his own, as well as fooling his followers through miracle work. It irked Navalar that the songs and poetry of Ramalinga, which he found lacking in the spirit of the orthodox canon, had gained a measure of popularity and were commonly sung in Shaiva shrines. Whereas Ramalinga did not quite view the Shaiva canon as fixed, Navalar attempted to give it a greater fixity by insisting on the use of standardised temple rituals.

Not surprisingly, the Tamil-speaking elite, whether in the Madras Presidency or at Jaffna, disagreed more with Ramalinga than with Navalar. At the time, the *vellalar* community was seeking upward social mobility through forging close social links with brahmins. For instance, they claimed the right to wear the *purul* (sacred thread) and the right to study the *shruti* (Hindu canon). Navalar's ideas especially appealed to this upwardly mobile community: what gave his position an edge was his tendency to accept a fixed Shaiva canon and the sectarian rejection of deities other than Shiva. Not surprisingly, Ramalinga found the work of Navalar to be a greater threat compared to that posed by the Christian missionaries.

Although both Ramalingar and Navalar led movements that were seemingly marginal to those led by the upper-caste, Western-educated intelligentsia, in a sense they, too,were modern movements in their own right – though they treated modernity differently. For them modernity arrived not through the replacement of one set of values or practices by another but by revisualising and refashioning the modalities of change. They were also modern inasmuch as they were self-conscious movements acutely aware of contemporary challenges and conceding the necessity for change. For lack of a better expression, these could well be called movements of 'vernacular' reform. Notwithstanding their internal differences, both Ramalinga and Aramuga Navalar are today acknowledged as the progenitors of the Tamil *Eelam* (homeland).

NARAYAN GURU AND RELIGIOUS MOVEMENTS
AMONG EZHAVAS IN KERALA

Similar attempts at formulating a more humanitarian religion also occurred in late nineteenth-century Kerala. However, Narayan Guru (1856–1928) and the movement he led was in some ways different. For one, the Guru belonged to neither the brahmin nor the intermediary caste but to the ritually marginalised sub-caste of the *ezhavas*, which gave the movement in Kerala a more radical and defiant edge. Second, Narayan Guru came to be eventually respected not only by low-caste Hindus but also by some Muslims and Christians. The Guru himself developed an interest in various religious traditions even outside Hinduism. In 1923, he organised an inter-faith religious conference at one of his *ashrams* at Alwaye, on the banks of the river Periyar. On his brief visit to Sri Lanka in 1926, he came to appreciate the thought and practices of the local Buddhists. One of his works, called the *Anukampadashakam* (Ten Verses on Compassion), has songs in praise of the Buddha, Adi Shankaracharya, and Jesus Christ. He also wrote verses in praise of Hindu deities like Kali, Ganesha, and Subrahmanya (Kartikeya). This eclectic quality in his religious thought appears to have been influenced by a contemporary sage and social reformer, Chattampi Swamikal (1853–1924), who belonged to the highly respected Namboodiri brahmin community. Swamikal was an Advaitin, a believer in the nondualist philosophy of Adi Shankara, but he was also attracted to Sufi mysticism. It is interesting that both Swamikal and the Guru should employ nondualist philosophy to preach their radical social and spiritual message; this separates them from the philosophical dualism adopted by both Ramalinga and Navalar. Narayan Guru found the devotional culture of *bhakti* valuable but preferred to integrate this with the philosophical unity underlying Advaita Vedanta.

1967 Indian postage stamp of Narayan Guru (1856–1928).

This strengthened his message of humanitarian universalism and rejection of caste discrimination.

His active contestation of caste privileges placed him in opposition to local brahmins, some of whom were high-placed Namboodiri brahmins. In 1888, he became the centre of a controversy after consecrating a Shiva icon. When the local brahmins furiously challenged an *ezhava*'s right to carry out this holy act, the Guru is known to have famously retorted that the Shiva icon in question belonged not to the brahmins but to the *ezhavas*!

With the help of a gathering number of followers, Narayan Guru next devoted himself to organisational consolidation. Arvipuram, where he had controversially consecrated the Shiva icon, became the site of the Narayana Dharma Paripalana Yogam (1903), the nucleus of the new religious movement. This was followed by the establishment of the Sarada Math in 1912 and the setting up of schools for the depressed classes at Sivagiri. It was here that both Tagore and Gandhi called on him in 1916 and 1925 respectively.

In the 1920s, Narayan Guru was also involved in another controversy, which raged over the question of permitting *ezhavas* and other low castes to enter local Hindu temples. Between

1924 and 1925, with the support of Gandhi and the Indian National Congress, there began the Vaikom Satyagraha over entry to the Mahadeva Temple (currently located in the district of Kottayam). The Vaikom movement met with some success in arousing a greater social awareness, which encouraged Gandhi himself to experiment more fully with the moral and political method of *satyagraha* (quest for truth). However, entry to temples elsewhere, as in Travancore, was not allowed until the Temple Entry Proclamation of 1936, issued by the young local ruler, Maharaja Chithira Tirunal, in defiance of his mother, the Queen Regent. The Proclamation, however, had little effect on the neighbouring princely states of Cochin and Calicut, where civic disabilities imposed on the depressed castes could be ended only after India attained independence in 1947.

The Guru denounced arrogant truth claims made by various religious traditions and greatly supported the principle of *ahimsa* (non-injury to all forms of life). His ethical teachings resemble those preached by the Vedantin Swami Vivekananda before him. Neither would distinguish happiness experienced by the self from that given to others. The Guru observed: 'The happiness of another is the happiness of mine, and my happiness is the happiness of others too'.[35] His most dramatic and significant message was that of upholding the unity of all humanity, overlooking distinctions of caste and creed: 'Of the human species is a brahmin born as a pariah too. Where is the caste distinction then among the human species?'[36]

Narayan Guru was a learned man who authored over sixty works, large and small, in Tamil, Malayalam, and Sanskrit. He also had the good fortune of leaving behind active and

---

35 Narayan Guru, *Atmopadesha Shatakam* (Instructions Given to the Self in One Hundred Verses) (n.d.).

36 Narayan Guru, *Jati Nirnayam* (A Critique of Jati) (1914).

competent disciples like Dr. Padmanabhan Palpu (1863–1950), the first *ezhava* to enter the Medical Service of the Travancore state, and the gifted Malayali poet and writer Kumaran Asan (1873–1924). The Guru's first major biographer, Nataraja Guru (1895–1973), was a disciple whom the Guru encouraged to travel to the West for higher studies.

RELIGION AND REFORM IN THE PUNJAB

The Punjab (literally, 'land fed by five rivers') was the major centre for one of the most important Hindu religious reform movements in colonial times, the Arya Samaj. This reformist body was not born in the Punjab but had its greatest popularity in this region. It is interesting, too, that a good number of Hindu Punjabis, rather than seek a prophet of their own, preferred to gravitate around the life and work of a Gujarati brahmin, Mul Shankar, who later assumed the monastic name of Swami Dayanand Saraswati. It was the Punjab that produced the most important Arya leaders in India. The Brahmo Samaj did enter this province earlier, but it was soon overtaken by the more dynamic Aryas. Conversely, the Arya Smaj had very few supporters in Bengal and was unable to displace the Brahmo influence.

The Arya Samaj (literally, 'Society of the Nobles') was established at Bombay in 1875 under very different circumstances. Dayanand entered the Punjab only two years later, around 1877, and did not stay in the province for long. However, his very presence and preaching transformed Punjabi society in significant ways, affecting not just the Hindus but also the local Sikhs and Muslims.

In 1849, the Punjab, hitherto the site of the Sikh Empire, had been one of the last territories to be added to British India. Under the British, it comprised five distinct regions or territories: Delhi, Jullundur, Lahore, Multan, and Rawalpindi.

Three major religious communities made up the bulk of the population of the Punjab: Hindus, Muslims, and Sikhs. Of these, Hinduism had been numerically weakened by conversions to Sikhism, Islam, and Christianity. By the third quarter of the nineteenth century, the Muslim population in the province exceeded that of the Hindus. However, the community that made the greatest gain numerically was the Christian, by successfully targeting the ritually defiled castes among the Hindus and Sikhs. In its reformist zeal, the Arya Samaj was eventually to target all those communities which had attempted to wean away the Hindus.

The Punjab had once been the site of early Brahmanical religion, but by the modern era, the brahmins had clearly lost political and social influence to the intermediary merchant castes of *banias*, *aroras*, and *khatris*. By the close of the nineteenth century, literacy among the *khatris* was higher than that among brahmins. The intellectual awakening and movements for social and religious reform in modern Punjab produced very few leaders who were brahmins by caste.

Early Attempts at Reform

The coming of British rule to Punjab constituted not merely a political revolution but also a social and intellectual one. A new social factor that became visible in nineteenth-century Punjab was the arrival of a migrant population, mostly from Bengal. These were upper-caste Bengali Hindus with a command of the English language and anglicised ways of life. They filled up the bulk of the subordinate posts available to Indians in the local administration and also produced the earliest crop of professionals: journalists, teachers, writers, publicists, and lawyers, who contributed significantly to the birth of modern Punjab. With this class arrived the first modern reformist body in the province, the Brahmo Samaj.

Some of the early Hindu Punjabi reformers, like Kanhaiya Lal Alakhdhari (1809–1882), had spent their student life in Calcutta, where they had obviously been influenced by the Brahmo Samaj. Of Kanhaiya Lal it was said that the man persistently wore European-style shoes, preferred to use the Sanskrit-derived Hindi word *bhojan* (meal) over the more common Urdu-Persian equivalent, *khana* (meal), and had no scruples about discussing Hinduism before non-Hindus. He was the author of two early reformist tracts, *Chirag-i-Hakikat* (Light of Truth, 1853) and *Shan-i-Marifat* (Light of Knowledge, 1858), which emphasised the virtues of an enlightened, humanistic education. Kanhaiya Lal briskly toured the Punjab, trying to propagate a liberal and progressive Hinduism. In 1873, he established the Niti Prakash Sabha (Society of Moral Enlightenment) in Ludhiana. To him goes the honour of first openly combating local conservative figures like Pundit Shardha Ram Phillauri (b. 1837), an acknowledged leader of orthodox Hindus who called themselves the 'Sanatanists' (literally, 'those who uphold the unchanging, or *sanātana*'). Kanhaiya Lal's campaign against the orthodox first split Hindu society in modern Punjab into warring camps.

In the Punjab, Brahmo reformism preceded that of the Arya Samaj by over a decade. The centre of Brahmo thought and activity was the Lahore Brahmo Samaj, founded in 1863, with branches subsequently opened at Rawalpindi, Amritsar, Multan, Ropar, Shimla, and Dera Gazi Khan. Brahmo leaders based in Calcutta regularly travelled to the Punjab: Keshabchandra Sen in 1867 and the Maharshi Debendranath Tagore thrice, in 1867, 1874, and 1875.

The Brahmos propagated their reformist ideas and values through numerous tracts and journals. In this context, the life and career of Nabinchandra Ray (1838–1890) is of particular interest. Nabinchandra was associated with the

Lahore Brahmo Samaj and served as its first minister. Like Kanhaiya Lal Alakhdhari, he battled the orthodox party in the Punjab, but his more lasting contribution was to bring modern education to Punjabi girls. Quite significantly, he chose to work not in his native language, Bengali, but in Hindi and Sanskrit. In 1866–1867, he founded the Jnanpradayini Sabha (Society for the Dissemination of Knowledge) which ran a Hindi journal called the *Jnanpradayini Patrika*, the first Hindi-language journal in the province. His best-known work, *Lakshmi Sarasvati Samvad* (A Dialogue between the Goddesses Lakshmi and Sarasvati, 1869), was an important publication on several counts. First, Nabinchandra did not allow his iconoclastic Brahmo religious sentiments to get in the way of suitably instructing Punjabi Hindu girls. In the book, the two Hindu goddesses agree on the view that a good life depends on successfully acquiring knowledge. Part II of the work introduced entirely new subjects to girls like geography and meteorology. Nabinchandra's daughter, Hemantakumari Chaudhurani (1868–1953), edited the *Sugrihini*, the first Hindi journal run by a woman.

Swami Dayanand Saraswati and Raja Rammohun Roy

Along with Rammohun Roy, Swami Dayanand Saraswati may justly claim to be the greatest social and religious reformer among colonial Hindus. Both, incidentally, were brahmins; this created in them an added urgency to reform a society which they found to be visibly degenerate. The organisations that they created have survived to this day and now have a global presence. Although the two men had much in common, they also displayed acute differences; a broad comparison of the two figures might be instructive here.

Rammohun appeared at a time when the Hindu intelligentsia was deeply affected by the rushing tide of new ideas imbibed through Western education. Comparable changes in the Punjab occurred about two generations later, when Hindus were beginning to be more cautious about just what to receive or not to receive from the West. Unlike Rammohun, Dayanand never mastered English or communicated in that language. However, each of them made a conscious effort to learn a language other than their own for more effective public communication: Rammohun learnt English and Dayanand, Hindi. Second, unlike Rammohun, Swami Dayanand chose a monastic life over that of the householder. Third, in their attempt to locate the 'authentic' sources of Hinduism, they chose to focus on different texts. While Rammohun relied almost exclusively on the Upanishads to the exclusion of Vedic Samhitas, the religious world of Dayanand Saraswati was based on the Samhitas, with little attention paid to the philosophy of the Upanishads. Fourth, in advancing their reformist agenda, they both emerged as polemicists, battling both non-Hindus and their fellow religionists, though Dayanand carried this much farther than did Rammohun. They were unanimous on two fundamental issues concerning the state of contemporary Hinduism: first, they insisted that certain practices like idolatry, the worship of 'false' gods and goddesses, and relying on the ritual services of the priestly class had to be taken out of Hindu thought and practice; second, they argued that reason and sound moral judgement had to be treated as the very foundation of all religious life. Finally, Swami Dayananda, more than Rammohun, was critical of the social and cultural inequities created by caste. He was also more patriotic in his expression; he argued more aggressively that, apart from resisting the West, Indians had also to aim at self-rule. To a great extent, this is explained by the historical context in which he lived and worked.

DAYANAND: THE MAN AND HIS MISSION

Swami Dayanand (born Mul Shankar) belonged to an affluent and respectable brahmin family of Kathiawar (Gujarat). His father, who served in the local administration, was a Shaiva in his religious persuasion, and an important episode connected with the early religious life of Dayanand was related to the worship of Lord Shiva. Once, when keeping a long vigil at a Shiva temple, he found, much to his horror, mice freely running over the holy icon of Shiva. This made him wonder if even the greatly revered and mighty Lord was powerless to prevent such sacrilege and pushed him to the conclusion that what the Hindus commonly and unquestioningly worshipped were actually 'false' gods.

Alarmed by the sense of detachment in their son, his parents tried to get him married and settled in a householder's life. Mul Shankar resisted this move strongly, running away from home twice in succession, the second time successfully. The next few years he spent largely wandering through the countryside, unable to find his true spiritual calling until he came upon a blind ascetic at Mathura by the name of Swami Virjanand, whom he accepted as his *guru*. Virjanand was a *yogi* and scholar of Sanskrit grammar who instilled in the young pupil two important ideas that stayed with Shankar throughout his life. First, Virjanand made him acutely aware of the fact that contemporary Hinduism stood badly in need of reform. Second, he taught him *yoga* and impressed upon his new disciple the value of studying classical grammar and philology to succeed in this enterprise. This primarily meant mastering Vedic literature and the Sanskrit lexicon.

Much of Dayanand's life hereafter was spent in touring upper India, including the North-Western Provinces (coinciding with present-day Uttar Pradesh and Uttaranchal), Haryana, the Punjab, and Rajasthan. He also visited the presidencies of Bombay and Bengal, which, as we shall see, produced important changes in his life and career. His visit to Bengal in 1872–1873 led him to important conclusions concerning his life as a Hindu reformer and publicist, and it was at Bombay, in reacting to what he deemed to be gross caricatures of Hinduism, that he established the Arya Samaj in the year 1875.

The greater part of Dayanand's missionary life was spent in the Doab – that is, in the fertile belt falling between the rivers Ganges and Yamuna. Departing from the company of his *guru*, Virjanand, in 1866, Swami Dayanand reached the important pilgrim town of Haridwar; here he distributed free copies of one of his earliest tracts, the *Bhagavata Khandana* (1864), in which he disputed the substance and the authenticity of the *Bhagavata Purana*, a text seminally important to Vaishnavas. At this time, however, the Swami was disadvantaged by not belonging to any Hindu *sampradaya* (sect) or organisation and, at Haridwar, being only one of the several hundreds of Hindu ascetics visible. Also, since he addressed the public in Sanskrit, only a limited number of people effectively understood him.

In 1870, he was invited to a religious disputation (*shastrarth*) at Benares, one among several that he attended in his life, on the subject of idol worship. Dayanand defended himself ably, but his orthodox opponents tricked people into wrongly believing that the Swami had been defeated in argument. The Swami pondered over his future mission as he made his way to Calcutta, the capital of British India. Even though the disputation at Benares had not gone in his favour, reformers in that city appreciated the Swami's courageous attempt at fighting the orthodox. Thus, the *Hindu Patriot*, a Calcutta-based paper, made the following remark on 17 January 1870: 'We have come to believe that the golden age of India has not completely come to an end'.

In Calcutta, he met the most prominent Brahmo leaders of the day, including Debendranath Tagore and Keshabchandra Sen. His experiences in an intellectually alive Calcutta proved to be different from the sleepy brahmin-dominated life in the Gangetic plains of upper India. On the whole, the experience here proved to be valuable in three ways. In the first place, it taught Dayanand to better define a reformed Hinduism in relation to other world religions like Islam and Christianity. Second, it was also here that he became aware of pressing social issues like female education and widow marriages. Third, it demonstrated to him the strength of organisations. The two factors that were to dramatically change Dayanand's life thereafter both originated in Keshabchandra. Keshab asked him to give up the *sannyasi's* traditional attire of the loincloth, especially when making public appearances, and to switch from Sanskrit to Hindi when addressing audiences in North India. Both of these Swami Dayanand quickly accepted. His first speech in Hindi was delivered when he visited Benares a second time in 1874.

Both legs of his tour of the North-Western Provinces helped Swami Dayanand to arrive at major conclusions about the reformed Hinduism that he wished to propagate. He now rejected ornate rites and rituals and categorically disapproved of idol worship and the worship of multiple gods and goddesses. Further, he publicly violated caste practices by disregarding taboos regarding food and drink: he would readily agree to eat and drink at the hands of lower-caste men and at places considered unsuitable for partaking of meals. After 1875, he also encouraged his followers to give up meat eating. By the 1880s, diet was one of the critical issues that split the Arya Samaj into rival camps.

The most critical question, however, that engaged Dayanand during these years was that of identifying the 'authentic' sources of Hinduism; at Kanpur, on the river Ganges, he settled on a list of twenty-one such sources, mainly comprising the

Vedas and other ancillary texts. Collectively, these texts were given the name of *parameshvararishirachitani* ('texts composed by God and the holy sages'). He made a conscious attempt to familiarise himself with other religious traditions. A copy of the *Gospels* was obtained from one Rev. Scott, and he had the Koran translated into Hindi. Like Rammohun before him, the Swami dismissed Puranic religion as grossly spurious, with its talk of miracles, mythology, and *avataras*. Like the Raja, too, he preferred an activist and affirmative approach to religion (*pravritti*) over ascetic renunciation or withdrawal (*nivritti*). This may partly explain why he never paid as much attention to the *Gita*, with its message of disinterested action (*nishkama karma*), as did several Hindu thinkers in his time and later.

It was in the summer of 1875 that Swami Dayanand commenced writing his *magnum opus*, the *Satyarth Prakash* (Light of Truth). The first edition of the work was published in Benares in 1875, containing only twelve chapters, without the final two chapters dealing with Islam and Christianity. These were added to the revised edition of 1882.

Sometime in 1874–1875, Dayanand met some Bombay merchants who apprised him of the 'decadent' religious life in that province. It is from them that he would have gathered information on the Swaminarayanis and of the crusade launched by the Bombay reformer Karsondas Mulji against the Pushtimargis of the Vallabhacharya sect. Presumably, it was also from them that he heard of Mahadev Govind Ranade and of the Prarthana Samaj. Apparently, Dayanand was drawn to such information and felt that Bombay represented a promising field of work. On arrival in Bombay, his supporters organised a series of public lectures and discourses, but without much success. Nevertheless, the local orthodox camp considered the visiting Dayanand to be a greater threat than the local Prarthana Samaj. Significantly enough, at Bombay, supported by a small but active body of followers, Dayanand framed the

Madam Helena Petrovna Blavatsky (1831–1891) standing behind
Henry Steel Olcott (1832–1907), middle seated, in Bombay, 1881.

working principles of a new organisation which they called
the Arya Samaj. The choice of the word 'Arya' was significant;
it reflected a growing discomfiture with the term 'Hindu',
unpopular with some on account of its being coined by non-
Hindus. At the time, the number of rules was twenty-eight,
which looked complex and unwieldy; about two years later, at
Lahore, they were reduced to less than half that number.

Swami Dayanand was in the Punjab for about 15 months,
and as many as forty-three branches of the Arya Samaj were
opened during that time, beginning with the principal centre
at Lahore, which was the work of Dayanand himself. Until
the 1880s, Lahore remained the nucleus of reformist activity
for both the Brahmos and the Aryas. Over time, however, the
Brahmos lost out to the Aryas. In 1879, a little before he left for
Rajasthan, the Swami also met and temporarily joined forces
with the newly formed Theosophical Society, established by the
American army officer Col. Henry Steel Olcott (1832–1907)
and the enigmatic Russian Madam Helena Petrovna Blavatsky
(1831–1891). The Theosophists were attracted by Dayanand's

knowledge of yogic practices and by his imposing personality; initially, the Swami even trusted them enough to have his autobiographical fragment published in their journal, *The Theosophist* (1879–1880). However, the alliance broke down in 1882 over the question of defining a working relationship. In all probability, Dayanand was suspicious of the esoteric nature of Theosophical spiritualist practices. The Theosophists, on the other hand, resented the idea of working entirely under the wing of the Aryas.

In June 1882, Dayanand reached Rajasthan, where his mission was more political in nature than religious. It was here that he experimented with the task of disseminating among the Rajput princes his thoughts on a new Indian moral and political order. Dayanand's stay in Rajasthan, as is well-known, was short; an untimely death claimed him rather painfully and dramatically. It is now commonly believed that he was poisoned at the behest of a dancing girl, a favourite of the Maharaja of Jodhpur, who felt threatened by the moralising discourses to which the Swami subjected the Maharaja. It was simply unacceptable for Dayanand that a Hindu ruler should succumb to the wiles of a woman – and a common courtesan at that. Before his death, Dayanand had managed to establish two important institutions that served the Arya Samaj well in the years to come: the Vedic Yantralay (Vedic Press), set up at Ajmer for the publication of Vedic texts, and the Paropkarini Sabha (Philanthropic Society), which was entrusted with the printing of his own works.

Dayanand's Religion

Swami Dayanand Saraswati is most commonly associated with the Vedic revival, whose uniqueness in the late nineteenth century becomes apparent when one recalls how the Brahmo Samaj had already repudiated the Vedas as a revealed scripture.

A 'Vedic golden age' was very much a part of Dayanand's thoughts. For him, the Vedas were eternal and divine in origin, and upon this 'Truth' stood the very sanctity for reform. Some scholars have compared Dayanand's cry of 'Back to the Vedas' with Martin Luther's cry of 'Back to the Bible'. For Dayanand, the Vedas were the repository of all knowledge; he was prepared to stretch this argument by suggesting that they also contained the seeds of scientific knowledge and technology. In addition, and contrary to claims made by contemporary Western scholars and their Indian followers, Swami Dayanand refused to believe that Vedic religion was polytheistic.

The *Satyarth Prakash*, Dayanad's *magnum opus,* is a combination of theological and moral discourses. It also provides rules on the everyday life of the Hindu, covering issues like marriages, conception, and birth, and essential rules of conduct to be followed by householders: self-control, abstinence from moral vices, cleanliness and hygiene, celibacy for the student, the education of boys and girls, frugality, freedom to travel to foreign lands, and ritual commensality regarding matters of food and drink.

In religious matters, his ideas and instructions are quite clear. In the manner of Rammohun, Dayanand denied any intention of founding a new religion, insisting that he was only recovering that which had been buried under a huge debris of blind faith, irrationality, and superstition. The *Satyarth Prakash* speaks of a designer God who efficiently crafted the world and all life within it. God had no origin in time and was omnipresent, merciful, and just. Since he was all-pervading, he was *ipso facto* formless. The last feature ruled out the concept of *avataras,* but Dayanand did concede that God could be both *saguna* (with attributes) and *nirguna* (without attributes) at will, if only on account of his infinite power. Dayanand recommended that certain literary and religious texts were to be scrupulously avoided; the list includes Kalidasa's *Raghuvamsha,* the works of the poet Magha, Bharavi's *Kiratarjuniya*, all Tantric texts, the *Yoga Vasishtha Ramayana* and *Panchadasi* among Vedantic works, and all Smritis barring that of Manu. In keeping with reformist intentions, Dayanand held that the minimum age of marriage should be twenty-five and sixteen years for Hindu men and women respectively. He approved of widow marriage in principle but preferred abstinence and the adoption of *niyoga*, or the levirate, for controlling sexuality in women and immoral relationships. The practice of *niyoga*, which had fallen into disuse for several centuries, later became a matter of embarrassment for the Arya Samaj – some Aryas were even forced to oppose it. Idolatry, in Dayanand's opinion, originated with the Jains, and the cult of the Vaishnavas he believed to have originated less than two centuries before among sweepers and scavengers! Predictably enough, he was harsh on the Pushtimargis and the Swaminarayanis. The Brahmo Samaj and the Prarthana Samaj were praised for their role in resisting Christianity but also accused of not being sufficiently 'Hindu'. Two lengthy chapters were reserved for his critique of Islam and Christianity. The Christian account of creation Swami Dayanand dismissed as pure fable and, commenting on Mathew 6:9–13, he remarked that people who started by thanking God for their daily bread had to belong to a rather underdeveloped society. The Koran he refused to accept as a revealed work. The *Satyarth Prakash* took the human species to have originated in Tibet, but, true to his interest in science and observed phenomena, Dayanand summarily rejected the idea of the Sun revolving around the Earth.

No less than twenty-five works, big and small, are attributed to Swami Dayanand; some are now untraceable. Between 1864 and 1876, he produced at least four extremely polemical tracts disputing one or another Hindu philosophical school. In addition, he produced two major commentaries on the *Rig* and the *Yajur* Vedas (*Rigvedabhashyabhumika* in

1877–1878 and the *Yajurvedabhashya*, a part of which was published posthumously). A relatively lesser-known work, but one which had an impact on contemporary Indian politics, was *Gokarunanidhi* (1881), a tract advocating the protection of cows and the ending of slaughtering cattle for food. This issue was to become a major irritant in Hindu–Muslim relations in the late nineteenth and early twentieth centuries. To this must be added the fact that in much of North India, the Arya Samaj was perceived as a body openly hostile to the Muslims. A tract published in Lahore in 1929 called Dayanand himself 'the principal foe of Islam in India'.

Swami Shraddhanand (1856–1926).

A Punjabi Arya, Pundit Lekh Ram (1858–1897), produced over thirty anti-Muslim tracts and pamphlets before he was assassinated by a Muslim fanatic; another Arya, Munshi Ram (1856–1926), who later took the name of Swami Shraddhanand, also fell to a Muslim assailant (see next section). In this context, it is important to note the work that the Arya Samaj carried out in the Punjab and elsewhere in India in reclaiming Hindus who had been converted to either Islam or Christianity.

The Arya Samaj in the Punjab After Dayanand

After Dayanand, the Arya Samaj in Punjab expanded rapidly. There were 32 branches in the Punjab alone in 1883, 200 in 1885, and 265 in 1886. This calls for an explanation. In hindsight, it may be justly argued that the Arya Samaj provided Punjabi Hindus with a cultural meaning to their lives and projected itself as a movement for social progress. It created space for an ideology shared by an organised body of followers. Dayanand's appeal for a Vedic revival attracted a class of Hindu Punjabis who may well have taken some pride in the fact that their homeland was once the seat of the early Vedic civilisation. Some of the ideals or values encouraged by the Swami also appealed to the hopes and ambitions of the upwardly mobile intermediary mercantile castes in the Punjab. Swami Dayanand himself was bold, robust, courageous, aggressive, and virile of body and mind; this image apparently attracted a cross section of Punjabi youth who were somewhat disenchanted with the Brahmos, with their meekness and anglicised ways of thinking. After the 1880s, the average Punjabi found the Bengali Brahmo far too cosmopolitan and insufficiently absorbed in national culture.

Interestingly, though, it was not disagreement over social reform or even religious doctrine that caused disunity among

Mahatma Hansraj (1864–1938).

Aryas – even the more conservative among them supported widow marriages and the education of the girl child. Rather, major differences within the community occurred over the question of diet and a suitable education for young boys and girls. By 1886–1887, the Aryas were divided into two rival, though not yet formally separated, parties. These were called the 'College Party' and the 'Mahatma Party' respectively after the social and cultural ideals they followed. The College Party, led by men like Mahatma Hansraj (1860–1938), Lala Lal Chand (1852–1912), and Bhai Jawahir Singh (1859–1910), and drawn mainly from the Western-educated intelligentsia, believed in modernisation and adapting themselves to Western values or ideas. By the 1880s, they controlled the movement for secondary and higher education in the Punjab and started what came to be called the Dayanand Anglo Vedic scheme of educational institutions, which survive today. Their rivals, the Mahatma Party, by contrast, accepted the more traditional side to Dayanand's teachings and insisted on a vegetarian diet and a more traditional education. After a formal split within the Arya movement which occurred in 1892–1893, the two camps steadily drifted apart. In 1902, one of their prominent leaders, Lala Munshi Ram, started the Gurukul movement at Haridwar, which imparted traditional education under a strictly controlled environment. Boys were admitted here at the early age of eight and remained with the institution until they had attained the age of twenty-five. They were given a traditional education but were also introduced to the rudiments of Western knowledge. They were dressed in saffron-coloured garments (traditionally associated with Hindu and Buddhist monks), brought up in strict seclusion, and not permitted to be with any member of their family or with the opposite sex. By 1907, twenty-five students had been enrolled in the institution. Eventually, Munshi Ram came to be involved with the *shuddhi* movement, which cost him his life – he was murdered in 1926. After Pundit Lekh Ram, he was the second Arya missionary to fall victim to a Muslim assassin.

Swami Dayanand's Critics

In the Punjab, as elsewhere in India, the growing popularity of a reformed religion, at least among the Western-educated Indian intelligentsia, was met with a conservative reaction. However, reformers cannot always be differentiated from their opponents by their class origins or ideology: conflicting ideas and practices could be found within each. In both Bengal and Maharashtra, both critique and defence of

153

traditional Hinduism came from practically the same social group: the Western-educated middle classes.

However, even those who had not formally received a Western education were aware of the changes occurring around them and reacted to them. In the Punjab, this class of people is exemplified by two brahmin individuals, pundits Shardha Ram Phillauri (1837–1881), of whom we have already briefly spoken, and Din Dayalu Sharma (1863–1939). Neither met Dayanand in person, but both actively fought his ideals and objectives. Pundit Din Dayalu's activities took him beyond the Punjab; he was instrumental in organising a body of orthodox Hindus called the Bharat Dharma Mahamandal, which planned to operate on a pan-Indian level. However, we shall mainly be examining the life and career of Pundit Shardha Ram here.

Shardha Ram, the son of a priest, himself performed the functions of a priest in his early life. Thereafter, he was engaged by local missionaries of the Presbyterian Church to assist with the translation of Christian texts. This is reminiscent of Arumuga Navalar's work in the Jaffna Peninsula. It is possible, that like Navalar, Shardha Ram gained some familiarity with Christian doctrines and used this familiarity to contest missionary propaganda. Reportedly, in 1853–1854, when touring the Indian state of Kapurthala in the Punjab, he successfully dissuaded the local ruler from converting to Christianity. In 1867, with the assistance of a friend, Munshi Yamuna Prasad, he set up an organisation called the Hindu Sabha which aimed at countering all alien attacks on Hindu society and culture. In subsequent years he lectured extensively on the need to respect the Hindu religious canon. It was in the course of such work that he met Kanhaiya Lal Alakhdhari; for a time the two even worked towards a common cause, but they drifted apart when Alakhdhari formally joined the Brahmo Samaj.

In 1876, Shardha Ram authored his magnum opus, *Dharma Raksha*, which, as its name suggests, was a treatise on the defence of Hinduism allegedly under attack from Christians, Muslims, and 'renegade' Hindus. After 1877, he had to meet the challenge from Swami Dayanand. Shardha Ram closely followed Dayanand's itinerary in the Punjab, trying to counter the Swami's arguments and continued attacking the reforming party even after Dayanand had left the Punjab. In 1880, he established a Vedic school at Phullaur, his birthplace, and another institution of higher learning called the Gyan Mandir, at Lahore.

Little is known of Shardha Ram's life after this time, but in the context of Hinduism in colonial Punjab, he may be justly called the best representative of what came to be known as 'Sanatanist ideology'. The word *sanatan* was rarely used in Bengal or Bombay with their strong traditions of innovative reform. By the term *sanatan*, Shardha Ram implied two things: first, the belief that the religion of the Hindus was essentially a collection of certain core, unchanging ideas or values, and, second, that in religious life, faith mattered more than reason.

Shardha Ram was a staunch defender of the caste system, and, uniquely, he maintained that the Hindu religion was limited to the *dvijas* (the twice-born, i.e. the first three varnas of brahmin, *kshatriya*, and *vaishya*). He was even prepared to publicly address a person from an inferior caste as *neech admi* (low-born). This clearly sets him apart not only from the Aryas and Brahmos but also from many Hindu conservatives who were willing to socially emancipate the lower castes, albeit on their own terms.

'Dayanand Unveiled':
Shiv Narayan Agnihotri and the Dev Samaj

Another staunch critic of Dayanand was Pundit Shiv Narayan Agnihotri (1856–1929), who even authored a book called *Dayanand Unveiled*. Agnihotri was by birth a high-ranking brahmin, educated at the Engineering College at Roorkee. Early in his life he was influenced by the religious views of Shiv Dayal Singh (1818–1878), the founder of the Radhasoami movement. The latter taught him Vedanta and encouraged him to join the Brahmo Samaj at Lahore, which he served as Honorary Minister between 1875 and 1882. In 1882, he decided to quit his employment and become a full-time Brahmo missionary. At some stage in his life he was influenced by the work of Fredrick Booth-Tucker (1853–1929), who brought the ideals of the Salvation Army to India. By 1887 he had become disenchanted with the Brahmo Samaj and started an independent movement in Lahore which was called the Dev Samaj.

Agnihotri took the Dev Samaj to represent a special divine dispensation. Like the Brahmos, he upheld the idea of a personal God, rejected transmigration, and remained greatly obsessed with the idea of atoning for sin. In his view, *moksha* ('liberation', in Hindu terminology) was not the cessation of the cycle of births and deaths but the conquest of sin. Agnihotri did not believe in the concept of a religious source book and acknowledged other religious systems only insofar as they conformed to the principles laid down by the Dev Samaj. This made the office of the leader hugely powerful, and Agnihotri claimed absolute and undisputed authority over his followers. On 4 October 1892, *Dharma Jivan*, the journal of the Samaj, stated that 'He [Agnihotri] and his mission are not two things but one'. Members were required to bow down reverentially in the presence of their leader (who was given the name Satya Deva (True God)) and to entirely trust in his words.

Agnihotri took religion to represent an evolutionary process; reportedly, this came to him through reading Herbert Spencer, and *Natural Law in the Spiritual World* (1883) by the biologist Henry Drummond. The point, however, was that this evolutionary process was believed to have come to an end with him and the organisation that he had founded. Such authoritarianism was later to affect the movement badly. In 1917, Agnihotri took upon himself the combined roles of messiah, soothsayer, reformer, arbitrator, and spiritual leader. The Deva Guru (as he now called himself) was likened to Jesus himself, having the power to grant deliverance from sins, settle disputes, and act as an infallible guide to his followers in their everyday lives.

Like the Brahmo Samaj, the Dev Samaj was essentially a body of literate men and women and its record for carrying out progressive social reform was quite impressive. Agnihotri encouraged inter-caste dining, the education of females, and widow marriage. He is believed to have married a widow himself. However, in the Punjab its popularity and numerical presence was relatively weak compared to that of the Arya Samaj; on the other hand, like the Arya Samaj, it contributed towards gradually pushing the Brahmos out of reckoning. In 1891, the Dev Samaj had only 12 members compared to over 14,000 Aryas and 128 Brahmos; in 1921, they numbered 3,597 compared with 223,000 Aryas and only 405 Brahmos. Educational institutions associated with the Dev Samaj survive even today at certain places in the Punjab but in a form that fails to catch public attention.

CONCLUSION

In this chapter, we have examined in some detail developments occurring in the Madras Presidency and in the North Indian state of Punjab. Both these regions were influenced by developments that had earlier taken place in Bengal and Bombay but also reveal some unique features of their own. In the Punjab, for example, a sharper distinction than in Bengal was often made between the purely intellectual values of Western education and its culturally objectionable aspects. Also, the English-educated Punjabi developed deeper roots in the indigenous tradition and was sooner drawn into violent, anti-colonial political movements: some Aryas developed links with armed revolutionary organisations. They were also more embroiled in communal politics than were reformers from Bengal or Bombay.

The cultural renaissance in the Madras Presidency was less significant than that in the two other presidencies. It was the work of a body of intellectuals which was both numerically weaker and less articulate in its response to commonplace social or religious issues. Madras produced far fewer reformist figures of all-India fame. It was only in the early years of the twentieth century that the region was rocked by an active social and political spirit, which mainly disputed brahmin hegemony and caught the attention of elites elsewhere. Local figures like E. V. Ramasamy Periyar (1879–1973) reinforced the critique of caste and religion that was also to be manifested in Maharashtra under B. R. Ambedkar. The success of the 'non-brahmin movement' in the Tamil-speaking regions divided public attention and weakened both the cause of social reform and nationalist politics in the region.

There was also a greater and more persistent spirit of provincialism in this region. A case in point is the movement for effecting changes to the traditional Shaiva canon, which used very distinctive communicative strategies, preferred the vernacular over English, and was never as cosmopolitan in its outlook as were the Brahmo or Prarthana Samajes. Notwithstanding their internal differences, both Ramalinga and Navalar as interpreters of the Tamil Shaiva Siddhanta laid the foundations of a distinctive Dravidian culture, quite distinct from that predominant in the north. The only exception to this trend was the work of Narayan Guru in Kerala, which reveals a broad eclecticism. This eclecticism partly followed from the fact that the Guru adopted the ideology of philosophical non-dualism; this tied him to the work of cosmopolitan figures like Rammohun and Vivekananda, who similarly saw an overlap between a sense of philosophical unity and the sociocultural.

DISCUSSION TOPIC:
REFORM HINDUISM IN THE MADRAS PRESIDENCY AND THE PUNJAB

- Would you agree with the view that models of 'Reform Hinduism' varied between provinces of British India?

- Analyse the nature of the religious movements seeking to reform Tamil Shaivism in the Madras Presidency. How were these different in nature from other reform movements in the region?

- Compare Raja Rammohun Roy and Swami Dayanand Saraswati as Hindu reformers.

- Compare the social and religious views of Swami Dayanand and the Arya Samaj.

Further Reading

J. N. Farquhar. *Modern Religious Movements in India*. New York: The Macmillan Company, 1915.

Kenneth W. Jones. *Socio-Religious Reform Movements in British India*. New Delhi: Cambridge University Press, 1994 (esp. Chapters 4 and 6).

Amiya P. Sen (ed.). *Social and Religious Reform: The Hindus of British India*. New Delhi: Oxford University Press, 2006.

Richard Weiss. *The Emergence of Modern Hinduism: Religion on the Margins of Colonialism*. Berkeley: University of California Press, 2019.

Pl. 6.
Tom. I. Pag. 31.

P. Sonnerat pinx.

Poisson Sc.

VEUVE INDIENNE.

A late eighteenth-century French engraving of the plight of the Hindu widow.

IV

MAJOR ISSUES IN HINDU SOCIAL REFORM: THE WOMAN QUESTION AND THE INEQUITIES OF CASTE

In Chapter 2 we attempted to provide a general understanding of the ideas and intentions underlying the concept of 'reform'. However, that chapter was directed more at understanding attempts to reform the Hindu religion rather than Hindu society. Historically speaking, this is the right narrative sequence to adopt since attempts at reforming the former preceded those seeking to change the latter.

This chapter will address social issues consequent on religious reform. A reformed religion, after all, would best work in a suitably reformed society. However, the reform of Hindu society naturally faced many challenges, not all of which could be satisfactorily resolved or, for that matter, even analysed with an appropriate seriousness; thus, the scope of social reform in India was more narrowly defined than in the contemporary West, where it was wide in scope and application. In nineteenth-century India, for reasons related to the structure of Hindu society and its everyday practices, reform was practically limited to two major issues: issues related to women – that is, the 'Woman Question', in the contemporary idiom – and oppression committed in the name of caste.

THE PRIMACY OF RELIGIOUS REFORM

When confronted with the moral and intellectual challenges thrown down by the West, the Hindu mind initially responded not with cultural counteraggression but by developing a critical attitude towards itself, and its attention first focused on the matter of religion. There are three possible reasons why, with the Hindus, the agenda of religious reform took precedence over the social.

First, the Hindu intelligentsia of this period came to believe that the site of social reform, too, lay in religion. In other words, they believed that it was by suitably altering religious beliefs and practices that one could bring about appropriate changes in the proper conduct of men and women in modern society. For instance, the most influential of Hindu thinkers and reformers of this period believed that the inequities of caste would disappear once people accepted the idea of their common origin in God. They also came to realise that many regressive social ideas and practices had their origins in religious literature. It therefore became important to re-examine and reinterpret the religion of the Hindus to make it conform to new social ideas or values. In their attempts to bring about changes in social practices, Hindu reformers like Rammohun, Ranade, and Ishwarchandra Vidyasagar drew upon Hindu *shastras* or scriptures in the belief that doing so would more easily overcome orthodox resistance to change and win the support of their countrymen. That the nature of Hindu society and culture was deeply religious and held the key to any meaningful social transformation was an idea that the Orientalists of the eighteenth century did much to propagate: the idea found easy acceptance among Western-educated Hindus and the traditional Hindu literati alike.

Second, the spontaneous concern with religious reform was, on one level, a natural reaction on the part of the Hindus. In the eighteenth and early nineteenth centuries, European observers or commentators were relatively more harsh in their condemnation of 'heathen' (by which they meant the Hindu) religious 'superstition' and 'bigotry' than of forms of Hindu social organisation. For such people there was obviously something especially revolting about worshiping the 'hideous', bloodthirsty goddess Kali or the reverence shown to inanimate objects made of clay, wood, or stones. By comparison, the caste system, though unjust and oppressive, was found to be more complex and to work in more subtle ways. Further, European evangelists were known to turn a blind eye to the oppressive side of the caste system if it helped them secure a larger number of converts. It was often the case that ties of caste within a certain community led to mass conversions, although conversion did not necessarily end caste discrimination.

Finally, given the inherent doctrinal flexibility within Hinduism, religious experimentation proved to be easier than attempts at changing everyday social practices. In Bengal, even orthodox Hindus agreed with Brahmo reformers when the latter drew attention to the strong traditions of monotheism and iconoclasm within traditional Hinduism. Differences between Hindus and Brahmos developed primarily over social issues like gender relations, conformity to caste rules, or questions of observing the rules of ritual purity and pollution. Some Hindus took Hinduism to be much less a cohesive religion than a particular form of social organisation. In effect, this alerted Hindu reformers to the necessity of carrying out important changes in the social sphere too. Modernity, they realised, had to rest equally on reformed doctrines and on more just and equitable social relationships.

THE TWIN ISSUES
IN HINDU SOCIAL REFORM

Though seemingly unrelated, the two issues of women and caste were connected in some important ways. For instance, issues like female education or legalising the remarriage of Hindu widows had a bearing on the caste question. Could lower-caste girls be admitted to schools run for or by the upper castes? Could the Hindu widow marry outside her caste? These were delicately complex questions which eluded simple or hasty answers.

It is on the whole true that both these issues were on the agenda of Hindu reformers in much of British India, though most visibly in the three presidency towns of Calcutta, Bombay, and Madras. Yet it cannot be denied that these were not pursued or agitated with the same seriousness everywhere, and conditions even within the three presidency towns differed substantially. Such differences were largely determined by the specific social formation of a region and by its cultural past. For reasons not yet fully understood, Bengal did not experience the same degree of social friction or hostility in the name of caste as did the presidencies of Bombay and Madras.

In Bengal, upper-caste domination was not exclusive to or even largely the work of brahmins, and this may have followed from certain facts peculiar to its known social history. For one thing, at some point in time, cultural habits and ways of life had become so un-Brahmanical in this region that brahmins from North India had to be settled in this province to initiate a degree of brahminisation. Further, Bengal had never produced a brahmin ruling dynasty in its early history and had fallen to Muslim conquest by the thirteenth century. Both of these factors appear to have had a bearing on how everyday life of the Hindus was organised in this province.

Western India, by comparison, was ruled for a long time by the Marathas, and in the early nineteenth century the British took over power from the ruling brahmin dynasty of the Peshwas, who had established their rule over 100 years previously. Thus, brahmin social dominance in Maharashtra drew support from brahmin political power. However, notwithstanding the more successful Brahmanical control in these regions, Hindu women were allowed a greater degree of social freedom in Madras and Bombay than in Bengal. Several Brahmo reformers from Bengal who toured these two provinces in the course of their missionary work testified to the fact that Bengali Hindu women suffered a greater degree of social persecution than those in Bombay and Madras. This may have followed from the fact that although brahmin power itself was weak in Bengal, Brahmanical culture in general was more pervasive and powerful; support for the latter came from the more numerous and influential intermediary castes like the *baidyas* and *kayasthas*. This would explain why in Bengal it was the brahmin Rammohun who agitated against the inhuman practice of *sati*, while the non-brahmin Radhakanta Deb was most vociferous in its defence. In the eighteenth and early nineteenth centuries, Bengal, more than any other region, became the object of strong criticism from colonial officials and Christian missionaries on account of two particularly inhuman social practices which targeted women: *sati*, whereby upper-caste Hindu widows either volunteered or else were forced to burn themselves on their husband's funeral pyre, and kulinism, a polygamous system common to brahmins and upper-caste Hindus, in which a male could take any number of wives yet hold no responsibility for their upkeep. Both *sati* and polygamy were practiced elsewhere, but they took especially regressive forms in ethnic Bengal.

The 'Woman Question' and Its Embedded Issues

The 'Woman Question' grew out of the increasing concern that Western-educated Hindus began to show towards the gross ill-treatment of Hindu women. Only exceptionally did someone not belonging to this class show any concern about this issue. By virtue of their modern Western education, the new Hindu intelligentsia agreed with the view that the state of civilisation in any country could be reasonably judged from the way it treated its women. Hence, many educated young men showed an increasing sensitivity towards this issue and pressed for an improvement in the social status of women. Not all of these men were formally connected with reforming bodies, but they generally stood behind the larger cause of the emancipation of women. As the reformer from Maharashtra, Mahadev Govind Ranade, once observed, it was necessary for men to speak up for women and children since they could not speak for themselves.

In hindsight, the Woman Question may be said to revolve around six interrelated issues, each of which eventually became a major agenda with the aspiring Hindu reformer: prohibiting the practices of female infanticide and the self-immolation of Hindu widows under *sati*, promoting the education of girls, enabling Hindu widow marriages, ending polygamy, and determining a socially just and medically safe age of (conjugal) consent between married couples. It is important to understand the vital connections between these issues. For instance, if Hindu widows were not to perform self-immolation, this begged the question: could the widow then opt to remarry? Similarly, so long as men could enter into multiple marriages, this aggravated the widowhood problem: the death of one man could at one stroke create numerous helpless widows doomed to lead a miserable life.

The education of women had an important bearing on the question of when to marry off daughters: imparting even basic education to girls would require pushing up the minimum age of marriage. Further, if a girl was to be educated, one might have been naturally led to ask, could she have the freedom to choose her own marriage partner?

British Initiatives on the Problem of Female Infanticide

Of the six issues, female infanticide was the one in which Western-educated Hindus showed the least interest, largely because it was a somewhat isolated phenomenon prevalent in only certain regions of India located far from the metropolis and common among certain castes only. However, Dr. Bhau Daji (1824–1874), a medical practitioner from Bombay and one of the few Hindus to show any interest in the issue, did make the pertinent observation that women themselves were complicit in such heinous crimes, a factor perpetuated by the sheer lack of education among them. The legal abolition of female infanticide was almost exclusively the work of British administrators. It was never promoted with the same frequency or intensity as were other issues related to women.

The Problems Concerning Female Education

The least controversial issue was female education, to which even the Hindu orthodox extended their support, albeit on their own terms. Radhakanta Deb, mentioned above, and easily the most conservative Hindu figure when it came to woman-related reform, was himself a champion of educating girls and even sponsored a supportive booklet authored by the pundit Gourmohan Vidyalankar. Three other eminent traditional Hindu scholars or pundits of the period supported the cause of female education: Ishwarchandra Vidyasagar (1820–1891), the well-known social reformer and educator and principal of

Ishwarchandra Vidyasagar (1820–1891).

Calcutta Sanskrit College, and his colleagues Madanmohan Tarkalankar (1817–1858) and Taranath Tarkavachaspati (1806–1885). When in 1849, John Elliot Drinkwater Bethune (1801–1851), president of the Council of Education for Bengal, opened the Bethune Girls School in Calcutta, pundits Madanmohan and Taranath promptly admitted their daughters to that school, even in the face of some opposition. Ishwarchandra opened rural schools for girls at his own expense and arranged for girl-students to be transported to the Bethune School in private horse-drawn carriages. The carriages had suitable Sanskrit verses inscribed on them, encouraging the education of girls. Providing such transportation proved to be helpful to this enterprise and demonstrates how Hindu society in nineteenth-century Calcutta was more averse to exposing girls to public gaze than to giving them a basic education. However, Vidyasagar's effort in the field of female education eventually failed since the government itself was reluctant to financially support his plans in the long run. The progress of female education everywhere was slow and lacked both social and state initiatives – yet, by 1882, two Hindu women had graduated from the modern Indian University of Calcutta. One of them was to become a registered medical practitioner.

Rammohun's Crusade Against the Cruel Rite of Sati

Far more complex and controversial were moves to intervene in matters related to marriage and the conjugal life of Hindus. The controversy related to some major issues, each of which had an important bearing on a woman's rights as an individual and on her place in society. The first issue to turn into a matter of public controversy was *sati* (literally, 'chaste Hindu woman'). The practice has a long history: it is mentioned in the Hindu epic, the *Mahabharata*, and presumably was practiced down the ages, albeit not as frequently as reported in early colonial India. More cases came to light in British India on account of the increasing circulation of newspapers and journals which kept watch on such occurrences and reported them regularly.

Sati was the practice that enjoined the upper-caste widow to throw herself into the funeral pyre of her husband in order to affirm and demonstrate her chaste thoughts and faithfulness to his memory. At the time, *sati* was reported from many regions of India, but mostly from Gangetic Bengal, where its occurrence increased sharply between 1815 and 1818. In Brahmanical culture, the wife was called the *ardhangini*, in whom the husband was said to reside even after his death. Since a part of the wife's body belonged to her deceased husband, a second marriage for the widow was deemed to be an act of infidelity. Until 1856, the high-caste widow had no choice but to accept self-immolation, or else lead an extremely miserable

A late sixteenth-century painting showing a Hindu princess committing sati *in the presence of Emperor Akbar.*

life as an outcast, spurned by her community and viewed with the greatest suspicion. In contemporary Hindu culture, since women were taken to be by nature promiscuous and sexually vulnerable, the unprotected, helpless widow was even more so. The act of *sati*, therefore, was seen as an honourable way for the woman and wife to avoid the sexual gaze of strangers and overcome her own weaknesses of the flesh.

European observers and commentators took *sati* to be a form of widow murder, especially in view of the coercion often exercised by her family members to end her life. In theory, the act of *sati* was deemed to be voluntary, and, indeed, pregnant women and women with very young children were spared the ordeal. On the other hand, according to the testimony of the police and British magistrates who were often present at the site of immolation, widows were literally thrown back onto the fire when they lost courage and tried to flee. One reason for this behaviour from relatives was sheer greed for the property inherited by the widow from her deceased husband, which would then pass to his relatives if the widow herself perished in the flames. For Christian missionaries, this barbaric act only pointed to the serious need for reforming the heathen. For a long time, the colonial state itself was reluctant to intervene in the matter, limited by its own declared policy of non-intervention in the customary rites and practices of its subjects. However, changes in the ideology and of the ruling classes in Britain itself prepared a more congenial environment for change. Happily, the move to abolish the practice was strongly supported by early Indian reformers like Raja Rammohun Roy and even a traditional pundit by the name of Mrityunjay Vidyalankar (1782–1819), who was employed at Fort William College in Calcutta. Rammohun was cautious in his approach; he advised the then Governor General, William Bentinck, to gradually weed out the practice through more effective policing rather than outright legislation. However, the government, keen to live up to its self-declared reputation of a progressive social agency, pushed for legislation – though only after it was convinced that changes in Hindu law or social practice would not foment rebellious thoughts in its subjects. The law prohibiting *sati* was passed in 1829. For colonial officials, the interests of the empire were always placed above all else. Even so, Bentinck's 'Minute on Sati' carries a strong humanistic appeal and a sense of public indignation that is worth quoting in brief:

The first and primary object of my heart is the benefit of the Hindu. I know nothing so important of their future condition and the establishment of a purer morality, whatever their belief and a more just conception of their belief in God. The first step to this better understanding will be the disassociation of religious belief and practice from blood and murder.[37]

Two relevant observations need to be made in the context of Rammohun's anti-*sati* campaign. Rammohun authored tracts in both Bengali and English, arguing that self-immolation by the widow had no support in the Hindu legal texts and that a life of *brahmacharya* (self-denial and celibacy) was the morally and socially preferable option. In support of this argument he cited Manu, taken to be the most important of Hindu lawgivers, but conveniently overlooked the fact that many other texts still recommended that the woman turn into the heroic *sati*. More importantly, Rammohun altogether overlooked marriage as an option available to the grieving widow. His advocacy of a life of *brahmacharya* for the Hindu widow actually added to the difficulties of reformers after him who found marriage to be a more humane and practical option. Rammohun also reinforced the older trend of tying social legislation to scriptural support. On one hand, this was no doubt a tactical decision which presumed that as far as the Hindu orthodoxy was concerned, the sanction of the *shastras* themselves would minimise the opposition to any legal innovation. On the other hand, this method took away from the purely rational and humanitarian side to any act of social reform and fight against social injustice. The orthodox party in Bengal and elsewhere did not accept

---

37 William Cavendish Bentinck's Minute of 8 November 1829.

the legal abolition of *sati*; it even challenged the Governor General's decision before the Privy Council in Britain. A body called the Dharma Sabha, entrusted with the defence of the Hindu tradition, and considered by some scholars to be India's first proto-nationalist institution, was founded under the leadership of Radhakanta Deb and submitted a petition to the Privy Council. Rammohun himself was in England during the subsequent debate in the council and was greatly relieved when it was rejected, albeit by a slender margin.

An early nineteenth-century etching depicting a widow being led to the funeral pyre of her husband.

Ishwarchandra Vidyasagar:
Alleviating the Plight of Hindu Widows

The problems arising in relation to woman-related reform were most dramatically manifest in the effort to legalise the marriage of Hindu widows that climaxed in the 1850s, best exemplified by the work of Vidyasagar. In Bengal, widow marriage was practised among certain lower castes but was taboo for upper-caste society. In Maharashtra, rules were more relaxed for even upper castes. The Peshwas are known to have allowed such marriages in return for a fee.

Several factors contributed to the plight of the upper-caste Hindu widow. Recurring droughts, famines, and epidemics, and the poor state of public health and hygiene generally, contributed to a high rate of mortality in British India. The fact that the husband was ordinarily far more advanced in age than his wife contributed to this problem. But while a man who lost his wife to any of the above causes was free to remarry, such a possibility was strictly denied to the widowed upper-caste woman. Hindu orthodoxy came to identify an ascetic widowhood with the most cherished values of Hindu society. In the campaigns concerning both *sati* and widowhood, what was debated was not so much the fate of the Hindu woman as the Hindu tradition itself. The strength and endurance of Hindu society was made to rest on the self-denying widow who observed lifelong vows of chastity and held the memories of her departed husband to be sacred and inviolable. Perpetual widowhood, in other words, was an important constituent of Hindu patriarchy.

In the nineteenth century, what stirred the conscience of the reformer was the abject life that the upper-caste widow was forced to lead, even if she were only a child. Brahmin widows in particular were expected to abstain from all non-vegetarian food, go without food and water on certain 'auspicious' days of the month, wear only coarse clothes, and even have their hair shaved. Such an intolerably hard life was inflicted on her only so that she might suitably prepare her body and mind for a life of utter restraint and self-denial. Reformers like Vidyasagar were moved by the cruel, undignified, and dehumanising treatment of the Hindu widow. He also shared the general concern that fellow Hindus felt towards the way she was likely to be socially and sexually exploited. This had some foundation in fact. Young widows were often misled by suitors with promises of a happy married life and family, then subsequently either abandoned, sold to brothels in major towns, or simply left to languish and die. Some fell prey to the lust of family members and were ultimately left with no choice but to end their own lives out of a sense of sheer helplessness, outrage, and shame.

Vidyasagar's earliest social reform campaign starting in 1850 was an essay on the issue of preventing early marriages among girls. This had a bearing on widowhood since early marriages only prolonged a life of suffering in the event of the husband's untimely death. At the time, however, his appeal was based more on reason and utility than on prescriptive *shastras*. The fact that the essay was hardly noticed may have persuaded him to switch to the tactical ploy of citing the approval of Hindu legal texts. Vidyasagar found such support for widow marriage in the law book of the *smriti* writer Parasar, who prescribed marriage as one of the options available to the widow. What strengthened the reformer's hand was the fact that Parasar described himself as the appropriate lawgiver for the degenerate age of Kali (*kaliyuga*), coinciding with the modern age. Rammohun, as noted above, did not prescribe the marriage of widows; in part, this may be attributed to his exclusively relying on the ordinances of Manu.

However, Vidyasagar's reading of the contemporary Hindu mind proved to be a gross error: notwithstanding approval from certain lawgivers, the orthodoxy simply rejected widow marriages on the grounds of what they called *deshachar* (established social custom). In the subsequented heated war of words between the reforming party and the opposition, numerous tracts were produced and publicly distributed. On the whole, though, the supporters of widow marriage were vastly outnumbered by the opposition. About ten times the number of signatures was collected from opponents than from supporters. However, the government, though initially reluctant to intervene, ultimately agreed to pass a law enabling Hindu widows to legally marry. Its position was strengthened by the knowledge that such marriages were permitted in some Hindu law books, if not all. The ruling class also had great regard for Vidyasagar as an eminent scholar, educator, and undaunted social reformer. The law was passed in 1856 and in essence simply enabled the widow desiring to marry to tie the matrimonial knot without fear of social persecution. However, it also placated orthodox sentiments by denying the marrying widow any rights in the deceased husband's property. At the time, many may have expected this clause to encourage widow marriages since members of the husband's family clearly stood to gain from the widow's forfeiting property rights. Yet the power of entrenched tradition proved far stronger and, though legally possible, the marriage of widows proved to be a social failure. For a long time, Vidyasagar had to bear the expenses of such marriages and, over time, this led to his incurring colossal debts. But there were other valuable lessons. Vidyasagar discovered to his horror how some men married a widow only to abandon her soon thereafter; others simply failed to honour their commitment, still others took more wives. Under the Act of 1856, the first widow marriage was held on 7 December 1856, involving two brahmins: Srishchandra Vidyaratna, once a student at the Sanskrit College, and Kalimati Devi. On the whole, the entire widow marriage campaign in Bengal proved to be far less successful than in Maharashtra, the Punjab, and coastal Andhra. In the marriage involving Kalimati Devi, no male family member could be found to 'give' away the daughter, as was customary, and Srishchandra atoned for his 'sins' after his wife died prematurely. Far fewer widow marriages were celebrated in Bengal, turning the aging Vidyasagar cynical and into something of a misanthrope.

The strength and resilience of the Hindu orthodoxy should by no means be underestimated, but the failure of the widow marriage campaign in Bengal partly arose from Vidyasagar himself and his methods. The case for Bengal looks all the more unsuccessful since, unlike in Bombay or South India, reformers in this province did not have to put up with the wrath of Hindu authority figures like Shankaracharya. In Maharashtra, Gopal Hari Deshmukh Lokahitawadi had to publicly atone for having attended the marriage of a widow. Both Viresalingam Pantalu in coastal Andhra and Mahadev Govind Ranade in Bombay had to suffer excommunication for having supported the reforming party on this question. In the Punjab, on the other hand, the Arya Samaj was able to arrange a good number of widow marriages.

In hindsight, it may be argued that Vidyasagar might have better succeeded had he confined the campaign to the marriage of child widows who had not consummated their marriages. Virginity in a wife was a virtue on which the Hindu tradition insisted, and this discouraged the marriage of women widowed in adulthood. But what made matters worse was Vidyasagar's insistence that widow marriages follow the same set of rituals as were ordinarily followed in the case of young girls. His intentions are clear: he was keen to give widow marriages the same social status as any other marriage; however, this proved to be unrealistic and had the effect of sending the wrong signals to the orthodox camp, whose position hereafter hardened. Colonial ethnologists give us to believe that even among castes which traditionally permitted widows to marry, the married widow had to put up with certain social disadvantages. She could not, for instance, serve food in communal meals. Reformers in Maharashtra proved to be wiser and more realistic in this matter since they devised two sets of marriage rituals, one for the virgin child widow and another for the adult. It would also appear that Vidyasagar somewhat hastily staked his campaign on a single legal text (of Parasar) whereas Ranade and his compatriots in Bombay discovered several more. Relying on Parasar alone may have weakened his case during the legal disputations that followed. Nor would Vidyasagar support widow marriages without recourse to Hindu marriage rituals. For instance, he refused to support the marriage of a Brahmo by the name of Gurucharan Mahalanobis to a widow unless he agreed to follow Hindu rituals; unsurprisingly, Gurucharan declined to comply. Vidyasagar was equally averse to widows marrying under Act III of 1872 since the latter provided for purely civil marriages, without regard to the religion of the marrying parties. He did nothing to encourage inter-caste widow marriages and such marriages are known to have taken place solely among Brahmos.

By the early years of the twentieth century, support for widow marriages was surprisingly emerging from a different quarter – from people who generally leaned to the side of the Hindu right. Anxieties were now expressed about the demographic decline of the Hindus, particularly compared to Muslims. In the Punjab, as we have earlier noted, the Arya Samaj was able to launch successful campaigns aiming to take back into Hindu society Hindus who had converted to either Islam or Christianity. In Bengal, Swami Vivekananda had expressed fears about the decline as early as 1899. Such people were of the view that one way of addressing this problem was to further encourage widow marriage among Hindus.

The Failed Campaign Against Hindu Polygamy

In his lifetime, Vidyasagar was involved with two other important social reform campaigns which make him the quintessential reformer regarding woman-related reform. One issue was the question of multiple marriages among Hindu men. Although common elsewhere, in Bengal this acquired particularly repressive forms. By the tenth or eleventh century, it was common for men, especially of the brahmin or *kayastha* castes, to take multiple wives, regardless of their age or social standing. This practice was generally known as the *kulin* ('of high pedigree') system and was built upon a detailed classification of brahmins or *kayasthas*, based on their acknowledged ritual purity. Over the years, this led to a system whereby the ritually highest-placed brahmins could be enticed by offers of money to marry into families placed lower on the scale. For these families, such marriages obviously meant an upward movement in the social and ritual hierarchy. *Kulin* men were so highly prized that fathers agreed to marry their daughters to them regardless of the number of wives they already had. Thus there arose a situation whereby a senile, eighty-year-old male could be married to a woman as young as ten and count her among the two dozen wives to which he was already married. From a list of such marriages in district Hooghly (West Bengal) that Vidyasagar himself prepared, some *kulin* brahmins were known to have over 100 wives. In many instances, the husband never met the wife after the wedding night but continued to demand an agreed sum of money from the wife's family. The *kulin* husband had no responsibility for feeding or clothing his wives, nearly all of whom spent the rest of their lives with their parents, virtually abandoned by their husbands. A good number of them scandalously eloped with young men and were never heard of again, or else pimped out in Calcutta brothels. Some were tempted into entering illicit relationships then either abandoned or killed when they conceived a child. The worst feature of all, however, was that when a *kulin* brahmin male died, his death instantly converted all his numerous wives into helpless widows, doomed to the most despicable life.

Vidyasagar had greater success, by contrast, in persuading fellow Hindus to petition for a law prohibiting polygamy; among his supporters were influential public figures, rich landlords and petty rulers, journalists, lawyers, and authors. However, in this instance, it was the government which went back on the support and enthusiasm it had shown earlier. Its reading of the several pro-reform petitions was that whereas the Widow Marriage Act of 1856 was in the nature of an enabling act only, the move to end polygamy amounted to a direct intervention in Hindu social and legal usages, contrary to official policy. Looking back at those years, it is quite obvious that by this time the government was only too aware of the storm created by the uprising of 1857, with rebels clearly angered by laws prohibiting *sati* and legalising the marriage of widows. No social legislation was attempted by the colonial state for nearly forty years following 1856.

The Highly Controversial Age-of-Consent Legislation

Towards the closing years of his life, Vidyasagar was involved in yet another public controversy concerning women, in this instance touching upon the sexual exploitation of child brides. Under existing law, the husband, usually an adult male, could not be punished for sexual cohabitation with the wife if she happened to be above ten years in age. In 1889, a particularly disturbing case came to light in Calcutta of a forty-year-old man, Hari Mohan Maiti, causing the death of his eleven-year-old wife, Phulmoni Dasi, through forced intercourse. Though the man was not legally at fault, this case alerted the government and concerned reformers to the persisting problems relating to Hindu conjugal life. It was therefore proposed the Penal Code be amended by marginally increasing the minimum age of marital consent from ten to twelve. In effect this meant that sexual cohabitation with girls under the age of twelve amounted to rape, punishable under law, even in the case of the husband. Not surprisingly, this caused shock waves among the Hindu orthodoxy, which viewed it as a grossly unjust intervention in the customary social life of the Hindu. There was a state of near revolt in Calcutta and Bombay, with prominent vernacular newspapers and journals writing passionately against the move. Massive protest meetings were held in major Indian cities, involving even housewives and children with the anxious cries of 'Hindu religion in danger'. The orthodox rested their objections on the rite of *garbhadhan*, which enjoined Hindu parents to marry off their daughter before she showed signs of puberty. This resulted in girls marrying at the absurdly young ages of eight or ten. Getting a girl married at the age of eight (called *gauridan*) was considered especially meritorious, assuring the father a place in heaven. This was yet another instance of a social malpractice finding support in Hindu religion. When the government sought Vidyasagar's opinion on the matter, the pundit objected to the proposed bill to amend the Indian Penal Code not on matters of principle but procedure. His recommendation was that instead of fixing the age of consent by age, it was more justly linked to a girl actually going into menses. There was substance to his argument since even the proposed changes would fail to protect a girl from male brutality once she had attained the age of twelve. The government did not heed his advice, perhaps again in deference to the power of the Hindu orthodox. The Age of Consent Act became law in 1891.

Initiatives Taken by Women Reformers

No survey of the Woman Question would be complete if it failed to mention the role played by Hindu women themselves. Some Hindu figures, like Swami Vivekananda, preferred that the task of carrying out woman-related reform be left to women themselves. In hindsight, this appears to have some merit since women were perhaps better equipped to understand the true nature of their problems. Though few women were directly involved in such reform, there were some important exceptions when women seized the initiative for themselves.

One of the early figures in the field was Savitribai Phule (1831–1897), wife of a reformer from Maharashtra, Jotiba Phule. She was taught at home by her husband and subsequently joined him in his several projects, including the running of a school for lower-caste women, founded in 1848. In modern India, she was perhaps the first female educator in administrative control of an educational institution. Tarabai Shinde (1850–1910), who received her basic education from her parents, eventually emerged as a feminist writer and activist, best known for her work *Stri Purushanchi Tulana* (A Comparison between Men and Women, 1882). The 1880s

1998 Indian postage stamp of Savitribai Phule (1831–1897).

Kadambini Ganguly (1861–1923).

proved to an important time for advancing the cause of female education and professional advancement. By 1886, India had two women trained in Western medicine, Anandibai Joshi (1865–1887) and Kadambini Ganguly (1861–1923). Of these, the former died rather early and could not practise medicine; the latter was the first woman in the entire British Empire and in all of South Asia to practise it. A third woman, Rukhmabai (1864–1955), also emerged as a qualified doctor. That year, Haimabati Sen (1866–1932?) earned her medical degree from Campbell Medical College in Calcutta. Haimabati was widowed in early life but married again and raised a family. She left behind an important memoir which strongly asserted a woman's autonomous rights, independent of any connections with either her parental family or that of her husband. Rukhmabai was better known in contemporary India for a different set of reasons. In 1885, there commenced a case in Bombay involving herself and her husband, Bhikaji, which yet again cast an important light on the issue of conjugal rights in Hindu life. Rukmabai had refused to live with her husband and to give in to his sexual demands. When Bhikaji approached the judiciary for the restitution of his conjugal rights, the European judges trying the case were initially sympathetic to the defendant, arguing that English law on this subject could not be applied to cases involving Hindus. This produced a huge public controversy, with the nationalist press in Bombay coming out in support of Bhikaji and alleging that Rukmabai's insubordination and independence of mind had resulted from her being educated in the Western way. The court's ruling eventually went in Bhikaji's favour, but the marriage was subsequently annulled and Rukmabai took up the study of medicine in the UK, emerging as a registered medical practitioner in 1894.

A contemporary woman activist who embodied courage and compassion was Pundita Ramabai Dongre Medhavi (1858–1922), a learned woman of the brahmin caste upon whom Calcutta University conferred the honorary titles of Pundita and Saraswati in 1878. Her scholarship of the classical Hindu tradition was profound, but she applied this knowledge to modern concerns. Her study of scriptures led her to denounce the strongly patriarchal system of the Hindus, which she articulated in her books, such as *Stri Dharma Niti* (1882) and *The High Caste Hindu Woman* (1887). Even in her early life, Ramabai broke convention by marrying a non-brahmin. Widowed soon after marriage, she spent a lifetime promoting women's education and rehabilitating destitute children and widows. She converted to Christianity in 1883 when in England and thereafter travelled to the United States to work for the cause of Indian women. The Arya Mahila Samaj, Mutkti Mission, and the Sharada Sadan were the three institutions she founded in the 1880s to successfully advance her social work. The Pundita was a close friend of Rukmabai who faithfully stood by her at a time when she was widely denounced and persecuted by the Indian press.

Pundita Ramabai Saraswati (1858–1922).

QUESTIONING CASTE

All societies resort to creating and perpetuating identities by which to define and understand interpersonal relationships. For this purpose, they may choose to use class, caste, gender, religion, or ethnicity, or even a varying combination of these. There is, however, the possibility of one or more of these identity markers being more powerful or influential than the rest. Generally speaking, the functions of class have been more pronounced in Western societies, partly because the latter have not had anything closely resembling caste. In India, by comparison, class and caste intersect in complex ways, at times in opposition to one another. Thus, a man from the highest-placed brahmin caste may not belong to a superior class. In certain regions of India, brahmins are among the poorest of people, mainly because their traditional means of livelihood are now lost to them. However, it is not uncommon for a man to be privileged both in terms of class and caste. Membership of a superior class may enable a man to improve his social or ritual status; conversely, people belonging to higher castes enjoy certain advantages over lower castes which are useful in the making of a superior class.

Until recently, a man born into an upper caste was more likely to benefit from the various social and economic opportunities that his society provided, and material success would then reinforce his caste standing. In modern India, one of the strongest objections to the caste system arose in the visible mismatch between economic success and social standing. The iron rules of caste, based on birth as they are, would not allow alterations in the social order. Under these circumstances, the accident of birth mattered more than personal merit or abilities. On the other hand, communities of caste which had materially succeeded for some reason naturally aspired to a higher social status by virtue of their material wealth or influence. Peasants or cultivators belonging to a depressed caste would naturally aspire to relocate themselves on the social or ritual scale once they had turned into prosperous farmers. This was often very important in matters of everyday life. Wealth could not in every case erase altogether social stigma traditionally attached to a caste. Even in contemporary India, a poor brahmin may decline to marry his daughter to a man from an inferior caste, regardless of what material benefits this might bring to his daughter or to himself. This is because social pedigree or ritual rank is often considered more valuable than economic wealth or professional standing.

In India, caste has also been a very pervasive institution. Contrary to what people elsewhere might think, the caste system, though originating in Hinduism, practically affected even Indian Muslims, Christians, and Sikhs since these religious communities largely comprised converts from Hinduism. Indeed, it is somewhat ironic that even those Hindus who embraced Islam and Christianity in the name of protesting caste discrimination carried the caste system with them when they converted. Scholarly studies have proved that the caste system also operates among Muslims and Christians notwithstanding their overt declarations of egalitarianism. In South India, lower-caste converts to Christianity have often been kept out of churches or congregations identified with intermediary castes or upper-caste converts. At this level, caste differences obviously become markers of power, which is common to any form of social organisation.

The Intertwining of Religion and Caste: Ambedkar's Debate with Gandhi

In India, another subject of continuing controversy was the interrelationship between religious doctrine and social organisation. This produced acutely conflicting readings or perceptions. Early European observers of India, as well as near-contemporary Indian thinkers like Bhimrao Ambedkar (1891–1956), have argued that the caste system drew sustenance from Hinduism. This view argues that if the Hindus practised oppression in the name of caste, this was not because they were grossly unjust or particularly regressive in character but because they were deeply religious. Hence, a set of reformers have argued, albeit with subtle differences between them, that in order to overcome caste discrimination, one had either to

*Bhimrao Ambedkar (1891–1956) at
Columbia University, New York City, c. 1916.*

provide Hinduism with a different doctrinal basis or else do away with that religion altogether. Such views have been contested by another set of reformers, who found caste to have no basis in religion. In 1936, answering charges made by Ambedkar, Gandhi argued that caste had nothing to do with a spiritual life and that the origin of caste was not something that would concern him at any time.[38] This echoes the earlier views of Swami Vivekananda who had said that caste differed from religion by its very nature

---

38   The debate between Gandhi and Ambedkar occurred over a pamphlet that Ambedkar authored, called *Annihilation of Caste* (1936). Gandhi's rejoinder appeared in the journal *Harijan*. There is an interesting history to this encounter. Ambedkar had been invited to speak at Lahore under the auspices of the Jat Pat Todak Mandal, a body run by Punjabi Aryas, seeking caste reform. Eventually, the organisers of the talk went back on the invitation and pressed Ambedkar not to deliver his talk, obviously under pressure from the local orthodox. An enraged and offended Ambedkar then went on to produce the *Annihilation*.

and functions. Whereas caste represented a social principle or practices that were bound to change with time, religions were by nature fixed, eternal, and immutable.

Closer examination reveals both these perspectives to be problematic. Ambedkar's recommendation that Hinduism be given a new doctrinal basis looks far more realistic than that of E. V. Ramasamy Periyar, the radical activist from South India who wished to do away with religion altogether. In the nineteenth century, the religious reformation launched by the Brahmo Samaj and the Prarthana Samaj did make some inroads into caste orthodoxy. For one, some reformers, like Ranade, were prepared to risk excommunication for the sake of advancing a more rational religion and equitable social practices. The Brahmo Samaj appointed non-brahmins like Keshabchandra Sen as ministers, did away with the office of the priest, and encouraged inter-caste marriages; some Brahmos, like Ramtanu Lahiri (1813–1898), who happened to be brahmins even cast off their sacred thread. This was a far cry from the days of Rammohun himself, who, despite his strong social reformism, retained the sacred thread even on his deathbed. However, there is no denying the fact that caste drew sustenance from religious scripture and the caste hierarchy, in turn, supported religious orthodoxy. For instance, the theoretical justification of *varna* and *jati*[39] lay in

---

39 The term *varna* literally means 'colour' but, in early India, it also denoted the fourfold classification of Hindu society into brahmins, *kshatriyas*, *vaishyas*, and *shudras*. All those ranked lower than the *shudras* were socially marginalised and constituted the so-called 'untouchables', whose very sight or company was ritually polluting This *varna* classification was originally based on occupation and on social or political functions. Over time, *varna* gave way to the more complex system of *jati* ('caste'), which is endogamous. *Jatis* are numerous and may be subdivided into *upajati* (sub-castes).

religious texts and this made it especially difficult to dispute or change these as cultural practices. Similarly, it was the caste system which affirmed brahmins in the position of priests and lawgivers. Priesthood was often hereditary. This made their social and ritual power or privileges quite unassailable.

Lower-Caste Challenges and Upper-Caste Reactions

In regions like Bombay and Madras, with their significant presence of lower castes and 'untouchables' and a fairly old history of caste contestation, matters intensified with the growth of a new social and political consciousness, progressively derived from Western education. Lower-caste boys or girls who were not admitted into schools run by the upper castes sought the education offered by missionary schools, where they imbibed new values of social justice and liberty and learned to critique High Hinduism, with its discriminatory practices. Jyotiba Phule, in Maharashtra, is an eminent example of this transformation from merely fighting social injustice to actively securing social justice as a human right. He was educated in a school run by American missionaries and soon developed an aggressive and adamant attitude towards upper-caste projects. In 1873, he founded the Satyashodhak Samaj (literally, 'community of truth seekers') with the aim of spreading this new consciousness widely among the labouring, agricultural, and artisanal classes. Lower-caste reformers like Phule expected the colonial state to more directly help reduce discriminatory practices and expressed disappointment when it was found not to do enough. Phule could read English and was greatly influenced by the writings of the American political activist and philosopher Thomas Paine. By one estimate Phule authored over a dozen tracts and pamphlets in which he articulated his ideas and opinions on a wide range of subjects. Predictably, these were polemical

Jyotiba Phule (1827–1890).

in nature and often their underlying intention was simply to shock upper-caste society. Some of these ideas found their way into two of his best-known works, *Gulamgiri* (Slavery, 1873) and *Shetkaryacha Kasab* (Cultivator's Whipcord, 1881), in which Phule launched a vitriolic attack on the brahmin's privileges in both religious life and secular calling. *Gulamgiri* likened the indignity and the oppression inherent in the caste system to that suffered by slaves in pre-modern economies. The work also challenged the claim that Aryans were the original settlers of India; to the contrary, it argues that the British had arrived in India to free the land of 'Aryan tyranny'. This work focused on the several problems facing the ordinary cultivator and of the oppression he faced in the hands of the landlords, moneylenders, and colonial officials. On one level, Phule also anticipates Ambedkar's later arguments about producing a significantly reformed religion for the Hindus. His *Sarvajanik Satya Dharma Pustak* (The Universal Book on True Religion;

1889, 1891) speaks of a religion that was more rational and universalist in nature, freed of all forms of discriminatory thought and practice. Phule's ideas and campaigns had the support of the Maharaja of Kolhapur in western India, who himself belonged to a depressed caste. The state of Kolhapur reserved jobs for non-brahmins and was willing to openly dispute Brahmanical privileges. When the local brahmins, offended by the Maharaja's moves, refused to anoint him as the ruler in the prescribed Vedic way, the Maharaja retaliated by withdrawing subsidies to all brahmin scholars in the state.

The Hindu orthodoxy in Bombay and Poona was naturally displeased with the radical questioning of the traditional social order and of the ways in which life had been traditionally conducted. Here it is important to bear in mind that by the late nineteenth century, nationalist politics, deeply influenced by a Hindu counteraggression, was largely in the hands of brahmins and other upper castes. In 1892, speaking before the Bombay Industrial Conference, the brahmin Bal Gangadhar Tilak (1856–1920), an orthodox Hindu and militant politician, expressed great dissatisfaction over attempts to launch caste-related reform.[40] His objections were twofold: first, he defended the caste system as a rational and natural social arrangement, but, second and more importantly, he was unhappy that social issues like caste should be agitated in a colonised country like India. Any preoccupation with social reform issues, he warned, would take away from a sustained campaign for securing greater political rights for Indians. Given the enormous difference in social rites and customs in India, attempts to reform society would lead only to further disunity. Political agitation, on the other hand, aimed solely at

---

40 The title of his talk was 'The Hindu Caste from an Industrial Point of View' (1892).

Bal Gangadhar Tilak (1856–1920).

the British, was bound to unite Indians. In a very important sense, this brings out the inner conflicts developing within Indian social movements. After 1895, the annual sessions of the political body, the Indian National Congress, and the social reform body, the Indian Social Conference, could not be held simultaneously or on the same site. By that time, politicians were reluctant to engage with social reformers. It was only after 1920 that the All India Congress Committee agreed to take up social questions.

The Birth of Caste Associations

The continuing critique of caste did produce certain positive, but rather unexpected, results. Rather than weaken the caste system, such criticism made it more active in various ways, albeit in a modified form. Many prominent castes in North India now took it upon themselves to enter the field of social reform, in which they achieved commendable success. People realised that the power and influence of caste could also be put to positive uses. In the 1880s, several castes like the *kayasthas*, in the United Provinces and Bengal, *khatris* in the Punjab, *nairs* on the Malabar coast, *prabhus* and *oswals* in Bombay, the *kunbis* of Berar and *jats,* scattered in much of present-day Haryana or the Punjab, turned their caste associations into reformist bodies. The Kayastha Conference was begun in 1887, the Vaishya Conference in 1891, and the Nair Conference in 1903. In Rajasthan, the local British Resident, Col. C. K. M. Walter, persuaded Rajput princes to agree to certain pressing social reforms under the banner of what came to be called Walterkrit Rajputra Hitkarini Sabha. Such bodies tried to raise the minimum age of marriage for girls, discouraged the giving and taking of dowries, furthered modern education, encouraged widow marriages, and willingly took back into their communities Hindus who had violated caste taboos by travelling abroad. On occasion, they did this by threatening offenders with excommunication – exactly the opposite of what had happened during earlier attempts at social reform. In Bengal, even the greatly marginalised caste of the *namashudras* (previously called *chandals*) organised annual conferences after 1881 in which they actively debated issues specific to their community. Such efforts gained ground partly because the new leadership in these caste associations was increasingly being taken over by younger, Western-educated men.

The Politics of Caste

The politicisation of caste became most apparent in South India, principally in the Tamil- and Malayalam-speaking areas. Here, lower castes were subjected not only to social exploitation but also certain indignities: they were made to pay a number of illegal tolls and taxes and, as examined in previous chapters, were prevented from moving about publicly or visiting Hindu shrines. In Travancore, on the west coast, women belonging to the lowly placed Shanar and Nadar communities were not allowed to wear anything above their waist so as to distinguish them from the upper-caste Nair or Namboodiri women. Around 1813, this led to an agitation which continued for the next forty years. In the temple towns of present-day Tamil Nadu, such as Madurai, Ramnad, Sivakasi, and Tinevelly, washermen were allowed to wash clothes only between midnight and the early hours of the morning so that they would not come into contact with upper castes.

As in other regions in India, the spread of Western education among the lower castes of South India helped promote a new language of rights, and, over the years, this turned into a demand for greater social, professional, and political concessions from the government. Caste reform in South India relied more on gaining political power for the entire community rather than setting personal examples of dedicated work and self-sacrifice. In comparison with other regions of India, lower-caste consciousness thus took a militantly anti-brahmin stance here. One of the early manifestations of this spirit was the creation of the Justice Party in 1916, so named because it had the explicit aim of securing justice for the oppressed. It demanded more jobs for non-brahmins and politically challenged the nationalist politics of the Congress Party in the name of both particular interests and provincialism. Not surprisingly, the Justice Party opposed Gandhian movements, which had an all-India character. It also refused to accept Hindi as the national language of India, arguing that the history and culture of South India had always been different from those of the north. The separatist

'Dravidian movement' was born of this agitation. It viewed the history of India in polarised terms, as a contest between Aryan and Dravidian cultures; for a time, this considerably weakened nationalist politics represented by the Congress. In 1925, S. Ramanathan founded the Self Respect Movement, which spread to the Tamil diaspora; its undisputed leader in India was E. V. Ramasamy Periyar, whose social and political vision was quite revolutionary in its intent.

The Colonial State and the Caste Question

In British India, several factors kept caste alive. In fact, some scholars argue that caste differences actually hardened under colonial rule because of certain measures undertaken by the government itself. However, this is only one side of the story: the system was equally strengthened because that suited Indian interests too. At best, the social reform campaigns of the nineteenth century produced structural shifts or adjustments within the caste system, but they never aimed at dismantling it altogether. For instance, many lower castes, rather than challenge the caste system and the principles on which it was based, preferred to emulate the ways of the upper castes solely to win greater social recognition. This was clearly a case of the social or ritual status of a certain caste not being in harmony with its material or professional success. The Indian sociologist M. N. Srinivas has called this the process of Sanskritisation, by which the lower castes adopted certain ideas, practices, or lifestyles of the upper caste in order to press claims for being relocated higher on the social or ritual scale. Thus, in the closing years of the nineteenth century, several lower-caste communities, which had earlier allowed their widows to marry and had no scruples about eating beef (strictly prohibited for upper-caste Hindus), began to discourage such practices. Hence, their effort was not to challenge the caste system itself but to manipulate it for purposes of upward social mobility. Similarly, lower-caste movements used their growing political and social consciousness not to break down the system itself but to insist on certain social or economic concessions on the basis of their caste standing. So long as they continued to benefit from the reservation of jobs or seats in educational institutions on such a basis, they naturally saw no cause for disputing the system.

Arguably, certain institutions created by the British did contribute towards lessening the rigours of caste. Modern state-funded schools, colleges, and universities were institutions where all Indian students had right of admission and the opportunity to imbibe modern notions of social advancement. Modern education did contribute towards some form of social levelling and allowed students from upper and lower castes to better appreciate the social and cultural habits of one another. However, the fruits of such education could not be obtained beyond a certain limit, given the restricted prospects of modernisation under colonial rule. Similarly, the coming of the railways to India diffused to some extent social segregation in the name of caste. Railway coaches were classified according to the travelling comfort they provided, not on caste criteria. The practical result was that, irrespective of their caste, people were forced to travel together, thereby reducing the rigours of caste. A reformer from Bombay once remarked that the Parsi soda water seller at the Bombay railway station would be more effective in dismantling caste than 100 learned papers. Yet this could, of course, all have been a temporary phenomenon: presumably, people went back to their old ways and habits once they reached their respective destinations!

On their part, the colonial government also perpetuated caste when it suited them. The Census in British India was perhaps the most potent instrument for practising discrimination in the name of caste. It was used to reserve jobs for designated castes and, in this way, the rulers played off one caste community against another. The Census certainly made Hindus more conscious of their caste standing so long as they stood to gain or lose from their defined status. The Census bred keen competitiveness between castes, each of which was keen to secure its share in government patronage. In order to lessen the political risk to itself, the British ruling class also adopted the opposite policy of labelling certain communities as 'criminal tribes and castes'. These communities were viewed with suspicion and denied any state support or patronage. In certain cases, the British arbitrarily created laws that determined which communities could own land and which could not. The Punjab Land Alienation Act of 1900 created considerable friction between the landed classes and the landless for precisely this reason. The colonial state often claimed to have brought equality before the law to India; such equality was never manifest in practice, however, partly because the lower castes, who were disadvantaged in many ways, could not effectively challenge the upper castes in long-drawn-out legal battles, which were always expensive and did not put the contesting parties on an equal footing.

Conclusion

In the nineteenth century, social reform was meant to complement religious reform for the important reason that a reformed religion could not possibly take root in an archaic society. The two were also interconnected in other ways. Meaningful changes in social practices could not have taken place without some reference to Hindu religious texts or law books. The opposition to the law allowing widow marriages would have been far greater than it actually was had Ishwarchandra Vidyasagar not been able to cite the support of certain law books. That apart, the passage of social legislation became easier once the government itself realised that what they were attempting was not wholly contrary to the Hindu *shastras*. This freed them from the charge of unduly meddling with Hindu social and religious practices. In the nineteenth century, this objection was indeed a grave one; people suspected not only the foreign government but also non-Hindus like the Parsi reformer from Bombay, Behramji Malabari, who was in the forefront of woman-related reform. However, it could be reasonably argued that the real issue at stake was the question of empowerment. Many politically sensitive Hindus opposed laws relating to women not because they were opposed to reform but because the act of lawmaking was not left to them. The demand for greater political representation of Hindus came up every time some social reform issue was agitated. Further, though many agreed with the necessity of improving the status of women, they differed significantly in their approach or methods. Some were gradualists and preferred to bring changes over a long period rather than rush into reform work. Others left it to women themselves, arguing that it was women who understood the problems of fellow women best. Still others were conservatives and only reluctantly agreed to side with reform.

Effective reform was often defeated or slowed down by the fact that not all laws had the backing of social acceptance. After 1856, it was legally possible for widows to marry, yet very few widow marriages were celebrated, especially considering the great effort and energy put into the movement. The cause of reform and reformers was also often weakened by failing courage and the incapacity to withstand social pressures. There was always the question of sustained moral courage on the part of the reformer: the thirty-one-year-old Madhav Govind Ranade, the champion of widow marriages in Maharashtra, married a thirteen-year-old virgin when his first wife died, pleading his inability to turn down his mother; the Indologist R. G. Bhandarkar went back on his plans to marry off his widowed daughter; and Kashinath Trembak Telang, a scholar who rose to the position of Vice Chancellor of Bombay University, had his daughter married off when she was only seven. The social opposition to widow marriages was reflected in contemporary vernacular literature. In Bengal, the novelist Bankimchandra Chattopadhyay produced popular novels in which a scandalous love affair between a man and a widow ends in disaster. In his highly acclaimed novel *Saraswatichandra*, the Gujarati novelist Govardhanram Tripathi (1855–1902) quite dramatically demonstrates the limitations in supporting widow marriages. Baba Pandamanji's Marathi novel, *Yamuna Paryatan* (1857) depicts a widow marrying, but only after she converts to Christianity; this novel quite openly displays a religious rather than social zeal. Regarding polygamy, in Bengal, prominent thinkers like Bankimchandra opposed Vidyasagar's move to end it. Bankimchandra did not dispute the social injustice inherent in the system but felt that intervention by an alien government and non-Hindu social crusaders like Malabari was far from desirable. Female education did not necessarily push up the average age of marriage or leave women the freedom to choose their partners in marriage. Many girls' schools failed because the parents refused to keep their daughter unmarried after a particular age; continuing with education after marriage was an unlikely possibility.

The social spread of the movement to mitigate caste discrimination was not as great as that of the 'Woman Question'. In some provinces like Bengal, the work was more symbolic in nature than substantive. On the other hand, Sanskritisation work proved more successful here, with lower castes claiming higher ritual rank than they were customarily granted. This not only kept the institution of caste alive but also had a regressive effect on certain social issues. As has been pointed out, certain lower castes actively adopted the ways of upper castes, preferring to marry their daughters early or discourage widow marriages. Even Brahmos, among whom woman-related reform was most successful, were guilty of backtracking. Thus, Ramtanu Lahiri, who gave up his sacred thread, would not marry his daughter to a non-Brahmin. Keshabchandra Sen gave his daughter in marriage before she had attained the legal age of marriage set by provisions he himself had created. This was also true of some members of the Arya Samaj in the Punjab: their journal, *Arya Patrika*, reported how Arya reformers were reluctant to dine with *chuhras* (local scavengers) and *chamars* (leather workers). In South India, protests against upper-caste domination was motivated as much by material interests as by ideological critiques of the system. In this region, lower-caste movements were soon drawn into politics since they realised that, ultimately, contesting upper castes was a matter of matching their social and political power. This weakened the purely social dimension of their movement.

Finally, social reform work was affected by the colonial environment in which it was placed. The British claimed to discourage or fight caste discrimination but ended up reinforcing it in some ways. What also cannot be overlooked is the inverse relationship between the advancing politicisation of Indians and the record of successful social reform. Hindu nationalism frowned upon all social reform work on the grounds that such work only led to disunity among Indians, given the wide variety of social ideas or practices present in Hindu society. On the contrary, political agitation directed against the common enemy (the British) was expected to bring greater solidarity and unification. It was not until the arrival of Gandhi on the Indian scene that Hindus began to realise that mere political freedom without the simultaneous creation of a more egalitarian social order would be quite meaningless.

DISCUSSION TOPIC:
WOMEN AND CASTE

- How would you define the 'Woman Question' in colonial India? What range of social issues did it cover?

- In what ways was social and religious reform among Hindus interconnected?

- From what social disadvantages did Hindu widows suffer? Why did the law permitting widow marriages fail to become popular?

- How would you explain the fact that instead of collapsing as a system, caste continued to flourish in British India?

Further Reading

J. N. Farquhar. *Modern Religious Movements in India*. New York: The Macmillan Company, 1915 (or subsequent editions).

C. H. Heimsath. *Indian Nationalism and Hindu Social Reform*. Princeton: Princeton University Press, 1964.

Lata Mani. *Contentious Traditions: The Debate on Sati in Colonial India*. Berkeley: University of California Press, 1998.

Andrea Major. *Pious Flames: European Encounters with Sati, 1500–1830*. New Delhi: Oxford University Press, 2006.

Amiya P. Sen (ed.). *Social and Religious Reform: The Hindus of British India*. New Delhi: Oxford University Press, 2006 (esp. Sections 1–3).

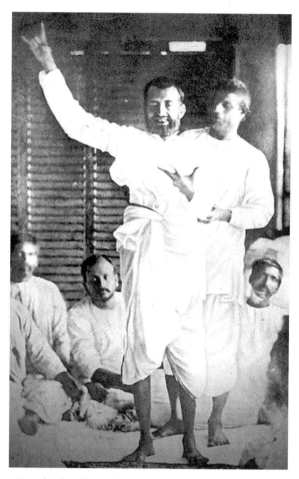

Ramakrishna Paramahamsa at a gathering in the house of Keshabchandra Sen in Calcutta, c. 1879.

V
AGGRESSIVE HINDUISM:
ECUMENICAL, EVANGELIST,
AND EXPANSIVE

The 1880s mark an important watershed in the development of colonial Hinduism. To a great extent this was influenced by the rapid rise of a political consciousness among the Western-educated Hindus, who had been exposed to new Western concepts of the nation-state and of nationalism. This nationalism was spurred by the arrival of a full-blown colonialist capitalism that was acutely exploitative, thoroughly subordinating India's economic and financial interests to Britain's global empire. At the same time, Indians were increasingly subjected to racial slurs and public indignities, faced shrinking employment opportunities, were victims of recurring famines and floods, and denied even a reasonable voice in self-determination. Such factors explain the birth of the Indian National Congress in 1885, which set itself the task of analysing and publicly articulating the grievances of the colonised.

Not surprisingly, this rising nationalism affected the ways in which Hindus looked at themselves. Hinduism itself was increasingly politicised and political demands were cloaked as religious expressions. By 1882, Bankimchandra, whose life and work we have already examined, had popularised the famous song 'Bande Matram' (Hail the Mother), which spoke of freeing the enslaved motherland in evocatively religious language. Bankim invoked imageries of the Divine Mother and of her Power to vanquish evil forces – by which he meant the colonisers. The Hindus now increasingly perceived themselves as a nation, sometimes unmindful of the fact that India was a plural society and home to several non-Hindu communities too. Undoubtedly, then, Indian nationalism, after the 1880s, was strongly influenced by the cultural world of Hinduism. The Congress itself was dominated by Hindus alone for a long time, thereby creating sectarian and communal schisms within Indian nationalism. This was to have far-reaching implications.

This chapter intends to show how Hinduism rapidly transitioned from resisting intellectual and cultural attacks

Abinindranath Tagore's iconic painting Bharat Mata *(1905), depicting India as a Mother Goddess, inspired by Bankim's novel* Anandmath *(1882).*

on itself to exhibiting various forms of counteraggression against its critics. In 1905, Sister Nivedita (born Margaret Elizabeth Noble, 1867–1911) authored a tract, 'Aggressive Hinduism', which, rather than apologetically defend Hindu thoughts and practices, exhorted the Hindus to take the battle to their adversaries. It no longer mattered what others thought of Hinduism, the Sister argued; rather, it was time for Hindus to declare what they thought of others. A few years later, another spokesperson for Hinduism, writing in the Anglo-Hindi journal *Mahamandal Magazine*, the organ of an orthodox Hindu organisation called the Bharat Dharma Mahamandal (Federation for the Protection of Dharma in India), argued that Hindus had erred in displaying tolerance towards other religions.

Nivedita, born of Irish-Scottish parentage, was the best-known disciple of Swami Vivekananda, referred to above, and her tract of 1905 was modelled on a famous speech that the Swami had delivered on his return to India in 1897 from his successful missionary tour of the West. Titled 'The Common Bases of Hinduism', this speech represented a passionate cry for fostering Hindu unity, aimed at both self-strengthening and fighting persistent Western attacks on Hinduism. The following is an excerpt:

> Mark me, then and then alone you are a Hindu when the very name sends through a galvanic shock of strength. Then and then alone you are a Hindu when every man who bears the name, from every country, speaking our language or any other language, becomes at once the nearest and dearest to you. Then and then alone you are a Hindu when the distress of anyone bearing that name comes to your heart and makes you feel as if your own son were in distress. Then and then

alone you are a Hindu when you will be ready to bear
everything for them.[41]

Clearly, this was an adventurous, assertive, and aggressive
Hinduism that was on the rise. Here it is relevant to remember
that it was Vivekananda who, at the World Parliament of
Religions in 1893, had put Hinduism on the world map and
aroused considerable Western admiration and interest in
it. Some of this rubbed off on to his missionary campaigns
back home. On his journey back to India, the Swami was
accompanied by several English and American disciples; to
the politically subjugated but now self-assertive Hindus,
this represented a cultural conquest of the West of which
they felt they could be justly proud. At the Parliament of
Religions itself, the Indian contingent was one of the largest.
More significantly, this was a platform from which Hindus
appeared to speak with a united voice. In Chicago, the Hindu
Theosophist Gyanendranath Chakravarty (1861–1936)
represented three other bodies: the Vaishnava organisation,
Hari Bhakti Pradayini Sabha of Kanpur, and two orthodox
bodies, the Varnashram Dharma Sabha of Delhi and Sanatan
Dharma Rakshini Sabha of Meerut.

This chapter will discuss at some length the assertive
and dynamic face of colonial Hinduism, which combined, as
suggested by its title, the qualities of ecumenism, evangelism,
and expansiveness. Though seemingly contrary, these were
operatively well-orchestrated strategies. The chapter will
show how some leading Hindu thinkers of the late nineteenth
century were able to combine cosmopolitanism with a just

---

41 Swami Vivekananda, 'The Common Bases of Hinduism', in *The
Complete Works of Swami Vivekananda*, vol. 3. Mayavati Memorial
Edition. (Calcutta, 1973).

*Sister Nivedita (1867–1911), right, with the Ramakrishna's wife
and spiritual consort, Sarada Devi (1853–1920), left.*

pride in their own culture and to counter the work of Christian
missionaries with missionary propaganda of their own.
Western-educated Hindus consciously appropriated certain
features distinctive to Western Christianity. They published
and popularised texts, frowned upon the offices of priest and
guru, and promoted the idea of a united Hindu organisation,
active missionary work, and the use of a common source book.
As the above excerpt from Swami Vivekananda suggests,
their intention also was to create a new, globalised, and self-
confident Hinduism that could brook no criticism.

The Growth of Hindu Ecumenism

We have earlier taken note of the doctrinal flexibility possible within Hinduism, allowing Hindus to simultaneously cultivate religious cultures of very different kinds. Most Hindu temples in the pre-modern era (as also in the modern) housed more than one deity, even when the temple was dedicated to only one. It would not at all be unusual for a Vaishnava temple to also have icons of Shiva and the Devi on display. For European observers initially, such multiple religious affinities was a source of some wonder. From the Hindu perspective, however, this made sense. Traditionally, Hinduism was able to combine respect to several divinities but allegiance to one. The preferred divinity was called the *ishta,* or the religious ideal. It must also be borne in mind that, particularly in traditional Hinduism, a definite conception of some deity mattered less than the separation of spiritual life from the profane. So long as Hinduism remained at heart an individuated, *moksha*-centric religion, salvation for the individual was the key concern. Such traits changed in modern India when Hindu religious life began to increasingly acquire a congregational character.

Interestingly, eclecticism in Hindu life co-existed with recurring sectarian quarrels, as between Vaishnavas and Shaktas in Bengal or Vaishnavas and Shaivas in southern India. For a long time, the Hindus of the pre-modern era did not identify Muslims as Muslims, which is to say that they were not viewed as a distinct religious community. Rather, the common tendency was to use their ethnic label. There are numerous references in medieval Hindu literature to the Turushkas (Turks) or Pathans, and even the generic albeit derogatory labels of *mleccha* or *yavana,* commonly used for Muslims. However, this did not indicate so much their variant religious practices as the belief that they belonged to a 'barbarous', non-Aryan race. It would not be misleading to say that at bottom the concern was more social and ritual in character than purely religious. Dining with the *mleccha* was certainly taboo, in contrast to listening to his religious discourse. In the early sixteenth century, the Bengali Vaishnava reformer Chaitanya had extended religious dialogues with wandering Pathans and had reportedly converted them to Vaishnavism. One of his closest followers was a Muslim by the name of Haridas. When 'Yavan' Haridas died at Puri, Chaitanya, notwithstanding his brahmin birth, personally laid him to rest by the seashore. In the pre-modern era, apparently, Hindus more readily distinguished theists from nontheists than classify theists themselves into distinct religious communities. For a Hindu, being a worshipper of God was in itself more important than determining who exactly he worshipped. Arguably, this was consistent with his orthopraxy.

There is an interesting point about Hindu ecumenism that could be mentioned here in passing. Not all religious traditions were able to translate a philosophical pluralism into acknowledgement or accommodation of rival traditions. Jainism, for example, adopts the philosophy of *anekantavada*, or the theory that 'Truth' is, by its very nature, diverse and open-ended. In practice, however, the Jains continue to live as a discrete religious community and are not particularly known for interacting with other religious traditions born in India or elsewhere.

Brahmo Experiments in Religious Universalism

In colonial India, the man to first speak of religious cosmopolitanism was undoubtedly Raja Rammohun Roy. Rammohun was a scholarly eclectic and a modernist in his self-understanding. For example, he learnt several Asian and European languages only so that he might be able to study the scriptures in the original and not rely upon commentators, each of whom presented a tradition in the light of their own limited understanding. In terms of methodology, this was modern. He studied religions also with the intention of drawing attention to common foundations of religious belief, cutting across time and tradition. This was a religious universalism by subtraction, inasmuch as it discarded elements of belief or practices which were suspected to have been corrupted over time. To this purpose, he also authored a work called *Universal Religion* in 1829.

Rammohun also believed in a constructive dialogue across religions. We do know of the deep influence cast upon him by certain rationalistic schools within Islam. Christianity he found to be abounding in moral excellence, a quality that he wanted Hindus to creatively appropriate into their lives. However, Rammohun overlooked the fact that religions were also founded in particular cultures and an effective separation of the two was not easy to achieve. For example, his 1829 work, though professing to deal with universal religion, ends up citing only Hindu sources. Rammohun consistently critiqued caste and blamed this on the lack of unity and patriotism among Hindus, yet, as we have seen, he personally never gave up the sacred thread of the brahmin, even on his deathbed. His natural pride as a Hindu-brahmin also led him to consider Hinduism (albeit a reformed version of it) as being spiritually superior even to Christianity, which he otherwise deeply admired. When in England, he drew attention to the fact that Christ was an Asiatic and how all major religions of the world had taken birth in Asia. In the years to come, this was to be the source of Pan-Asiatic sentiments and a way of contesting European political and cultural hegemony in the modern world.

The Trust Deed of the Brahmo Samaj that the Raja framed in 1828 was broadly catholic and cosmopolitan, allowing various worshippers to come together on a common theistic platform. However, both Rammohun and the Brahmo Samaj after him also proved somewhat exclusionary inasmuch as they disallowed any form of image worship or the worship of multiple gods and goddesses. Rammohun himself conceived the Brahmo Samaj as the meeting ground for all theists and maintained that no one could be disallowed entry into the Brahmo place of worship on grounds of his or religious belief. Yet the Trust Deed forbids carrying any idols or images into the prayer room for Brahmos.

Over time, the critical rejoinder that contemporary Hindus offered on this question was twofold. First, they claimed that the common man could not possibly envisage 'higher' but abstract conceptions of God and was hence forced to use icons and images as an aid to worship. It was presumed that in time, 'crude' idolatry would lead to the use of more sophisticated forms of worship. Second, Hindus also strongly asserted that it was not the image itself that was worshipped but the God who resided within it. A third argument also began to be increasingly offered by Hindus: to say that God could not appear before the devotee in a particular form was unduly limiting the limitless potency or power of God. On this question, interestingly, Rammohun and Vivekananda, though both Vedantists, thought differently. Vivekananda, as we shall presently see, had none of the Raja's contempt for giving human form to a transcendent God or for worshiping multiple divinities. His position was simply that Hinduism, best represented by the school of Advaita Vedanta, had the quality of accommodating diverse ideas and practices under a common religious and philosophical framework. At the time, Vivekananda's position certainly looked more pragmatic and popular and Rammohun's somewhat unrealistic and utopian. For example, Rammohun revolutionised Hinduism by granting the esoteric knowledge of the Vedas to even *shudras* and women, but overlooked how, given their ignorance and lack of education, these were the very classes that were most likely to unquestioningly follow conventional religious ideas or practices. However, Vivekananda's differences with Rammohun may be attributed to yet another reason. By the time Vivekananda emerged as a spokesperson for Hinduism, the Hindu's tone in response to his critics was far from apologetic. In some ways it had already gone back on the idea of reform.

The Brahmo Samaj after Rammohun appears to have moved in two contrary directions. On the one hand, it vigorously contested the work of Christian missionaries and prevented the possible conversion of many Hindus. On the other, some prominent Brahmo theologians visibly leaned towards Christianity. The most dogged opposition to missionaries came from Maharshi Debendranath, who disliked Christianity as much he disliked nondualist Vedanta.

Rajnarayan Basu (1826–1899).

For many Hindus, though, the religion of the Brahmos appeared to be something like an acceptable half-house. It was especially popular among men who had grown critical of their own faith but were unwilling to sever their connections with parental society. Some associates of Debendranath were among the earliest to express a form of Hindu nationalism, as for example Rajnarayan Basu (1826–1899), who delivered a hugely popular lecture in 1873 called *Hindudharmer Shreshthata* (The Superiority of Hinduism). Debendranath and Rajnarayan viewed Brahmoism only as an exalted form of Hinduism and not as a separate religion. The inclination towards Christianity, on the other hand, was most visible in the lives of Keshabchandra Sen and his cousin, Pratapchandra Majumdar, who, it may be recalled, were among those who had broken off from the conservative Brahmo camp led by Debendranath. Close association between Brahmos and Christians was developed mainly with the assistance of Unitarians in England and America. Brahmos were sent to England for higher theological training conducted in institutions controlled by the Unitarians. Predictably, such developments produced contrary effects. This helped Brahmoism to win international recognition; for instance, several Brahmo leaders were invited to represent India in the World Parliament of Religions at Chicago (1893). Nevertheless, Brahmos also came to be increasingly viewed as an alienated, anglicised group with little or no connection with Indian life. Some Hindu writers and journalists in Bengal parodied Brahmo social practices and forms of worship, much to the amusement of the growing body of literate but conservative Hindus.

Keshabchandra is also often remembered for his unique religious experiments around the notion of religious universalism. Keshab was not himself a scholar but encouraged the study of major world religions. Four of his close followers were commissioned to produce standard works on the life of Krishna, on the Buddha, on Christ and Christianity, and a translation of the Koran. He also believed that a universal religion could be synthetically created by fusing selected elements of thought and practice from various religions. Thus, the teachings of Moses could be combined with those of Chaitanya, or Hindu gods invoked alongside Christian saints or angels. When compared with the method adopted by Rammohun, this was Universalism by addition. In effect, whereas Rammohun had sought to identify the universals in religion, Keshab aimed at formulating a universal religion. To this experiment he gave the name of Naba Bidhan (New Dispensation Church). As an experiment, the Naba Bidhan failed eventually – again, because people associated religion with culture. A synthetically and somewhat arbitrarily fused body of thought or practices looked culturally unfamiliar to most people. The Naba Bidhan resembled a visually pleasing

Ramakrishna Paramahamsa (1836–1886).

Kali Temple, Kolkata, India.

bouquet of colourful flowers, but one arbitrarily put together and with no particular scheme of arrangement in mind.

The limits of such experiments were best demonstrated by a contemporary of Keshabchandra, the Hindu mystic Ramakrishna Paramahamsa, whom we briefly discussed earlier. Ramakrishna's experiments, too, were unique and not something that could be readily adopted by the common man, yet they had sufficient breadth and eclectic space to attract popular attention.

OLD-WORLD ECUMENISM

Ramakrishna was in essence a *sadhaka*, or a committed spiritual practitioner, groomed in the traditional Hindu way. The sources of his religious knowledge were essentially oral and not scriptural since he was at best a semi-literate man who could barely sign his name. However, his brahmin birth offered him certain advantages. For instance, as a brahmin he had greater freedom of spiritual association and could study the ways of any religious group he liked. In the years to come, his brahmin birth also helped secure his place as a teacher and religious counsellor to genteel society in urban Calcutta. Just as the food cooked by a brahmin was acceptable to all Hindu castes, a brahmin with demonstrated spiritual experiences was highly revered in the community.

Ramakrishna served as a priest in a temple located at Dakshineswar, a few miles north of Calcutta. Importantly, he began by serving this temple complex as a priest to Vaishnava deities Radha and Krishna and only later switched to the worship of the Shakta goddess, Kali. His family members, too, were Vaishnavas (his father, Khudiram, was a devotee of Raghubir, or Lord Rama) by disposition; such switching of religious affiliations was not unknown within Hindu families. As a *sadhaka*, Ramakrishna successively undertook training in Vaishnavism, Shaktism, Tantra, Vedanta, Sufi Islam, and Christianity, to varying degrees of depth. He had virtually no doctrinal understanding of Buddhism, Islam, or Christianity but claimed to have had mystical visions of the Buddha, Christ, and Mohammed.

In later life, Ramakrishna would explain his spiritual experiences as resulting from some intense and insatiable urge for God realisation, which, at times, drove him to the point of near lunacy. It was also his claim that he agreed to undergo such a wide range of spiritual training only to strengthen his conviction that all religions aimed at God realisation even though they adopted different paths to attain this objective. In Ramakrishna's view, religions were like several languages, each expressing the same phenomenon, albeit differently. It would have been highly monotonous, he once quipped, for a musician to stay with one musical note when there was the freedom to play several by turns.

It is important to realise that Ramakrishna's panacea for catholicity or ecumenism was not born out of his historical environment. Persecution and violent conflicts in the name of religion were not unknown to India, but these had never reached the scale or intensity experienced during the religious wars of medieval Europe. Ramakrishna's eclecticism strengthened rather than created a pre-existing trend in traditional Hinduism. It is equally important to acknowledge that he did not try to formulate a universal religion, either by subtraction or addition: an intellectual study of comparative religion would have never appealed to him. His aim was to encourage a yearning for God realisation in people regardless of the path they followed.

The important conclusions that Ramakrishna arrived at upon ending his *sadhana* may be summed up as follows:

- The foremost aim of human life was to attain God realisation. All else was secondary in nature or importance.
- Religions were created by God, not humans. This ipso facto denied humans the right to make any arrogant truth claims about the nature of God and religion.
- Humans could never truly understand God or religion. On the contrary, they could easily misinterpret both since their understanding of such matters was limited.
- 'Religious tolerance' was a meaningless and misleading expression. It falsely suggested that one person's religion was superior to that of another and that one person was somehow tolerating errors in the other.
- Salvation could arrive only through the grace of God and by leading a pious life.
- There were as many approaches to God as there were opinions, and a person was free to choose a path that suited or appealed to him or her the most.

• All religious paths led to God and were hence equally valid. However, some were less pure than others. A relatively impure path would also ultimately take a seeker to God, though not as readily.

The important feature of Ramakrishna's religious apprenticeship was that it respected existing religious boundaries. For him, these boundaries were not porous or penetrable: all religions had to be accepted in their totality and not selectively. Ramakrishna's training in Islam included eating food cooked in the 'Muslim' way, something otherwise despicable for a Hindu brahmin, and avoiding visiting the Kali temple where he served as a priest. In essence, such universalism was the very opposite of that practised by Keshab. However, Ramakrishna's universalism also had its limitations: although he freely associated with both urban reformist bodies and rural religious congregations thronged by peasants and artisans, he found faults with each. He was also critical of the Brahmo preoccupation with sin and sinning, a trait they had allegedly acquired from their association with Christianity, and he found the relatively free gender mixing within rural cults also quite disturbing and detrimental to religious life. In his view, 'newfangled' religions like the Brahmo Samaj and the Arya Samaj would not ultimately endure. What was infinitely superior and was there to stay for eternity was Hindu or Sanatan[42] Dharma. News of a Hindu converting to another religion pained him immensely.

---

42 The word *sanatan* means 'timeless' or 'eternal'. Readers will recall that there was a religious camp by that name in the Punjab which opposed the Arya Samaj. In this instance, the term is taken to refer to certain core, unchanging values which essentially defined Hinduism.

Swami Vivekananda (1863–1902).

THE CYCLONIC SWAMI

Within the framework of an assertive and self-confident Hinduism, Swami Vivekananda (whose pre-monastic name was Narendranath Dutta) occupies an important place. His life and work as a Hindu monk was marked both by cultural aggression and ecumenism, by an urge for *mukti* (personal salvation) as well as a commitment to altruism and improving the human condition. He freely admitted to Western audiences that his real purpose for travelling to the West was not to

223

preach religion or convert non-Hindus to Hinduism but rather to gather individuals and money for undertaking projects that would help reduce the poverty and ignorance among his countrymen. Vivekananda was truly a patriot and prophet combined in one.

Swami Vivekananda received a modern Western education in an institution run by the Church of Scotland in colonial Calcutta. Early in his life, he developed a pining for God realisation and kept asking well-known religious figures of his city if indeed they had 'seen' God, much to their embarrassment. Not one of them claimed to have had any such experience. This only deepened Vivekananda's anguish, until one day one of his European tutors in college, the Rev. William Hastie, suggested that he call upon Ramakrishna at Dakshineswar, whose mystical trances (*samadhi*) and instructive preaching and parables had already become the talk of the town. In their very first meeting, Ramakrishna startled the young man by claiming that he had met God in person just as intimately as he was meeting his interlocutor; from that day, the young Narendranath felt powerfully drawn towards the saint, whom he eventually accepted as his *guru*.

Vivekananda was initially a member of the Brahmo Samaj and his early lessons in religious cosmopolitanism were derived from this association. However, this was to be considerably strengthened in the company of his *guru*. Ramakrishna taught his favoured pupil the catholicity and forbearance to respect diverging religious opinions or truth claims but, more importantly, to make God realisation the prime purpose of his life. Vivekananda translated Thomas à Kempis's *Imitation of Christ* into Bengali, knelt before the altar of every chapel he entered, worshipped the daughter of a Muslim boatman of Kashmir as the Holy Virgin, and spoke of hoisting a 'Vedantic brain' atop an 'Islamic body'. As a member of the Brahmo Samaj he had once expressed revulsion at the fearsome Hindu-

Tantric goddess Kali; towards the closing years of his life, however, he wrote poems in her praise. In his time he was perhaps the only Hindu scholar-monk who commented on the four otherwise divergent paths of *jnana yoga* (gnosis), *bhakti yoga* (devotion), *karma yoga* (selfless activism), and *raja yoga* (meditative practices); he even tried synthesising them. He found no intrinsic fault with image worship and believed that even when indulging in such worship, people revealed not ignorance or superstition but only a relatively lower form of Truth. It was also his belief, therefore, that people proceeded not from ignorance to Truth but from Truth to Higher Truth. Swami Vivekananda had immense faith both in the spiritual potential in humans and in their socially transformative power. On the whole, however, he preferred that people subordinate the quest for personal salvation to the pursuit of the common good. His advice to Hindus had therefore a strong ethical content. Not surprisingly, he considered the compassionate Buddha to be his *ishta,* or chosen Ideal.

Partly on account his *guru*'s teachings, Vivekananda's thought always retained an accommodative breadth of interest. Though an Advaitin – a follower of the school of Acharya Shankara – he also strongly disagreed with the Acharya. This is reminiscent of Rammohun, who had similarly differed with Shankara. Vivekananda himself believed that Vedanta had to be given a more socially responsible face. Speaking at London in 1896, he coined the term 'Practical Vedanta', by which he tried to convey the idea that rather than be associated with monks or ascetics and remain isolated in remote hills and jungles, Vedanta had to come closer to everyday life and resolve recurring human problems. Thus, meditative practices and the spiritual angst could be made to co-exist with a firm commitment to social welfare. The first could be conducted in the secluded environment of a Himalayan hermitage, and the second, carried out in everyday life. It was thus that

Vivekananda founded in 1897 the Ramakrishna Math and Mission, combining the ideals of Hindu monasticism and the civic virtue of an ethical commitment to society. Monks of the Ramakrishna are seekers of personal salvation but remain deeply implicated in social and educational work, medical relief, or alleviating the human distress caused by famine and floods. In 1899, with the help of some English disciples, Vivekananda founded the Advaita Ashram at Mayavati, located in the Himalayan foothills, where, in keeping with the postulates of Advaita, no image of the Hindu gods, goddesses, or even of Ramakrishna is displayed. The Vedanta that Vivekananda espoused was thus more a course in social action than abstract dogma. In this sense, his reading of religion was very different from that of his *guru*, Ramakrishna.

Ramakrishna believed that a spiritual life was ultimately inconsistent with a worldly life and that seeking God realisation required progressive distancing of the self from everyday life in the world. The world in itself was illusory and caught humans in a snare. The lure of women (*kamini*) and wealth (*kanchana*) he took to be the greatest impediments to God realisation. Vivekananda, on the contrary, combined his monastic vows with service to humanity and firmly believed that religion was worth nothing if it could not wipe the widow's tears or bring food to the hungry mouth. He spoke contemptuously of priestly, exhibitionist Hinduism, which spent colossal sums of money on feeding and clothing inanimate divine objects while the 'living god' – the poor, sickly, and the starving – went without food, shelter, and basic human care. He disagreed also with his *guru*'s cynical attitude towards philanthropy or charitable work. It was Ramakrishna's belief that charitable work was only a cover for human self-gratification; his pupil, on the other hand, always counted on voluntarism and the value of social commitments. He tried to persuade both princes and

The Parliament of Religions in Chicago, 1893.

the common man to reveal altruism and a concern for fellow humans. There is an anecdote about how Vivekananda came down heavily upon some Hindu preachers who wanted him to support cow-protection societies. The Swami angrily retorted by saying that the human species needed greater protection than the bovine! In his early monastic life, the Swami flouted all norms of caste and ritual purity by accepting coarse bread from a scavenger and sharing a smoke with a ritually defiled cobbler. When in America, he reportedly ordered beef to his dining table and reacted angrily to his brother disciples advising him to follow a strictly Hindu diet. He admired French cooking, could recite verbatim from the pages of a Dickens novel, and habitually smoked cigars. Contrary also to his *guru*'s advice, Vivekananda socialised with women, took several European women as his close disciples, and, when in the West, wrote home enthusiastically about the social power and freedom that Western women enjoyed. All this made him a very untypical Hindu *sannyasi*.

However, with all his liberality, breadth of interest, and cosmopolitanism, Vivekananda was also a quintessentially Hindu monk who was out to establish a Universalism founded on Vedanta, an integral part of the Hindu tradition itself. He was extremely unhappy to hear of Hindu shrines being vandalised by Muslim invaders and irked by Christian missionaries targeting poor and disadvantaged Hindu families. When speaking before Western audiences, Swami Vivekananda simultaneously critiqued the very concept of 'tolerance' and pressed claims about Hinduism being the most tolerant of religions. Here is what he said on 11 September 1893, in his opening address before the World Parliament of Religions at Chicago: 'I am proud to belong to a religion which has taught the world both tolerance and universal acceptance. We believe not only in universal toleration but we accept all religions as true'.[43]

In subsequent lectures delivered at Chicago, he denied that there was any polytheism in India or that caste had any foundation in the religion of the Hindus. It is noteworthy that at the Chicago Parliament, while the Swami claimed to represent an entirely nonpartisan and universalist position, his discourse carried the spirit of evangelism. Interestingly, too, while Vivekananda himself claimed to speak for Vedanta, his admirers back in India took this to mean Hinduism in general. This is amply clear from what members of an audience told the Swami at the Indian princely state of Ramnad in South India: 'You have with an eloquence that is surpassed and in language plain and unmistakable, proclaimed to and convinced the cultured audiences in Europe and America that Hinduism fulfils all the requirements of an universal religion and adapts itself to the needs of men and women of all races and creeds'.[44]

---

43 Swami Vivekananda, 'Addresses at the Parliament of Religions', in *The Complete Works of Swami Vivekananda*, vol. 1. Mayavati Memorial Edition (Calcutta, 1973).

44 Swami Vivekananda, 'Reply to the Address of Welcome at Ramnad', in *The Complete Works of Swami Vivekananda*, vol. 3. Mayavati Memorial Edition (Calcutta, 1973).

Speaking at San Francisco on 8 April 1900, on his second visit to the United States, Vivekananda clearly suggested that Vedanta alone had the qualities fit to become the future world religion. In his understanding, two unique features of Hinduism made this possible: it had neither a historical founder nor employed the concept of a unified church. In hindsight, in making such claims, Vivekananda appears to have overlooked the fact that a good philosophy did not necessarily make an appealing religion and that operatively all religions had roots in specific cultures from which they could not be disentangled with any ease. Though no images or photographs of Ramakrishna himself are allowed in the Mayavati Ashram, the latter remains the major publishing site of the Ramakrishna Order, preaching and propagating the ideals of the saint himself and of his chief disciple.

Swami Vivekananda's mission shared the contemporary Hindu claim that only India, with its spiritual gifts to the world, could counteract the rank materialism of the West. But he also gave this theory a new historical twist. In Vivekananda's view, India's spiritual mission to the world was pre-Christian and had really begun with Emperor Ashoka. What might have also rattled his Western interlocutors in particular was the claim that it was the Buddha who had incarnated as the Christ and that all Christianity was Aryan in origin.[45] Buddhism he took to be no different from Hinduism; indeed, one of his lectures, delivered at Chicago on 26 September 1893, was called 'Buddhism, the Fulfillment of Hinduism'.

---

45 Vivekananda shared the theory that Christianity had been born on the island of Crete and was the work of Theravada Buddhist monks; he cited a mystical vision that he had en route to the West in support. The work *The Original Jesus* by Elman Grubner and Holger Kirsten, published as late as 1995, supports this view.

In the closing years of the nineteenth century, a controversy broke out between Shaivas and Buddhists over proprietary rights to the Bodh Gaya shrine. In this instance, both Vivekananda and Nivedita are known to have sided with the claims of the Shaiva Mahant against those made by the Buddhists. The Swami also dismissed the commonplace theory about the Aryan invasion of India and, in a way which clearly anticipated the views of the Hindu right in India, he took 'Hindu' to be an omnibus term covering other religious communities: 'Typically, the word Hindu covers not only Hindus proper but Mohammedans, Christians, Jains and other people.'[46]

Vivekananda often used the terms 'Hindu' and 'Indian' interchangeably, and perhaps not unwittingly. The following is what he told a correspondent of The Times: 'Educated Mohammedans are Sunnis, scarcely to be distinguished from the Hindus. The Great Akbar, the Mughal Emperor, was practically a Hindu'.[47]

Finally, Swami Vivekananda was one of the earliest Hindu thinkers to express some concern about the allegedly diminishing number of Hindus in relation to other religious communities in India. He expressed such fears to Nivedita sometime in 1899. A few years later, in 1912, Rabindranath Tagore argued that the term Hindu, unlike 'Muslim', was not really a religious label but an ethnic and cultural one. Given the fact that a very large proportion of Bengali Muslims were converts from Hinduism, Bengali Muslims actually qualified

---

46 Swami Vivekananda, 'Report on the Lecture at Jaffna, 1897', in *The Complete Works of Swami Vivekananda*, vol. 3. Mayavati Memorial Edition (Calcutta, 1973).

47 *Valuable Conversations with the Swami Vivekananda in England, America and India* (Calcutta, 1902). Author not known.

*Mahatma Gandhi (1869–1948), right,
with Rabindranath Tagore (1861–1941), left, c. 1940.*

to be called 'Hindu-Muslim', he added. Apparently, Tagore
was also apprehensive about the demographic 'crisis' allegedly
affecting the Hindus since he used this argument to sharpen
his critique of caste discrimination. The day was not far
ahead, he warned, when the Muslims will easily entice the
great-grandchildren of the famed Bengal pundits of Bhatpara
and Nabadwip[48] to convert to Islam by formally accepting the
Kalma (statement of faith).

---

48 Bhatpara, located on the banks of the Ganges, was an old Brahmanical
    settlement which specialised in *smriti* (Hindu law). Nabadwip, or
    Nadia, also a brahmin-dominated settlement, was famed for the study
    of the Nyaya school of Hindu philosophy.

GANDHI AND RELIGIOUS PLURALITY

In colonial India one of the most powerful voices promoting the idea of plurality and cosmopolitan feeling in religious life was Mohandas K. Gandhi. For him, the idea of one God did not imply that there must also be one religion. His own religious life was framed in the light of at least three older traditions of Jainism, Vaishnava *bhakti*, and nondualist Vedanta. He liked the philosophically open-ended quality (*anekantavada*) in Jainism, the devotional surrender to God among Vaishnavas, and the cosmic unity of all life posited in Advaita. The *Sermon on the Mount* was one of his favourite texts and among his closest friends were Christian missionaries like Charles Freer Andrews (1871–1940). His first biographer too was a clergyman in South Africa, Rev. Joseph Doke. In his *ashrams* he introduced common prayer meetings where scriptures from various traditions were read out and where inmates were encouraged to celebrate diverse religious festivals.

In his religious eclecticism, Gandhi approaches the life of Ramakrishna. However, he also turned out to be a greatly controversial figure, disliked by a good number of Hindus as well as Muslims. The former regarded him as a renegade out to appease Muslims: this ultimately cost him his life. Ironically, the Muslims too did not quite trust his eclectic credentials and saw him as a Hindu fundamentalist in the guise of a liberal Hindu. The major reason for this, of course, was that Gandhi was primarily a politician, deeply implicated in contemporary politics, of which perhaps the most frightening face was the eruption of communal violence affecting the life and property of both Hindus and Muslims. Although he personally kept away from exercising political power, he was always placed at the centre of political controversy.

What is interesting and important here, however, is the extent to which Gandhi internalised and expressed from time to time pre-existing concerns about social and political questions involving Hindus. For instance, whether consciously or unconsciously, Gandhi readily echoed certain key arguments earlier made by Hindus. He insisted that all religions included both truth and error, an argument going back to another Vedantin, Rammohun. Further, he denied that humans could ever have an adequate understanding of God and religion: all views on religion, he argued, were subject to a double filtration through, first, dependence on humanly created scriptures and, thereafter, reliance on commentaries written upon those texts, also the work of humans. To this he added that religion was essentially concerned with personal experience, something Vivekananda had described as *anubhava*. What Krishna, Mohammed, or Jesus had said did not matter unless one practically realised these as 'truths' in one's own life. It followed from these views that no religious tradition represented the whole truth about God. Rather, they each represented some special quality not found to the same degree in others. Thus, Christianity best represented love, Islam equality, Buddhism compassion, and Hinduism the cosmic unity of all life. It stood to reason, therefore, that people would only benefit from a constructive dialogue across religious traditions. This was not an intellectual exercise in the study of comparative religion but the acknowledgement that all religious paths ultimately led to God. Like Vivekananda, Gandhi considered the term 'tolerance' to be a merely gratuitous assumption. Since all major religions were fundamentally the same, this called for mutual respect, not mutual tolerance. Understandably, therefore, Gandhi too was quite averse to the idea of religious conversion, although he did not combatively resist it. On one level, Gandhi was also concerned about the numerical strength of the Hindus but, more importantly, with the show of Hindu unity. In the 1930s, he bitterly opposed the British move to define the depressed castes as separate electorates, arguing that these castes equally constituted a part of Hindu society. Clearly, this was aimed at preventing a schism within the Hindu community at a time when numbers mattered. Perhaps the most visible quality shared by Vivekananda and Gandhi was their great concern for the poor and the socially marginalised; here, Gandhi's coining the term *harijan* to denote the depressed castes strongly echoes Vivekananda's use of *daridranarayana*. The only difference in emphasis here is that while Vivekananda employed the category of an economic class (the poor), Gandhi preferred the more social category of the (deprived) caste.

Gandhi differed from Vivekananda on one other important issue: cow protection. On this question Gandhi was both firm and consistent; he went to the extent of claiming that protecting cattle from the butcher's knife and conferring on the cow the sacred status of 'Mother' was a quality that actually defined the Hindu. Also, he preferred the householder's life to that of the ascetic and here, once again, his views more resemble those of Rammohun. Being a politician, Gandhi ultimately sought a political resolution to the Hindu–Muslim problem and that concerning the depressed Hindu castes; however, the very scale and intensity of these problems defeated him.

THE VAISHNAVA REVIVAL IN COLONIAL INDIA

Broadly speaking, Hindu universalism in the colonial era took two discernible forms: the Vedantic and the Vaishnava. Both adopted missionary postures and undertook active proselytisation at home and abroad, and each claimed to represent the only 'authentic' religion of the Hindus and to exhibit the greatest historical continuity. Both perceived themselves as representing the recovery of a tradition that had fallen into disarray and disrepute. However, it should not be fogotten that this is but a synthetic division: philosophically, Vaishnavism was founded on Vedanta, albeit of a kind markedly different from Advaita, or nondualism.

In hindsight, it may be reasonably argued that in colonial India, one of these forms was more successful in capturing public attention than the other, at least initially. Interest in Vedanta connects figures as far apart in time as Rammohun and Radhakrishnan (who rose to the office of the president of India). For many Indian thinkers, Vedanta was quintessential Indian philosophy, rooted as it was in the Upanishads. In colonial India, the most prominent Vedantists, like Rammohun, Vivekananda, or the Punjabi, Swami Ram Tirath (1873–1906), were transnational figures. All three visited the West and won Western admiration. By comparison, the Vaishnava revival emerged relatively late. With a few exceptions, it was often limited to a particular Vaishnava *sampradaya* and largely confined to India. Gathering international interest in the cult of Krishna and swelling membership of Vaishnava organisations were later phenomena.

The best-known instance of international interest is the meteoric rise of the International Society of Krishna Consciousness (ISKCON) during the 1960s and 1970s. This organisation now rivals the global spread of Vedanta Societies established by monks of the Ramakrishna Order. Interestingly enough, while both are popular, the Ramakrishna Order and ISKCON are founded on predominantly different ideas and practices. One is based on individual spiritual practices, in line with the traditional Hindu quest for *moksha* or salvation; the other rejoices in collectivity and the display of religious emotion. One prefers meditative practices and does not display Hindu religious icons in its shrines and seminaries; the other openly espouses the worship of Hindu deities and encourages public displays of ecstatic *bhakti*. Of the two, the neo-Vedantic movement was more ecumenical: it celebrates both Hindu and Christian festivals; in contrast, the Vaishnava revival does not allow the worship of non-Vaishnava deities. There are, however, practical and important exceptions to these generalisations. While the Vaishnava revival valorised a monastic life, the Vedantists are given to singing of *kirtana* hymns and the ritual worship of certain Hindu icons. It is important not to overlook the fact that Vedanta actually has several subschools, some of which include a devotional community.

The history of this Vaishnava revival in modern India is long and complex; a brief mention of some representative figures and their contribution to this revival follows.

After its early formative history, the Vaishnava tradition in India developed over two stages. It grew phenomenally around the fifteenth and sixteenth centuries in the wake of the '*bhakti* movement' in much of northern India and the peninsular south. This originates in the work of the so-called 'Vaishnava Vedantins': Ramanuja, Madhva, Nimbarka, Bhaskara, and Vallabhacharya, all of whom disregarded Shankara's conception of an impersonal god and insisted on personalised worship instead. In a sense, this was a creative fusion of the *Vedanta Sutras* of Badarayana and the *Bhakti Sutras* of Shandilya and Narada. Their preferred deity and object of pious adoration was Vishnu or Krishna. By the sixteenth century, active Vaishnava *sampradayas,* or communities, were firmly established in the Mathura-Vrindavan region, the legendary birthplace of Krishna, widely celebrated in folk culture. This Vaishnava movement of the sixteenth century was marked by a massive cultural production of religious treatises, songs, poetry, drama, liturgy, libraries, temples, and pilgrim trails hitherto unparalleled in the history of India.

The second phase of the Vaishnava revival, in many ways connected to the first, occurred in the course of the nineteenth century, albeit amidst very different conditions. This revival was developed with difficulty, particularly in the face of hostility from early Hindu reformers such as Rammohun, who was dismissive of the Vaishnava tradition and doubted the veracity of Puranic literature on which much of Vaishnava religion was based. Ironically enough, however, the reformist Brahmos were among the first to convert to Vaishnava ways of life. In the 1860s, euphoric Vaishnava *bhakti* swept the Brahmo movement, leading adherents to hold *nagar sankirtans,* or public processions, marked by ecstatic devotional singing on the streets of Calcutta. Subsequently, this practice was adopted even by the (Christian) Salvation Army.

This revival was experienced at various places in colonial India. In an earlier chapter, we had occasion to speak of the

*An early twentieth-century painting of Chaitanya and Nityananda
leading a group chanting of the names of Krishna.*

Swaminarayanis in the Bombay Presidency, who were reviving Vaishnava ways of life around the same time as Rammohun was condemning it in Bengal. In Maharashtra, men like Ranade and Bhandarkar, whose lives and work have been discussed, spoke and wrote extensively on the Maratha poet saints and the thriving cult of Vithoba at Pandharpur. Their writing was to have an important bearing on the cultural awakening in Maharashtra and on Maratha provincialism. At the holy Hindu city of Kashi, the Hindi poet and journalist, Bharatendu Harishchandra (1850–1885), actively led a movement to nationalise Vaishnavism, which he took to be the 'only real religion' of the Hindus.

An even greater recovery of the Vaishnava tradition occurred in ethnic Bengal and was mainly the work of the Gaudiyas, Bengal Vaishnavas who swore allegiance to the medieval Bengali mystic Krishna Chaitanya. According to early ethnographic reports, about a quarter of the population in lower Bengal was already Vaishnava by the early nineteenth century. Over time, devotional communities under the name of Hari Sabhas sprung up in this province and in

Sisir Kumar Ghosh (1840–1911).

areas outside it with a substantial migrant Hindu Bengali population. The first association of lay Vaishnavas, called the Haribhaktipradayini Sabha (Society for the Dissemination of Vaishnava Bhakti), was founded in Calcutta by 1852. This was followed by a phenomenal expansion of the Vaishnava press and literature. Old Vaishnava classics were reprinted and made up a substantial part of printed books and journals annually produced.

Two aspects dominated this movement. First was the tendency to project the age of Chaitanya as a 'golden' period in Bengal's history, to see him as the Indian equivalent of the German reformer Luther, and to claim that a reformation of the kind witnessed in Germany had been replicated in India too. Some thinkers even coined the expression 'Hindoo Protestantism' to describe this. However, from being a mere social or religious reformer, Chaitanya had also increasingly turned into a cultural icon for the Hindu Bengalis, reflecting a sharpened political consciousness among them. New political meanings were now read into his life and work. For instance, his exhorting the people of Nadia to defy the local Kazi's orders prohibiting Vaishnava processions was interpreted as an early sign of peaceful noncooperation on the part of a politically oppressed people. In Bengal, the figure who best represented this interweaving of anti-colonial sentiment and religious revival was the political journalist Sisir Kumar Ghosh (1840–1911), who was also a pious Vaishnava and the author of two of the best-known biographies of Chaitanya, the multi-volume *Amiya Nimai Charit* (1894–1910) and the English-language *Lord Gauranga or Salvation for All* (1897).

This movement equally aimed at rescuing the popular Vaishnava god Krishna from missionary slander and from charges levelled by reformist Hindus. The life and deeds of Krishna now began to be seen in a historical light; this found its sharpest expression in the thinker and novelist Bankimchandra. In modern Bengal, Bankimchandra was the first to drive a wedge between the pastoral-playful Krishna of folk Vaishnavism and the rational, heroic figure from the epic *Mahabharata*. His purpose here was to dispute the many 'scandalous' misdeeds attributed to the juvenile Krishna in the Vaishnava religious classic *Bhagavata Purana*, which had become the source of much public criticism. For Bankim, Krishna was not only God incarnated as man but also the exemplary politician, diplomat, strategist, and the source of high philosophy, as in the *Bhagavad Gita*. His major argument here was that in descending to Earth in human form, God assumed the role of an ideal man only so that he would set the right example for humanity to follow.

The neo-Vaishnava movement in nineteenth-century Bengal saw the folk Krishna as a visible threat to both religion and morality: a 'lecherous' juvenile who performed strange and irrational miracles could be accepted neither as an ideal man nor as a God. For a long time, Bankim would not even accept the *Bhagavata Purana* as an authentic source for the life of Krishna. As many as twenty-six works on the life of Krishna, albeit reformulated in a 'rational' and 'reformed' light, were published between 1880s and 1903, all by *bhadralok* authors and apologists. This points to an important paradox within the modern Vaishnava revival. On the one hand, it aimed at making Vaishnavism a universal religion, regardless of considerations of caste, class, or culture; on the other hand, by rejecting very popular modes of worship, it created a sharper divide between 'high' and 'low' Hinduism. The Krishna of the *Mahabharata* was unknown in popular religious culture; no temples were dedicated to him nor were festivals held in his honour or exquisite poetry produced celebrating his life and deeds. Yet, for *bhadralok* society in Bengal, it became vitally necessary to distance itself from a thriving but morally suspect religion.

This was the first step taken by them towards 'authenticating' and sanitising the Vaishnava world.

The movement associated with Bankimchandra also attempted to join the provincial community of Gaudiya Vaishnavas with a pan-Indian one. This tendency may be said to have begun with the famed Vrindavan Goswamis in the sixteenth and seventeenth centuries. The Goswamis knew the local language (Brajbhasha) well but chose to write their works on Vaishnavism in cosmopolitan Sanskrit so that these could be the common property of educated, upper-class devotees anywhere in India. Equally, the Goswamis chose to write nearly as much on the Divine Krishna himself as on the human reformer, Chaitanya. Bankim's *magnum opus*, the *Krishnacharitra* (Life of Krishna, 1886, revised and enlarged edition, 1892) was a work that replicated this effort. Rather than support the cult that had grown around him, Bankim associated Chaitanya with an overly sentimental religion which only 'emasculated' the Hindus. In this, he was clearly influenced by the advancing Hindu nationalism which tried to link patriotic fervour with vigorous manliness. Theologically, Krishna was the Hindu answer to Christ, but he was also India's national icon. Undoubtedly, Bankim's work was an important step towards the nationalisation of the Vaishnava tradition.

ORGANISED EVANGELISM

To project Hinduism as tolerant, accommodating, and inclusive in its self-understanding was but one face of late nineteenth-century Hinduism. There was indeed a universalist resonance to some arguments offered in this context. Even in the 1880s, Bankimchandra had argued that devotion to the god Vishnu was not a religious commitment but a metaphysical acknowledgement of the underlying unity of all life. By this token, even Christians and Muslims could be counted among Vaishnavas and, in one sense, this was Hindu ecumenism at its best. There also emerged, however, a more combative Hindu face which tried to actively challenge non-Hindus. Later in this chapter, we shall have occasion to see how Vaishnava missions, too, were to join the Vedantic movement in this combative enterprise.

Understandably, Hindu aggression was directed at Islam and Christianity, to which the Hindus had lost the most by way of numbers. By comparison, neither Buddhism nor Brahmoism (far less the Jains or Sikhs) posed a threat to a buoyant Hinduism. By the nineteenth century, Buddhism had weakened considerably, notwithstanding a renewed interest in it both in India and in the West. Sir Edwin Arnold (1832–1904) translated important Buddhist texts into English and drew public attention to the state of neglect in several Buddhist shrines in India. This mission was later pursued by the Sinhalese Buddhist Anagarika Dharmapala (1864–1933), who founded the Mahabodhi Society in 1891. Buddhist manuscripts found in Nepal, Tibet, and elsewhere encouraged a new interest in the old Buddhist canon. Most Hindu spokespeople denied the autonomy of Buddhism as a religion. Vivekananda had a somewhat stormy relationship with Dharmapala as also with the Theosophists, who supported the Buddhist revival in South Asia. Here, we may recall how both Vivekananda and his chief disciple, Sister Nivedita, sided with the Shaiva Mahant at Bodh Gaya temple against the claims of the Buddhists. Buddhism in India became a potent force only in the 1930s, when the Dalits (depressed castes) took it up as an alternative to caste-ridden and socially oppressive Hinduism. B. R. Ambedkar was one of the eminent contemporaries to so convert.

The surge of Hindu aggression similarly took a toll on Brahmoism. A new pride in race sharpened the Hindu critique of the West and frowned upon the social and religious reform in which the Brahmo Samaj had been deeply implicated. As the space for such reform shrank, so did the popularity of the Brahmo Samaj. In the Punjab and the North-Western Provinces, as noted earlier, the Brahmos had long been dismissed as a 'denationalised' body. Such feelings came to be expressed even in Bengal as conservatism and cultural suspicion struck deeper roots in Hindu society.

Hindu reaction was partly directed at the work of Christian missionaries. Christianity was now the religion of the new ruling class, and in some ways, contesting one amounted to contesting the other. Also, it was the Hindus that Christian missionaries had targeted more than Muslims. The Hindus were not only more numerous but, in the eyes of the missionaries, suffered from several 'heathen' prejudices. Muslims, after all, could not be faulted on account of image worship, the worship of multiple gods or goddesses, or for practising caste discrimination – at least not in theory.

Hindu reaction to Christian propaganda was sharp and progressively acquired an aggressive character. In 1839, the Scottish Evangelist John Muir's classic *Matapariksha* (An Examination of Hindu Doctrines) had produced at least three well-known rebuttals from Hindu scholars based in Bombay and Calcutta. What is more interesting, however, is that this counteraggression included the expression of both doctrinal and cultural differences. Hindu pundits found it quite unreasonable that Christ, who was deemed to be the son of God, should be born of 'mean' parentage and be forced to die on the cross like an ordinary man. The pundits admitted that they did not disbelieve in the miracles associated with Christ, but found Hindu miracles to be decidedly superior. Long before the Arya Samaj took to reclaiming converted Hindus, various bodies in South India were actively engaged in such work. There were, for instance, the Patituddhar Sabha, founded in 1851, and the Hitaishini Sabha, founded in 1865.

The Shaiva reformer Arumuga Navalar, whose work was discussed in Chapter 3, wrote as many as twenty-five anti-Christian tracts. In the 1830s, fierce public debates were held by the sea at Bombay between the Scottish Presbyterian John Wilson (1804–1875) and Pundit Morebatt Dandekar, later the author of the work *Hindudharma Sthapana* (The Vindication of Hinduism, 1831). Some twenty years later, there was another round of hostility between the missionaries and pundits. Among the latter was now Vishnu Bhikaji Gokhale (1825–1871), a Chitpavan brahmin better known as Vishnubawa Brahmachari. Gokhale was a scholar who seriously tried to revive Vedic religion in Maharashtra in place of the folk and the Puranic. Many fellow Hindus took exception to his suggestion that the *kuladevatas* (family or tutelary deities) usually drawn from Puranic culture be replaced by the Vedic. In 1859, he produced a book (in excess of 700 pages) by the name of *Vedokta Dharmaprakash* (Light on Vedic Religion). It is not commonly known that this book anticipates Swami Dayanand's *Satyarth Prakash* in locating all secular and sacred knowledge in the Vedas. Modern inventions like the printing press and steam engines were claimed to be prevalent in Vedic times. However, Vishnubawa shot into greater prominence with a series of lectures he delivered by the sea in Bombay, aggressively refuting missionary projections of Hinduism. Reports on these exchanges were first published by the weekly paper *Bombay Guardian* between January and May 1857, just on the eve of the outbreak of the great Indian uprising, and subsequently by the Bombay Tract and Book Society as *Discussions by the Sea Side* (1857). It is not certain if such exchanges inflamed the passions of the rebels of 1857, but they did cause a great stir in Bombay itself; often the police had to be brought in to restore peace between agitated rivals. What also made Vishnubawa an important public figure

Kedarnath Dutta Bhaktivinod (1838–1914).

was the political treatise *Sukhadayak Karya Karini Nibandha,* translated into English by Capt. A. Phelps as *An Essay in Marathi on Beneficent Government* (1867). In this treatise, also taken to be based on old Vedic ideas, Vishnubawa tried to draw up plans for a model state and government based on the ideas of primitive communism. In his scheme, the state regulated all the important activities of the people, ranging from food production to education, marriage, old age pensions, etc., and both the production and distribution of essential commodities were based not on public demand but on actual needs. The treatise proved to be of merely academic interest, but one of Vishnubawa's arguments resonates with an idea that was soon to assume some importance. Since the *mlecchas* (by which he meant the Muslims) had Hindu ancestors, Vishnubawa argued, it was natural for them to return to the Hindu fold.

We have earlier argued how the Vaishnava tradition gradually acquired a political colour. However, not everybody agreed with infusing politics into religion: in this view, rather than contest the West or Christianity, it made better sense to win people over to Vaishnava ways. Further, Krishna, though associated with the Hindu tradition, was actually the Supreme God for all humanity. The man who vigorously adopted this path was Kedarnath Dutta (1838–1914), later given the honorific title Bhaktivinod, by which he is best known today. Dutta was a civil servant by profession, but at some point in his career, he developed a deep interest in Vaishnavism and renounced his secular life and profession. In 1869, in a public lecture he delivered on the *Bhagavata Purana*, Dutta strongly rejected the dominant reformist critique of this religious classic. Dutta's lecture was directed at interpretations (as, for instance, by Rammohun and Bankimchandra) which had debunked the 'licentious' figure of Krishna and questioned the very basis of image worship.

Both Sisir Ghosh and Dutta shared strong roots in the Chaitanya tradition but differed sharply over how best to propagate this religion. Whereas Ghosh made political capital out of Chaitanya's popularity among women and lower castes, Dutta found Ghosh's religion worryingly populist, thereby allegedly changing the very character of Bengal Vaishnavism. For Dutta, Vaishnavism was essentially the religion of the cultured classes. A pure Vaishnava had to be literate, respectful of the *shastras*, and morally chaste at all times. In Dutta's perception, Vaishnavism's good name had been sullied by the unregulated entry of the rabble, of renegade men and women who were neither capable of understanding the finer points of Vaishnava theology and aesthetics nor leading a morally upright life. This is a view with which even Bankimchandra too would have readily agreed. However, Bhaktivinod looked askance at both popular Vaishnavism and the power hitherto wielded by the class of brahmin-Vaishnava lineages, the Goswamis. Both these classes he found to be typically un-Vaishnava, albeit for a different set of reasons. He was keen to weed out the Sahajiyas, usually lower-caste singing minstrels who lived by begging and were reportedly utterly lax in their social and sexual lives. But Dutta soon also found himself at the head of a movement which challenged traditional Goswami claims on defining both Vaishnava theology and sacred geography. This amounted to subjecting genteel Vaishnavism to control by Brahmanical, upper castes rather than the brahmin alone and may have represented an intra-*bhadralok* contest for control and power. One of Bhaktivinod's important and enduring interventions was to declare Mayapur, across the river from Nabadwip, as the true birthplace of Chaitanya. This had the effect of splitting Bengal Vaishnavism into warring camps. Evidently, this struck at the roots of Goswami power and greatly affected their fortunes as custodians and interpreters of the Vaishnava tradition in Bengal. Dutta's movement attracted the upwardly mobile intermediary castes and classes and provided them greater cultural space. Patronage of the popular Vaishnava journal *Sajjanatoshini*, which Dutta founded in 1881, came mostly from the professionally successful classes: civil servants, lawyers, teachers, doctors, and journalists. Not surprisingly, Dutta spurned all attempts to give the Vaishnava revival a political orientation, remaining openly loyal to the colonial state.

For Bhaktivinod, it was promoting the specifically Vaishnava cultural and religious world that assumed greater importance than promoting the Hindu. For him, people of this world belonged to one of two categories: they were either Vaishnavas or non-Vaishnavas, either religious or nonreligious. Compared to the universalising claims of the Vedanta, this certainly looks sectarian. Paradoxically, however, this allowed Dutta to project the adoration of Krishna as a universally redemptive religion, aimed at securing personal salvation for the seeker and unrelated to any cultural pasts. For anyone willing to accept it in its true and 'uncorrupted' form, Vaishnavism was thus free, open, and accessible. Interestingly enough, this move to project Vaishnavism as the prime religion of the Hindus might have found tacit support in existing European scholarship. As early as 1805, the German Indologist Friedrich Schlegel had identified Vishnu as the central deity in the Hindu pantheon; subsequently, an influential body of thought represented by scholars like Albrecht Weber and Carl Maria Franz Lorinser drew instructive parallels between the lives of Krishna and Christ. Evidently, this encouraged the idea of promoting

Bhaktisiddhanta Saraswati (1874–1936) and disciples with the Governor of Bengal, Sir John Anderson, in the early 1930s.

Vaishnavism as a world religion. Premananda Bharati (pre-monastic name Surendranath Mukherji, 1858–1914), in 1902 the first Vaishnava missionary to visit the United States, not only built upon this parallelism but actually turned the intended parallelism on its head by insisting that Vaishnavism itself represented the fulfillment of Christ and Christianity. Bharati also contributed towards presenting a united front comprising both Vaishnavas and Vedantists before Christian evangelists in America. He is known to have worked in close partnership with Swami Abhedananda, a brother monk of Vivekananda who headed the Vedanta Society of New York, and the Vedantist from the Punjab, Swami Ram Tirath. This only demonstrates how a common cause could sink sectarian differences, however temporarily.

Bhaktivinod's son, Bimalprasad Dutta (1874–1937), who took the monastic name of Bhaktisiddhanta Saraswati, was a successful institution builder who made Mayapur a thriving centre of Bengal Vaishnavism which caught international attention. In some ways, Bhaktisiddhanta consolidated on the work begun by his father. Under him, for instance, the controversy regarding the relative place of brahmins and non-brahmins within the community of Vaishnavas assumed greater significance. Bhaktisiddhanta defined *adhikara* (religious qualification) in terms of a person's innate qualities and not his caste standing, although he remained as wary as his father about 'pseudo Vaishnavas' infiltrating the community and bringing the movement into disrepute. This strategy had the merit of socially broadening the Vaishnava revival: it was now Brahmanical but not Brahmanist. This made possible a subtle transfer of power from the brahmins to non-brahmin upper castes, a trend hinted at above. Regulating the entry of devotees to the Vaishnava Order continues to be as important an issue in current times as it was in the past. On the other hand, it cannot but be noticed that both Bhaktisiddhanta and his successor in office at ISKCON, Bhaktivedanta, were non-brahmins. Second, Bhaktisiddhanta paved the way for the progressive globalisation of the Vaishnava movement. The Chaitanya Math, which he founded at Mayapur in 1918, was the parent body for what later came to be known as the Gaudiya Math (founded 1920), now also with an international presence. His own disciple, Abhay Charan De (1896–1977), better known by his monastic name, A. C. Bhaktivedanta Swami, went on to establish ISKCON in 1966, which remains one of the globally most successful religious organisations to be born out of the Hindu tradition.

Barring the work of the Hindi poet Bharatendu Harishchandra at Benares, Vaishnava evangelism and organisational networks outside Bengal have not attracted much scholarly interest. The historian of modern Indian religion J. N. Farquhar has referred to the consolidation of the Madhva *sampradaya* in South India. This, too, was the work of English-educated professionals like Kanchi Subba Rao, who served as a deputy collector under the Madras government and founded the Madhva Siddhanta Unnahini Sabha (Association for the Strengthening of the Madhva Sytem). Among its wealthy patrons were the rulers of the princely Indian states of Travancore and Madras. It was around this time that Madhva's commentary on the *Vedanta Sutra* was translated into English and a standard biography of this medieval Vaishnava reformer came to be published. Similar developments occurred with respect to the Sri Sampradaya associated with Ramanuja. The scholar A. Govindacharya Swami, a resident of Mysore city, published Ramanuja's commentary on the *Gita*, a life of the Vaishnava reformer, and started the journal *Vishishtadvaitin*. Two organisations founded with the explicit purpose of disseminating the life and teachings of Ramanuja were the Ubhayavedanta Prasaratama Sabha and the *Vishishtadvaita Siddhanta Sangam* in Madras city.

The work of Bharatendu was associated with the Pushtimarga *sampradaya* of Vallabhacharya and his son, Vithalnath. Yet his vision for Vaishnava modernisation was rather nonsectarian. Bharatendu was an important office bearer of the Kashi Dharma Sabha, a body that busied itself with questions of ritual propriety among Hindus; this gave him certain organisational advantages. In 1873 he founded the Tadiya Samaj with the purpose of consolidating the local Vaishnavas, and in 1876 he authored the important treatise *Vaishnava Sarvasaya*, which aimed at producing greater integration among the various Vaishnava communities. As with the Gaudiya Vaishnava figures like Bhaktivinod, Bharatendu acknowledged the theological validity of image worship as well as its emotional functions for the Krishna devotee. He personally translated the *Shandilya* and *Narada Bhakti Sutras* with the purpose of spreading the cult of *bhakti* and ran vernacular journals which helped to spread his message.

Significantly enough, the religious movements launched by Kedarnath Dutta Bhaktivinod in Bengal and Bharatendu Harishchandra in Benares effectively contested two of the important postulates within modern Hindu reformism. First, their work strengthened the claim that, contrary to claims once made by men like Rammohun, Puranic religion was actually a fulfillment of Vedic religion because it offered the Hindu a richer and a more complete understanding of the nature and functions of God. Second, unlike the Brahmos and reformist Hindus, it held the ritualistic worship of divine images just as valid as the abstract contemplation on a formless God. What is especially interesting here is that the disapproval of image worship has now been effectively divorced from earlier Western critiques of such practices. ISKCON today has a substantial number of Western devotees who openly participate in the Vaishnava ritual calendar and the worship of Vaishnava icons housed in magnificent shrines.

CONCLUSION

This chapter has attempted to familiarise the reader with the history of organised Hinduism, which took birth around the third quarter of the nineteenth century. During this period the growth and dissemination of political consciousness among Hindus also led to the interpenetration of politics and religion. This new political consciousness worked in contrary ways. On one level, it aimed at uniting all Indians in a common anti-colonial struggle; on another, the increasing use of the Hindu religious idiom ruptured this political unity. Also, from a position in which they were essentially trying to defend themselves against their critics, Hindus progressively took to counteraggression, partly by altering their self-understanding but also through stronger rebuttals of criticism originating from both Hindus and non-Hindus.

Prima facie, this aggressive Hinduism manifested itself in ways that may look mutually contradictory but actually reveal an integrated strategy. Thus, from the point of view of Hindu self-assertion, both cosmopolitanism and cultural self-defence complemented each other, the first by highlighting the catholicity and tolerance said to be embedded in the Hindu tradition and the second by gathering greater internal strength with which to effectively confront critics. Such strategies were adopted by both the Vedantic revival in colonial India and the Vaishnava. Swami Vivekananda projected Vedanta as the religion eminently to become the future religion of mankind but remained in some ways a spokesman for the Hindus. Similarly, neo-Vaishnavas aimed at both better defining Vaishnavism within the framework of the Hindu tradition but also in creating an inclusive religion with transcultural potentialities.

Discussion Topic:
Ecumenical, Evangelical, and
Expansive Hinduism

- How would you describe the Hindu ecumenism practised by the Ramakrishna-Vivekananda tradition? Did it suffer from any practical limitations?

- What were the defining features of the Vaishnava revival in colonial Bengal?

- Would you agree with the view that Swami Vivekananda represented both an inclusive-accommodative view of Hinduism and one that was culturally insular?

- In what ways did the religious views of Ramakrishna differ from those of Brahmos like Rammohun and Keshabchandra?

- What was Mahatma Gandhi's understanding of Hinduism?

FURTHER READING

Vasudha Dalmia. *The Nationalization of Hindu Traditions: Bharatendu Hariscandra and Nineteenth-Century Benares*. New Delhi: Oxford University Press, 1997.

M. K. Gandhi. *What is Hinduism?* New Delhi: National Book Trust, 1994.

Brian A. Hatcher (ed.). *Hinduism in the Modern World*. London and New York: Routledge, 2016 (Chapters 4 and 5).

Ferdinando Sardella and Lucian Wong (eds). *The Legacy of Vaishnavism in Colonial Bengal*. London: Routledge, 2020 (Chapters 1–4).

Amiya P. Sen. *Chaitanya. A Life and Legacy*. New Delhi: Oxford University Press, 2019.

Amiya P. Sen. *Swami Vivekananda*. New Delhi, Oxford University Press, 2006 (Chapters 3–4).

Amiya P. Sen. (ed.). *The Indispensable Vivekananda. An Anthology for Our Times*. New Delhi & Ranikhet: Permanent Black, 2006.

Amiya P. Sen. *Ramakrishna Paramahamsa: The Sadhaka of Dakshineswar*. New Delhi: Penguin Viking, 2010 (Chapter 5).

Banaras Ghats.

VI
HINDUISM – COLONIAL AND THE CONTEMPORARY: AN OVERVIEW

There are broadly two ways of looking at history, which, purely for the sake of convenience, I will call respectively the tourist's and the aerial. Like the tourist closely exploring an ancient city, its worn-out stone-paved lanes and bylanes, ruined parapets, and crumbling corridors, history may be examined with an eye on small and intricate detail. This is comparable to the botanist scrutinising a prehistoric plant fossil under the modern microscope to determine its age or uniqueness. However, there also has to be, alongside, a panoramic view that encompasses it all, which sees the city as an organic whole, rather than losing itself in minute detail. This is possible only when we view a historical site from, say, a high rooftop. This view links the local topography to patterns of human settlements; it helps us to distinguish slums and modest huts inhabited by the poor from imposing, high-rise structures meant for the affluent. In short, it gives us clues to the social character of the city. It is helpful to use this analogy to understand contemporary Hinduism. A good part of contemporary Hinduism was born in colonial India but it is difficult, if not impossible, to understand contemporary Hinduism when entirely located within the historical framework or experiences of colonialism itself. We need to detach ourselves in time from the past only so that we may gain the correct perspective on matters. Distancing ourselves in time makes it possible to employ a telescopic vision as well as to understand matters with the advantage of hindsight.

Numerically, Hinduism is today the third-largest religion after Christianity and Islam. Roughly 16 per cent of the world's population are Hindus and are taken to practice Hinduism as their religion. Hindus constitute about 80 per cent of India's population; this is surpassed only by the Himalayan state of Nepal, where the ratio of Hindus to the total population is slightly higher. Hindus of Indic origin are also to be found, albeit in small minorities, in Pakistan, Mauritius, and Bangladesh. But these facts need to be qualified in at least three important respects. First, it is only in the last 200 years or so that using the term 'Hinduism' to describe a particular set of religious beliefs or practices has gained currency. Second, it is also over the same period that the term 'Hindu' has come to indicate a group of people practising a distinct religion called Hinduism: in our premodern past, the commonly known connotations of this term were perceptibly different. Third, although Hinduism originated in the Indian subcontinent, there are instances of this religion being practised even by non-Indic people, as in certain areas of Southeast Asia. This followed from trade contacts, travels, political conquests, or human migration across geographical and cultural spaces. Hinduism has also spread to Europe and North America, with many Hindu religious and cultural institutions and an active Hindu community settled in these areas. Britain, which has had strong historic ties with the Indian subcontinent in modern times, now has a substantial Hindu population comprising old migrants and their descendants.

This concluding chapter is divided into two halves. The first half will broadly summarise the major arguments and observations detailed in the preceding six chapters. The second half will be devoted to a brief but critical assessment of the ways in which colonial Hinduism relates to the contemporary. There are both significant continuities and discontinuities here that one must make a sincere effort to understand.

SUMMARISING COLONIAL HINDUISM

- Although the term 'Hinduism' is derived from the term 'Hindu', the historical association between the two is complex and was established only in recent times. For example, 'Hindu' was originally a geo-ethnic description rather than a religious one, which is to say that the Hindus began to be seen as a religious community only much later. The term 'Hinduism' is of even more recent origin. Scholars are now agreed that it came into vogue only during the late eighteenth century to denote a single religion that all Hindus were deemed to follow. It has been rightly argued that this was but an assumption shared by people of that time. European observers, for example, assumed that the faith of the Hindus was a 'religion' in the same sense as Christianity was, whereas in reality this was not quite the case. Historically, the Hindus have always been known to insist more on social than religious conformity; thus, departures from established caste practices were much less tolerated than differences over doctrines. This has led some scholars and observers to understand 'Hinduism' more as an orthopraxy than an orthodoxy. This feature sets Hinduism apart from Christianity.
- It has also been argued that 'Hinduism' was an entirely modern construct largely created by colonised Hindus themselves seeking a fixed and unified religious and cultural identity where there was none. This appears quite conjectural. There is reason to believe that this process of formulating a unified Hindu world view started in the

precolonial era. It is also important to acknowledge that often an underlying cultural consciousness is inchoate or indeterminate and does not carry a descriptive label for itself. In other words, it is entirely possible that the Hindus shared a common religious consciousness without also producing a sense of cohesive and close-knit religious community. The latter was undoubtedly sharpened with the coming of Muslims to India and the birth of cultural and political contestations between Muslims and non-Muslims.

- There is yet another apposite instance of this. Even in early history, Indians had tried to continually review and rework existing thought and practice with an eye on securing greater social equity and sophistication in religious thought and practices – this may justly be labelled as the work of social and religious reform. However, until about the nineteenth century, 'reform' was not the term used to describe these efforts; nor were people who initiated these changes known as reformers. This suggests that, although certain social or intellectual intentions existed among a people, these were not given a descriptive label until historical circumstances or our very categories of thought changed. Men like the Buddha, Kabir, Dadu Dayal, Nanak, or Chaitanya were not called 'reformers' by their contemporaries; this occurred only in modern times when human intervention and the very substance of social change began to be understood in perceptibly different ways.

- One of the significant problems that modern educated Hindus faced in the nineteenth century was meeting the moral and intellectual challenges thrown up by the contemporary West. This called for a new self-understanding; in colonial India, Rammohun Roy was again the first to respond to these challenges. For Rammohun, adopting the term 'Hinduism' was tantamount to modernising the religion of the Hindus and providing them with a sense of common social and religious identity. He found the Hinduism of his time to be full of irrational ideas, unjust social practices, and superstition. Caste differences, as he rightly alleged, discouraged a sense of unity and patriotism among Hindus. These antiquated features made him press for reform.

- A religious reformation required identifying the vital constituents of a religion, separating as it were, the grain from the chaff. After all, just what was one to reform? Rammohun and others after him believed that many ideas or practices that were a part of contemporary Hinduism actually did not belong to it. For the Hindus, this view encouraged serious research into their past with an eye on locating that which was 'pure' and 'authentic' in their tradition as against the spurious and the corrupted. Inspired by the British Orientalism of the late eighteenth century, Hindus began to talk of a 'Hindu golden age', which had been regrettably lost over time. The purity of the Hindu tradition now began to be measured in terms of its historically established age. It was thus that the Hindu intellectual and cultural awakening of the nineteenth century acquired notions of both reform and revival. Revival indicated the need to reinstate the ideal religion regrettably lost in time, and reform itself implied a return to an idyllic past.

- The challenge before colonised Hindus of the nineteenth century was to effectively negotiate modernity without dislodging themselves from tradition. Tradition represented the cumulative knowledge and accomplishments of a people, and, understandably enough, it also stood for a pride of race for people who had inherited a rich historical heritage but lost their political freedom. In the early nineteenth century, growing intellectual contacts between India and Europe planted certain new and significant ideas in the mind of the new Hindu intelligentsia who had benefitted from the spread of modern education. For instance, they readily accepted the idea that all nations had to strive towards modernity, breaking the shackles of unreason, prejudices, and superstitions of the past.

- The life and work of Rammohun blazed a trail for his successors, and what is generally known as the Indian Renaissance of the nineteenth century followed. This began in Bengal, the province in which British rule was first established, but soon spread to other areas in British India. Those associated with this movement were driven by the belief that fundamental changes in the day-to-day life of the Hindu had first to be brought about in matters of religion. Strictly speaking, they were not secular in their thought or habits and declined to make a sharp distinction between that which was religious in nature from that which was not. The watchword everywhere was 'reform', though effectively the social and intellectual nature of this awakening varied regionally.

- In Bengal itself, the departure from established ideas and practices came the earliest and took fairly radical forms. A group of students who called themselves 'Young Bengal' rejoiced in deliberately shocking orthodox opinion, and, even after them, Bengali reformers were prepared to sever their connections with parental Hindu society in the name of 'Truth' and 'Justice'. Members of the reformist body called the Brahmo Samaj considered themselves to be a separate community. They refused to perform image worship or revere multiple Hindu gods and goddesses, educated their women, celebrated inter-caste marriages, encouraged their widows to marry, and adopted a cosmopolitan outlook in matters of religious culture.

- By comparison, reformism arrived relatively later in other provinces of British India and revealed greater conservatism in social and religious matters. In the Bombay and Madras Presidencies, for example, caste was a far more important question than it was in Bengal. This might also explain why reform work in these provinces called for greater caution and were slower paced. Reforming societies in Bombay simply collapsed once news of members breaking caste taboos was mischievously leaked out. Further, there is no record of a 'Young Bombay' or 'Young Madras' ever taking birth. The radical content of reform in Bengal also explains why outside that presidency Bengalis began to be seen as 'denationalised' libertines. In the Punjab, Bengali migrants and their allegedly 'anglicised' ways of life were actively contested by the local Arya Samaj. Reform movements in the Punjab were characterised by two other important features. For one, they were less cosmopolitan compared to those developing in Bengal. Swami Dayanand, the founder of the Arya Samaj, was as much critical of existing Hindu sects and communities as he was of Islam or Christianity. Second, it was the Arya Samaj which first seriously contributed towards reclaiming those Hindus who had been earlier converted to Islam or Christianity.
- Reformist strategies differed between provinces of British India. In attempting to get the British government to pass new laws – as for instance the one legalising widow marriages – Bengal reformers relied far more on the sanction drawn from *shastras* (authoritative texts and scriptures). This is somewhat ironical since Bombay, the

Punjab, and coastal Andhra, which relied relatively less on this strategy, celebrated more widow marriages than did Bengal. Also, even within the so-called 'Woman Question', Bombay focused far more on settling upon a physiologically and morally correct age for marrying girls than it did on the question of widow marriages or polygamy. In South India, organised politics around the caste question often distracted from woman-related problems. It was thus that the brahmin and upper castes became a greater target for lower-caste agitators than oppressive husbands or, more generally, male sexual offenders. The other question that distracted from woman-related reform was Hindu nationalism. Hindu nationalism hardened social attitudes and discouraged the very idea of social or religious reform; the result was that by the early years of the twentieth century, meaningful social reforms were to arrive sooner in Indian princely states, as for instance in Mysore, Kolhapur, or Baroda, where nationalist agitation was far weaker than in British India.

- By the closing years of the nineteenth century, Hindu thought or action was characterised by what Sister Nivedita once called 'Aggressive Hinduism'. This was a potent combination of xenophobia, blind defense of tradition, and cultural aggression. The Hindus were now not merely defending Hinduism against Western attacks but challenging certain ideas or postulates associated with Western culture itself. In a sense, this was but a counter-Reformation that expressed some anguish about 'thoughtlessly' emulating alien ways of life at the cost of one's own but was also eager to take the battle to political and cultural adversaries.
- There was now, quite uncharacteristically, an evangelist Hinduism. This was atypical since traditionally,

Hinduism, unlike Islam or Christianity, was not a proselytising religion. A Hindu man or a woman was one who was born as such, not converted from some other religion. This began to change by the close of the nineteenth century, when aggressive Hindu organisations like the Arya Samaj began reclaiming Hindus converted to Islam and Christianity. By this time, the Hindus also began to express a greater concern over numbers. They were undoubtedly the largest religious community in British India but felt increasingly threatened by Muslims and Christians who were now rapidly multiplying in numbers. The question of numbers was important for yet another reason, since it often determined the share of material resources, jobs, or political offices that each community would be entitled to in British India. In the years to come this was to prove a major source of inter-community rivalry and tension.

- Broadly speaking, Hindu evangelism took two forms: the Vedantic and the Vaishnava. Both these sub-traditions claimed to be universal in character and best suited to the needs of the modern man. By the early years of the twentieth century, both Vedanta and Vaishnava sub-cultures were to establish their presence in the West and began to draw appreciative audiences. Importantly, both attempted to strengthen the concepts of altruism and moral activism within the religious life of the Hindus. *Seva* (social service) was an important feature of this new religious consciousness.

- In colonial India, the Vedantic revival arrived earlier in time and developed over two successive phases: the first was associated with Rammohun and the second with Swami Vivekananda. Both were based on a creative re-reading of traditional nondualist (Advaita) tradition whereby an abstract and somewhat passive philosophy was sought to be made more active, realistic, and socially responsible. Both Rammohun and Vivekananda treated Vedanta as an ecumenical or eclectic world view that could override bigotry and sectarianism. Keeping with their modernism, they also rejected the older tendency to keep religious knowledge restricted only to the upper castes and classes. The most important claim made by this revival was making Vedantic Hinduism a truly universal religion, transcending political and cultural borders and barriers. While the West had indeed advanced phenomenally in the domain of material culture, it was argued, the key to understanding human spirituality still lay with the Hindus. This made it possible for men like Vivekananda to assert that India and Hinduism had an important role to play on a global level by restoring in man his spiritual quest that would only perfectly balance the concern for his social and economic betterment.

• Interestingly enough, Vivekananda's Vedantic universalism drew upon the old-world ecumenism of his spiritual *guru*, Ramakrishna Paramahamsa. Sri Ramakrishna was a rustic and barely literate Hindu mystic but a gifted preacher who could communicate 'high' philosophical truths in the simplest language. His own spiritual life was dedicated to locating and affirming the truth that all religions ultimately led to God realisation. His catholicity found the very concept of 'tolerance' problematic, since it assumed that only one party was right and was simply tolerating flaws and shortcomings in others. Vivekananda quite creatively appropriated the universalism of his Master's message to build upon his idea of projecting a universal religion. In the long run, though, the Ramakrishna-Vivekananda tradition had a paradoxical effect on the Hindu mind. On the one hand, it created a new respect for non-Hindu cultures; on the other, it discouraged critiques of Hinduism itself. If all religions led to a common goal, what, if any, was the need for a Hindu to convert to another faith?

• As with the Vedantic revival, a new life was injected into Vaishnava devotional culture in the course of the nineteenth century; perhaps its most productive manifestation was felt within Gaudiya or Bengal Vaishnavism. By the 1880s, Vaishnava *bhakti* had become a potent medium for cultural self-expression among educated Hindus. Generally speaking, this found support in three distinct and yet in some ways interrelated movements. First was the revival of Krishna *bhakti* itself, partly as a reaction to the critique that had earlier emerged against image worship, the worship of an allegedly morally suspect Krishna himself, and the 'overly sentimental' or 'effeminate' culture embedded in popular Vaishnavism. Second, there was the serious and successful attempt at reviving and reinvigorating the cult that had developed around the medieval Vaishnava mystic Chaitanya. By the close of the nineteenth century, Chaitanya had become a symbol of both Vaishnava piety and Hindu cultural nationalism. The third trend was represented by a conscious drive to foist upon Vaishnavism a new theological and philosophical gloss. The first movement was best represented by the work *Krishnacharitra* by the Hindu thinker, Bankimchandra Chattopadhyay, whose mission it was to represent Krishna as an ideal moral and historical figure comparable to Christ. The second represented a phenomenal expansion of the Vaishnava literary space complemented by serious efforts to publicise the life and work of Chaitanya. Here it is important to remember that even the reformist Brahmos contributed significantly to this Vaishnava development. Brahmos were among the first to convert to neo-Vaishnavism and also the earliest to introduce typically Vaishnava practices into Hindu public life in colonial Calcutta, for example through devotional street singing (*nagar sankirtanas*). The third trend is represented by important Vaishnava writers and theoreticians like Kedarnath Dutta, also belonging to the genteel *bhadralok* class, who, through his abundant writings, propounded powerful theories related to a devotional culture. Bhaktivinod gave the neo-Vaishnava movement in Bengal new organisational strength and the ability to aspire to a global presence. Under his spiritual successors, the move to universalise Krishna *bhakti* grew in strength, now best represented by ISKCON.

Sri Krishna-Balaram Mandir was built in 1975 on the orders of Bhaktivedanta Swami Prabhupada.

• The spirit of reformist change also touched classes other than the Western-educated, and in this sense the changes under colonialism were quite far reaching. In the hinterland adjoining each of the three British Indian presidencies of Bengal, Madras, and Bombay, there emerged movements for social and religious change. They were led by people who were closer to traditional ways of life and sought to bring about change using the social and cultural mechanisms that tradition itself could offer; they were not a part of the new intelligentsia that India's modern universities were turning out. We have briefly studied three representative movements of this kind: the one in Gujarat led by Sahajanand (Swaminarayan), in Tamil-speaking areas by Ramalinga, and in rural Odisha by Mahima Swami and his disciple, Bhima Boi. Another important feature of these movements was that they were essentially patronised by rural people, most of whom were peasants, artisans, agricultural workers, or petty traders belonging to intermediary or lower castes with no formal education to their credit. The leaders of these movements actively used vernacular languages in spreading their message. Quite significantly, too, they preferred using evocative songs and poetry over prose disputations since their appeal was more to the heart than the head.

We may conclude this section with certain pertinent observations. The advancing tide of Indian nationalism, as noted earlier, generally weakened the agenda for social and religious reform. By the 1890s, the Indian National Congress, the largest Indian political body, refused to share its venue with the Indian Social Conference, which dealt exclusively with social questions. The understanding here was that, given the immense varieties within Indian life, deliberations on social or religious questions only weakened Indian unity. By comparison, nurturing a common political sentiment against the continuance of foreign rule could more effectively bring more people onto a common platform. One of the vital debates to emerge in the nineteenth century was over the question of whether or not to encourage social reform over the political. Some argued that political freedom for Indians would better resolve their social problems: when politically free, Hindus would be masters of their own house and would no longer have to depend on the will of an alien ruling class (the British) who neither fully understood problems concerning Hindu society nor possessed the moral right to intervene in the social and religious affairs of their non-Christian subjects. Predictably, the rival party argued, and not without reason, that in a country like India, with its complex structure and vast diversity, mere political freedom without also securing the social and economic emancipation of the people would be meaningless. Political independence could bring political equality between citizens but not a socially equitable society or restore to the common person their natural dignity, which had been steadily lost to centuries of continued injustice and oppression. Indian leaders like Mahatma Gandhi could see the colossal problems facing the poor, the sickly, and the undernourished in India and, like Swami Vivekananda before him, he argued that feeding the poor and providing them with shelter, a livelihood, and a basic education were the more pressing challenges before the Hindus and the citizens of a new nation. Both Rabindranath Tagore and Gandhi spent a part of their lives in rural reconstruction programmes, working in the interests of the common peasant and artisan because it was in its numerous villages that the real soul of India could be located. Vivekananda, Tagore, and Gandhi were all united in their critique of a traditional Hinduism that could not wipe the grieving widow's tears, provide food to the starving and sickly infant, bring the light of knowledge to the ignorant, or reject social inequities built around caste and class. They all rued the fact that fellow Hindus spent more time and resources on feeding their lifeless gods than the starving humans on the streets. For them, if God was to be found on Earth at all, he was most likely to be found residing among the poor and the downtrodden.

Belur Math is the headquarters of the Ramakrishna Math and Mission, founded by Swami Vivekananda.

Contemporary Hindu Religion and Society in Relation to the Colonial Past

During the course of the nineteenth century, Hinduism underwent important changes in religious ideas and social practices. On the whole, it could be said to have become more liberal, rational, socially sensitive, and utilitarian. An increasing number of educated Hindus no longer believed in the idea of an infallible source book or that it was revealed by God to man. More Hindus now disregarded the offices of the hereditary *guru* or the family priest, critiqued idolatry, ornate ritualism, and the worship of multiple gods and goddesses, and Hindu reformist movements of this period like the Brahmo Samaj, Prarthana Samaj, and Arya Samaj fought hard to discourage such practices. Hindus now more freely and more frequently travelled to foreign lands; they no longer believed that such travel was unjustified and violated social or religious conventions, or even that prohibitions regarding food and drink had anything to do with God realisation.

The legacy of many of these colonial developments in Hinduism endures. Today, urban, educated Hindus no longer make it a point to ask who might have cooked their food, and a greater proportion of them are now willing to enter into inter-caste or inter-community marriages. For the unbelieving Hindu, it is now possible to enter into a civil marriage, devoid of any religious ceremonies. The self-immolation of Hindu widows on the funeral pyre of their husbands (*sati*) has long been outlawed, upper-caste Hindu widows are now free to marry, girls can freely go to schools and colleges, no Hindu boy or girl can marry below a certain legally defined age, and Hindu males can no longer take a second wife while their first wife lives. New modes of travel that successfully emerged in British India, as for instance the railways, further contributed to weaken the institution of caste. Railway compartments were differentiated by the class of travel undertaken and by fares, not by the caste origin of passengers. No less importantly, the religion of the Hindus itself is now democratised: non-brahmins may write religious treatises, publicly participate in religious discourses, or dispute meanings given to a religious idea or an act by the orthodox brahmin. Religious wisdom is no longer the monopoly of a certain class of people and, contrary to previous practice, religious classics can now be openly propagated and publicised. Lower-caste Hindus and so-called 'untouchables', hitherto barred from entering any Hindu temple or shrine, can now do so without fear of discrimination. In recent times, many Hindu men and women have actively protested against discriminatory practices carried out in certain temples or holy shrines where women were disallowed entry.

In large measure, the growth and development of this new Hinduism was made possible by the coming of modern education through modern institutions of higher learning leading to a mental revolution, expanded communication networks, the growing importance of the printed word, and the spectacular growth of vernacular languages and literature. In all these areas, the colonial state and government played the role of an active agent. The success of the print media made mass education a reality. The translation of classical Hindu religious and moral treatises originally written in Sanskrit into commonly spoken languages allowed many more Hindus to become familiar with their tradition and suitably critique it; this could be justly compared to Germans being able to read the Bible translated from Latin into German. Reading and commenting upon Hindu sacred texts was no longer the monopoly of brahmins or even Hindus more generally.

While contemporary Hinduism does still have some roots in the ancient Vedic religion, such connections remain in place only historically, not as living cultural practice. Today, there are no active cults around the most important Vedic gods like Indra and Varuna, nor can we find temples dedicated to them; even Agni is more symbolised by the sacred fire that ritually purifies rather than revered as a deity to whom lavish Vedic sacrifices were once made. Over time, new gods have taken the place of the old, in keeping with new social and cultural requirements and new patterns of thought. Contemporary Hinduism has now occasionally introduced the services of female priests in place of male. On the occasion of marriages or other ritually important acts, enterprising Hindus have been known to substitute the formal reading of *mantras* by priests with audio presentations using electronic devices. This has not caused serious social objections, at least not in the larger cosmopolitan cities. Also, few Hindus still habitually consult the Hindu almanac before setting out on a journey or when organising some important family ceremony, nor do they follow food taboos in keeping with the ritual calendar. Death and disease are now understood more in medical terms than as some punishment inflicted by an avenging god or the consequences of wrongdoings perpetrated in some past life. To ward off attacks from measles or chicken pox, many more Hindus now prefer vaccination to praying before a deity for cure or relief. Even 100 years ago, such departures from norms and conventions would have been considered sacrilegious.

Certain things, however, have not changed at a comparable pace. A reverence for established customs and conventions still, at times, inhibits an acceptance of modern ways of life. Hindu pilgrim trails, fairs, and festivals continue to draw huge crowds and, shockingly, many continue to ignore issues related to hygiene and sanitation integral to such events. Quite

The annual chariot festival, ratha-yatra, *in Jagannath Puri, Odisha.*

Diwali celebrations.

Pilgrims gathering for Prayag Kumbh Mela in Allahabad, Uttar Pradesh.

recently, at the important Hindu gathering of the Kumbh Mela, several hundreds of thousands of pilgrims attending defied restrictions put in place by the state to combat a virulent pandemic that is, at the time of writing, still raging in the country. Some Hindus still view modern doctors and health workers with some suspicion.

While on the whole, gender relations in Hindu society are now more liberal than before and the status of women has generally improved, the girl child continues to be traumatised and victimised in several ways. City streets and urban work spaces are still not wholly safe for women professionals. Under the law, girls are equally entitled as boys to education and other services provided by the state; however, existing social prejudices discourage this in several ways. In the majority of Hindu households, less importance is attached to the educational or professional growth of a girl in relation to her brothers. A greater social premium is still put on the birth of a son than a daughter; the government has recently had to prohibit sex determination of the fetus to prevent feticide, which has a long history in certain Indian communities. And even though widows are now legally entitled to marry, Hindu society has silently but effectively discouraged such marriages. Numerous Hindu widows, abandoned by their family and friends, eke out a miserable existence in Hindu pilgrim centres like Benares and Vrindavan where they continue to be socially and sexually exploited.

Even today, only a few among urban Hindus are prepared to dispense with the services of a priest and *guru*. On the contrary, the presence of such people is believed to strengthen or endorse their social standing in the community. After the West took to the modern Hindu *guru* in a big way, this has become an even greater fad among the urban affluent in India. Countless *ashrams* are now run in the name of media-savvy *gurus*; their followers, both male and female, can be found in most Indian provinces. Many of these *gurus* may be identified with English-language Hinduism, are patronised by successful business houses in India and generous donors from the West, use modern technology to publicise themselves and their ideas, travel globally, and freely mix with women disciples. In their very demeanour they look very different from the modest, saffron-clad, shaven-headed traditional Hindu *sannyasi* who spends his life in the isolation of some obscure Himalayan retreat. Rather than choose the *sannyasi's* traditional life of a recluse, these modern *gurus* are generally eager to grab media attention through popular social platforms.

The hierarchical arrangement of caste, though weakened in some respects, persists in many other forms. It is still an important factor when negotiating traditional marriages or, more generally, in everyday relationships. Cases are still not uncommon, involving a boy and a girl marrying across caste boundaries, in which the couple are severely reprimanded even to the point of being executed by 'elders' in so-called 'honour killings'. While class divisions based on education or incomes are now quite powerful in themselves, caste continues to insidiously enter the everyday life of the Hindu. It is fragile in theory but still powerful in social practice.

Finally, in recent years, there has been a discernible political effort to 'Hinduise' India and to get Hindus to agree on the idea of a common culture that every Hindu is expected to share. There is now a greater insistence on just what kind of food Hindus should ideally consume, what cures he or she must seek to combat recurring ailments, or what a non-Hindu can and cannot do in a Hindu-majority India. Indeed, this campaign has met with great success. Hindutva or political Hinduism tends to be both unjust and exclusionary at the same time. It uses the terms India and Hindu interchangeably, a practice that justly invites objections from non-Hindus. Contrary to general perception, the ideology of Hindutva has a long genealogy which exposes certain cultural anxieties entertained by Hindus in relation to other religious communities. On the whole, though, it is reasonable to say that the prehistory of Hindutva is discernibly different from its contemporary forms. For one, the older notions of Hindutva were more cultural and self-reflexive in nature than communal and politically exclusionary. These did not necessarily perceive Muslims as the 'other'. In recent years, there also been intense and violent controversy around the government's attempts to define the parameters of Indian citizenship. It has been alleged, and not without reason, that such acts were meant to target certain religious communities. Such practices tend to violate the very plurality of the Hindu world view, and also overlook the fact that in history neither Hindus nor Hinduism have grown or developed in cultural isolation.

GLOSSARY OF KEY TERMS

Advaitin: Follower or practitioner of the philosophical subschool of Advaita (nondual) Vedanta, the foremost exponent of which was Acharya Shankara circa ninth century ce. In modern India, Rammohun Roy, Swami Vivekananda, and Ramana Maharshi are among the best-known Advaitins.

Astika: Commonly taken to mean 'theist' or 'theistic'. However, originally the term meant acknowledging the authority of the Vedas. The six Hindu schools of philosophy were taken to be astika since they acknowledged the authority of the Vedas even if some of them remained sceptical about the existence of God. By comparison, Buddhists and Jains were considered nastikas, i.e. those who did not acknowledge the Vedas as authoritative.

Avatara: Term related to avatarana ('descent of God to Earth'). In this sense the term needs to be differentiated from the Christian concept of 'incarnation'. Also, unlike Christianity, Hinduism allows multiple avataras. Used in relation to both Lords Shiva and Vishnu, though more commonly with the latter. Lord Vishnu is famously associated with the ten primal avataras (Dashavatara).

Bhadralok: Literally, 'genteel people'; a term that came to be commonly used in nineteenth-century Bengal for urban, educated upper-caste (or -class) males employed in some professional capacity. This class was typically associated with the professions of teaching, subordinate civil service, law, journalism, creative writing, printing, and publishing. Female equivalent of the term is bhadramahila.

Bhakti: Devotional sentiment, usually centred around a favoured deity; derived from root *bhaj*. In the phrase *bhakti yoga,* it also represents an acknowledged path to God realisation.

Brahmacharya: Commonly taken to mean celibacy in both males and females. In early India this represented the earliest stage in the life of an upper-caste male when undergoing formal studies with a *guru*. In Brahmanical Hinduism, *brahmacharya* is taken to produce special spiritual and ritual powers.

Brahmin: Ritually, the highest-placed *varna* (see below), although not always so socially. There are several subdivisions within brahmins whose standing and dietary habits vary regionally.

Dharma: Term with multiple meanings. Most commonly, 'moral order' or 'set of duties'; *dharma* may be specific to certain social groups such as women (*stridharma*) or a certain *varna* or caste (*kshatriyadharma*); it may also have a more universal meaning or application (*samanyadharma*), as in practising noninjury or being truthful.

Dvija: Literally, 'twice born'. Term applied to the three upper *varnas* of brahmin, *kshatriya*, and *vaishya*, the males of which are required to undergo a second ritual birth by means of putting on the sacred thread.

Jati: Commonly translated as 'caste', i.e. an endogamous social group defined by birth. Historically, *jatis* have always undergone positional changes, going up and down the social order through time. Their position within the hierarchy of castes is usually determined through conformity to certain prescribed social and ritual practices.

Kshatriya: Second of the four *varnas* in early India, placed immediately below the brahmins. Traditionally identified with the military and ruling classes, but in early India, some sages who appear in the Upanishads were *kshatriyas* by birth.

Moksha: Literally, 'salvation'; fourth and last stage in the so-called *chaturvarga* (fourfold objectives) in the life of upper-caste males.

Nirguna: Literally, 'that which has no property or attributes'. In Hindu Brahmanical thought, this term is applied to the Brahman or the Transcendent Absolute. The absoluteness of the Brahman lies in its very unchanging or inert quality which defies all description. However, there are schools of thought that choose to define the Brahman as *saguna* or God, to whom certain human qualities could be attached.

Puranas: Vast body of Hindu literature dating back to the early medieval period, covering matters such as religion, ritual, mythology, and dynastic history There are deemed to be eighteen major Puranas (Mahapuranas) and some minor Puranas (Upapuranas). These texts are intensely sectarian in character relating to the worship of Lords Shiva, Vishnu, and the Devi (primeval Mother Goddess).

Saguna: Literally, 'that which bears a certain quality or property'. Term usually attached to the Transcendent Brahman by *bhakti* schools of thought within Hinduism. Some schools of thought (for example, the Brahmo Samaj) abided by this conception of Brahman but would not grant it a human form.

Shaiva: Follower or devotee of Lord Shiva. Includes several sub-schools within this tradition.

Shakta: Follower or devotee of Shakti, the primeval Mother Goddess commonly known as the Devi.

Sannyasi: Hindu ascetic or world renouncer who is expected to sever all ties with society.

Sati: Literally, 'chaste wife'; also used to denote the Hindu widow who self-immolated on the funeral pyre of her dead husband.

Shastra: Text providing authoritative instruction, e.g. social and moral codes such as *Dharmashastra* and *Nitishastra*; also, specifically, scripture.

Shuddhi: Literally, 'purification'; in the late nineteenth century, the term was applied to the movement started by the Arya Samaj to reclaim Hindu converts to Islam and Christianity.

Shruti: Literally, 'that which is heard only', namely scripture. Vedic literature is considered *shruti* since, traditionally, it was learned by rote by select groups of Brahmins and never consigned to writing. All that changed in the nineteenth century.

Shudra: Fourth and last of the *varnas*. Shudras were not *dvijas* and hence could not wear the sacred thread. However, they were still considered ritually superior when compared to untouchables.

Upanishads: The philosophical and speculative, and chronologically latest, part of Vedic literature; a part of *shruti* and primary source of the Vedanta philosophical school. In many ways the Upanishads rebel against some of the fundamental idea or values of early Vedic religion. Some preceded the Buddha in time, while others were composed as late as the medieval era.

Vaishnava: Devotee or follower of Lord Vishnu or Krishna. The many religious views of the Vaishnavas are divided into *sampradayas* (schools of thought). The followers of Lord Rama also qualify to be called Vaishnavas but are not as numerous or well-known.

Vaishya: Third of the four *varnas* known in early India. *Vaishyas* were *dvijas* and hence could wear the sacred thread. Occupationally, they were traders, land owners, or rich peasants.

Varna: Social category based on birth and occupation. In early India there were four such categories: brahmin, *kshatriya*, *vaishya*, and *shudra*. Not to be confused with *jati* ('caste'), since a *varna* may represent a cluster of several *jatis*.

Vedas: Rich and ancient corpus of Brahmanical literature. The Vedas are four in number, with the *Rig Veda* generally taken to be the oldest. For a long time, this literature was accessible to brahmin males alone. Ironically, it was a brahmin, Rammohun Roy, who first declared that they ought to be made available to women and non-brahmins as well.

Vedanta: Either the end of the Vedas (Veda+*anta*); or the quintessence of Vedic thought. The latter definition is the more commonly accepted today. There are many schools of Vedantic thought, ranging from nondualism (Advaita) to dualism (Dvaita).

Zemindar: Literally, holder of *zemin* (land) (from Persian). The term dates back to the Indo–Muslim period in Indian history but was popularised after 1793, when the British initiated a system of land revenue collection in Bengal called the Permanent Settlement; hereafter, *zemindars* were deemed to be hereditary landowners, a position that they had not enjoyed earlier.

References

Abhedananda, Swami. *India and Her People*. New York, 1906.

Bhandarkar, Ramkrishna Gopal. 'The Position of the Prarthana Samaj in the Religious World'. 1903.

Brahmo Year Book, 1880.

Chattopadhyay, Bankimchandra. *Letters on Hinduism* (*c.* 1882). Reproduced in *Bankim Rachanavali* (Collected Works of Bankimchandra), vol. III, edited by J. C. Bagal. Calcutta, 1969.

Dalmia, Vasudha. 'The Only Real Religion of the Hindus: Vaishnava Self-Representation in the Late Nineteenth Century'. In *The Oxford India Hinduism Reader*, edited by H. von Stietencron and Vasudha Dalmia. New Delhi, 2007.

Farquhar, J. N. *The Primer of Hinduism*. London, 1911.

Farquhar, John Nicol. *Modern Religious Movements in India*. London, 1915.

Gorakh Bani, edited by Pitambardutta Barthwal. Allahabad, 2004.

Guru, Narayan. *Atmopadesha Shatakam* (Instructions Given to the Self in One Hundred Verses). n.d.

Guru, Narayan. *Jati Nirnayam* (A Critique of Jati). 1914.

Kolhatkar, Waman Rao Madhav. 'Widow Re-marriage'. In *Indian Social Reform. In Four Parts. Being a Collection of Essays, Addresses, Speeches etc* (with an Appendix), Part I, edited by C. Y. Chintamani. Madras, 1901.

Lipner, Julius. *Hindus: Their Religious Beliefs and Practices.* London: Routledge, 1994.

Marshall, P. J. (ed.). *The British Discovery of Hinduism in the Eighteenth Century.* Cambridge: Cambridge University Press, 1970.

Oddie, Geoffrey A. *Imagined Hinduism: British Protestant Missionary Constructions of Hinduism, 1793–1900.* California and London: Sage, 2006.

Roy, Rammohun. 'A Defense of Hindu Theism' (1817). In *The English Works of Rammohun Roy,* edited by Kalidas Nag and Debajyoti Burman, vol. 2. Calcutta, 1946.

Roy, Rammohun. *A Second Defense of the Monotheistical System of the Vedas in Reply to the Present State of Hindoo Worship,* 1817.

Roy, Rammohun. *Translation of an Abridgement of the Vedanta or the Resolution of all the Vedas etc.,* 1816.

Sen, Amiya P. *Rammohun Roy: A Critical Biography.* Delhi: Penguin Viking, 2012.

Sen, Guru Prosad. *An Introduction to the Study of Hinduism.* Calcutta, 1893.

Sen, Keshabchandra. 'Young Bengal, This Is for You'. 1860.

Speeches and Writings of Surendranath Banerjee. Madras: G. A. Natesan & Co., 1940.

Tagore, Debendranath. *Brahmodharmer Vyakhyan* (An Exposition on Brahmoism, 1861). Reprinted Calcutta, 1965.

Valuable Conversations with the Swami Vivekananda in England, America and India. Calcutta, 1902.

Vivekananda, Swami. 'Addresses at the Parliament of Religions'. In *The Complete Works of Swami Vivekananda,* vol. 1. Mayavati Memorial Edition. Calcutta, 1973.

Vivekananda, Swami. 'The Common Bases of Hinduism'. In *The Complete Works of Swami Vivekananda,* vol. 3. Mayavati Memorial Edition. Calcutta, 1973.

Vivekananda, Swami. 'Report on the Lecture at Jaffna, 1897'. In *The Complete Works of Swami Vivekananda,* vol. 3. Mayavati Memorial Edition. Calcutta, 1973.

von Stietencron, H. 'Religious Configurations in Pre-Muslim India and the Modern Concept of Hinduism'. In *Representing Hinduism: Construction of Religious Traditions and National Identity,* edited by Vasudha Dalmia and H. von Stietencron. New Delhi, 1995.

Index

MANDALA

An Imprint of MandalaEarth
PO Box 3088
San Rafael, CA 94912
www.MandalaEarth.com

Find us on Facebook:
www.facebook.com/MandalaEarth

Publisher Raoul Goff
Associate Publisher Phillip Jones
Publishing Director Katie Killebrew
Project Editor Amanda Nelson
VP Creative Director Chrissy Kwasnik
Art Director Ashley Quackenbush
VP Manufacturing Alix Nicholaeff
Sr Production Manager Joshua Smith

Text © 2024 The Oxford Centre
for Hindu Studies

Photographs © 2024 Mandala Publishing,
except for: pages xiv, 11, 36, 42, 45-46, 66, 78,
84-85, 88, 103, 108, 110, 118, 129, 131, 135,
146, 150, 152, 162, 170, 172, 184-185, 187,
190, 193, 195, 206, 208, 211, 216, 218, 223,
227, 231, 238, 248 (Courtesy Wikimedia
Commons); pages 18-19, 175, 237 (Courtesy
Wellcome Collection); pages 30, 71, 74, 219,
256, 268, 271, 275-276 (Courtesy Shutter-
stock).

ISBN: 979-8-88762-075-6
ISBN: 979-8-88762-134-0 (Export Edition)

Manufactured in India by Insight Editions
10 9 8 7 6 5 4 3 2 1

Library of Congress Cataloging-in-Publication Data
Names: Sen, Amiya P., 1952- author.
Title: Colonial Hinduism : an introduction / Amiya P. Sen.
Description: San Rafael : Mandala, [2024] | Series: The Oxford Centre for
    Hindu Studies Mandala Publishing series | Includes bibliographical
    references and index. | Summary: "In a tightly woven narrative,
    historian of modern India Amiya P. Sen traces the shifting
    self-understanding of Hindus in the light of the many challenges posed
    by the British colonial encounter, offering an accessible yet
    analytically rich book on the birth and development of modern Hinduism,
    which will be of interest to students and the interested general reader
    alike"-- Provided by publisher.
Identifiers: LCCN 2024020020 (print) | LCCN 2024020021 (ebook) | ISBN
    9798887621340 (hardcover) | ISBN 9798887620756 (hardcover) | ISBN
    9798887620763 (ebook)
Subjects: LCSH: Hinduism--India--History. | Hindu renewal--India--History.
    | India--History--British occupation, 1765-1947.
Classification: LCC BL1153.5 .S46 2024 (print) | LCC BL1153.5 (ebook) |
    DDC 294.50954/09034--dc23/eng/20240602
LC record available at https://lccn.loc.gov/2024020020
LC ebook record available at https://lccn.loc.gov/2024020021

ROOTS of PEACE   REPLANTED PAPER

FSC
www.fsc.org
MIX
Paper | Supporting
responsible forestry
FSC® C016779